The Unavoidable Hierarchy

Unavoidable Hierarchy provides an analysis of why, in virtually every organization, members advance or decline in standing for reasons that have little or nothing to do with their merit. Michael Hatfield explains how this dynamic can be observed and analyzed, and insights gleaned from the analysis.

With organizations struggling to meet the aspirations of their employees; ill-equipped or patently inappropriate individuals failing in executive posts and need for businesses to be at the top of their game, *Unavoidable Hierarchy* is a timely and important book for all managers, particularly those concerned with the human dynamics of the business.

Michael Hatfield draws on advancements in Game Theory, Network Theory, Organizational Behavior and Performance Management concepts to capture and evaluate the (previously unarticulated) influencing factors behind the game of corporate snakes and ladders. The resulting analysis will help you identify how these factors manifest as strategies and tactics within the organization, meaning that effective countermeasures can be derived from such an analysis.

Whilst these factors are likely to remain ubiquitous, the author's focus includes ideas and strategies for mitigating their impact and making changes at the level of both the individual and the organization.

Michael Hatfield, MBA, PMP, CCP, EVP works as a Project Leader for a nuclear laboratory in the American Southwest, and is the author most recently of *Game Theory in Management* (Gower Publishing, 2012) and *Things Your PMO Is Doing Wrong* (PMI Publishing, 2008). His blog, currently appearing on ProjectManagement.com, was named one of the 100 most influential project management blogs. Michael's popular column Variance Threshold was a regular feature in *PMNetwork* magazine for over a decade, and his work has been published in such diverse publications as *Project Management Journal, Cost Engineering, Gantthead, People on Projects, The Measurable News, Building Better Business* and the *Nuclear Weapons Journal*.

He has worked as an entry-level technician for the Air Force Weapons Laboratory's Electro-Magnetic Pulse (EMP) test sites, as the director of a National Laboratory's Project Management Office overseeing a budget of $1.3 Billion (USD), and many very interesting jobs in-between. Michael can be reached at varthold@aol.com, and blogs at http://www.projectmanagement.com/blog/Game-Theory-in-Management.

Refreshing. Insightful. Many "ah-ha" revelations. It's a front-row ride that will likely change your view of yourself, of those around you and your behavior going forward. The philosophies are expertly woven into stories. The reader emerges with a pragmatic awareness of self rarely proffered in business/project-related books.
                                   —Neal Whitten, President, The Neal Whitten Group

The Unavoidable Hierarchy

Who's Who In Your Organization, And Why

Michael Hatfield

Routledge
Taylor & Francis Group

LONDON AND NEW YORK

First published in paperback 2024

First published 2016
by Routledge Publishing
4 Park Square, Milton Park, Abingdon, Oxon OX14 4RN

and by Routledge Publishing
605 Third Avenue, New York, NY 10158

Routledge is an imprint of the Taylor & Francis Group, an informa business

Publisher's Note
The publisher has gone to great lengths to ensure the quality of this reprint but points out that some imperfections in the original copies may be apparent.

British Library Cataloguing in Publication Data
A catalogue record for this book is available from the British Library

Library of Congress Cataloging in Publication Data
A catalog record for this book has been requested

ISBN: 978-1-4724-6255-8 (hbk)
ISBN: 978-1-03-283727-7 (pbk)
ISBN: 978-1-315-54942-2 (ebk)

DOI: 10.4324/9781315549422

Typeset in Sabon
by Out of House Publishing

Contents

Figures

Tables

Acknowledgments

I have promised William C. Dowling, Professor of English at Rutgers University, but formerly of the University of New Mexico, a prominent place in the acknowledgments section of any book I ever write, since he taught me how to write and research like a true scholar, and I owe him a great debt for having done so. I am also grateful to my family, for putting up with my absences and distractions while researching, writing, and rewriting this book. Also, many thanks are due my sister, award-winning author Marcia Daudistel, for her insights and support.

Introduction

I know this has happened to you.

You are involved in some sort of organization, some kind of social interaction – it might be a club, a company, a faculty lounge, an election-night celebration – and a seemingly incomprehensible event unfolds. Someone is unexpectedly and unfairly ejected from the club, promoted in the company, denied tenure in the review committee, or elected over a far more capable opponent. You are hurt or elated, but confused just the same, as you turn to an associate, a question mark written on your face. Your colleague knows the question on your lips, shrugs, and looks off into the distance.

"It's just politics."

As if those three words could somehow substitute as an explanation for what you have just witnessed, a massive departure from a structure previously assumed to have had some connection to a meritocracy.

And, oddly enough, you accepted this so-called explanation, in a form of a tacit acknowledgment that only the naïve or very young could possibly adhere to the notion that merit, and merit alone, should ever be the sole (or even majority) arbiter of where we stand with respect to others in the world, or the world itself.

The world of politics is opaque indeed, and not just the electoral variety. Politics in the office, the board room, the faculty lounges, the classrooms and church choirs and thousands of other venues have profound impacts on the functioning of those organizations, but also on how we view ourselves and our relationships with those organizations. It simply will not do to walk away from any attempt to capture, to quantify the behaviors that lead to these seemingly detached-from-reality decisions that hold such a powerful sway over our day-to-day activities, over our very lives. Inky or not, these depths absolutely must be plumbed.

In the following pages I want you to accompany me on an intellectual journey into some very dark places, where we, as observers, look into the tactics, strategies, and decisions that create, maintain, or overturn the social constructs, the hierarchies to which we are all subject. Proceeding from the work of some truly brilliant minds, I believe we can discover some truths about the nature of these hierarchies, how they work or become dysfunctional, and why they succeed or fail. Perhaps more importantly, though, I believe we can also uncover why we are placed within these hierarchies as we are, and how that can be changed.

Understand, though, that this is a massive undertaking. If it were possible to bring forward a sufficiently advanced analysis that could be mathematically reduced to a formulaic set of tactics, it would allow us to further our placement within a given hierarchy, and we would all be rich, powerful, respected, or saintly, depending on the goals of the individual and social structure involved. I spent considerable time in my second book[1] overturning the notion that the future may be quantified, even in comparatively mild or overly broad ways, and this book does not contradict the previous analysis. A quick note before we get underway: in the ensuing pages, I use some fictional settings – stories – to help illustrate the notions I'm furthering. These stories aren't intended to serve as premises that support my conclusions. That tactic, employed by authors such as B. F. Skinner (*Walden Two*) and Eliyahu Goldratt (*Critical Chain*) strikes me as disingenuous. Those novels set up situations where their theories are employed in specific circumstances, and – wouldn't you just know it? – result in success for their protagonists, and that's not what I'm doing. The fictional settings I put forth help illustrate how interactions among those characters in perfectly ordinary situations can be more fully explained using the hierarchical structures I believe are prevalent in these and many analogous circumstances. All characters appearing in this work are fictitious. Any resemblance to real persons, living or dead, is purely coincidental.

In grabbing the untouchable, seeing the invisible, analyzing the unknowable, we can return from our journey of discovery, having accomplished the truly remarkable: knowing ourselves, and where we ought to truly stand with respect to the others we meet, and the universe at large. The implications of what we learn will influence our very destinies.

Note

1 Hatfield, Michael, *Game Theory in Management*. Farnham: Gower Publishing, 2012.

Chapter 1

Everybody Wants to Rule the World

Every man is said to have his peculiar ambition. Whether it be true or not, I can say for one that I have no other so great as that of being truly esteemed of my fellow men, by rendering myself worthy of their esteem.

Abraham Lincoln

Virtually all social interactions are hierarchical in nature, almost all of them unavoidably so. Did you go to a coffee shop today, and purchase a beverage? Odds are you stood in a line, which is essentially an ordering of who will be served and in what sequence, usually based on your time of arrival. Don't believe that the coffee queue is a hierarchy? Check the reaction of those in line if you were to attempt to stride to the front, and demand service out of sequence.

Like most hierarchies, the coffee queue's rules are not confined to the way they are nominally presented. Typically, in coffee shops located in Hollywood, California, a celebrity or movie star can expect to receive immediate service, regardless of the length of the line in front of them, and, for the most part, the people already in line are okay with this. Why should that be so? Are those who are particularly adept at pretending to be people they aren't more virtuous than others? Based on the typical life stories of famous actors and performers, the answer would have to be a resounding "no," unless you count multiple marriages, tattoos, extremely likely (if not verifiably known) use of illegal recreational drugs, and a willingness to appear on-camera without clothing as indicators of having led a virtuous life.

Then why are they treated the way they are?

The answer to that question is similar to the story of the discovery of the planet Neptune. William Hershel had discovered Uranus in 1781, and by 1846 it had almost completed one full orbit since the discovery.[1] However, Uranus was observed to have moved in a manner that could not be explained by Newtonian gravitational theory unless there was another gravity source in a more distant orbit acting on it. Urban Le Verrier predicted the location of where such a Uranus orbit-perturbing body would be, and on the night of September 23–4 of 1846, Neptune's existence was visually confirmed.[2] At the time the discovery was considered significant in the extreme, not only because astronomers were now aware of an additional planet in the Solar System, but because the discovery had essentially been made mathematically, with direct observation providing the confirmation.

This event also has a profound influence in our little investigative journey, in the mapping of the structures and other elements making up social constructs. When a hierarchy as simple and intuitive as first come first served is upended in the coffee house, and no one seems to mind, there is only one reasonable explanation: there's something else going on here, outside the stated parameters that had been expected. Some of those things might include:

- It might be "Wear Purple Day" at the coffee shop, and the line-cutting celebrity was the only one so clad.
- There are precise exceptions to the first-come-first-served rule, that you may be unaware of, but the celebrity was familiar with, and exploited.
- The celebrity may be blackmailing everybody in the line in front of you, effectively stymieing any objection they may have to being preempted in their coffee purchase.
- Or, there may be an alternate set of rules in play, rules that have not been openly articulated, but everyone (or, at least, the people in the queue) understands and accepts.

It's this last explanation that is most reasonable and, indeed, one that I think goes a long way towards offering an explanation for those social interaction events that, on their face, don't make a lot of sense. There simply must be other forces or structures in play and, while not having been articulated or otherwise made known, are universally acknowledged and followed.

So how, exactly, did all of these unstated structures and rules become so prevalent so as to impact almost every aspect of our lives?

To find this out, we will have to engage in a series of mental exercises involving what would otherwise be considered extreme circumstances. Let's start with the basics: the fundamentals of social constructs.

Consider two men confined to a common, natural environment. In order to survive, they can either cooperate with each other, or compete for available assets. Unless the men are identical twins, they will tend to have a significantly varied set of survival skills, meaning that their odds of survival greatly increase if they choose to cooperate and take advantage of the macro skill set. For the sake of clarity, let's borrow Daniel Defoe's characters Robinson Crusoe and the native he saves, Friday.

The moment Crusoe and Friday mutually decide to cooperate, they have entered into a social construct, or hierarchy. Because their survival skills are varied, some form of a division of labor that entails job assignment to the best performer is clearly indicated, if for no other reason than to conserve precious time and energy. If the Island of Despair (the name Crusoe gives to the island where he's shipwrecked) had been rich in natural resources and wild-growing/roaming foodstuffs, with a guarantee of non-intrusion by potential belligerents, then cooperation among the men would not necessarily have a bearing on their chances for long-term survival, if just living out their lives on the island was the plan. However, if *any* of those conditions were to change, or be recognized as non-workable from the beginning, then cooperation is clearly indicated.

So, Crusoe and Friday are cooperating. On what basis, exactly? Who gets to decide the division of labor? In the book the implication was that Crusoe should naturally be the leader of the two-man team, since he was educated gentry. But if we cast aside all such cultural elitism, Crusoe might have been the logical leader anyway: he had already been shipwrecked prior to being cast away on the Island of Despair, and had lived there on his own for some time prior to saving Friday from being eaten by cannibals. From those elements alone it would appear likely that the fictional Crusoe had the edge in demonstrating the skills needed to stay alive in a hostile environment.

Note that, even with cultural jingoism being eliminated from consideration, a hierarchy is already present, even if the basis for it has not been articulated, and even if it involves only two people. Also consider that, with the factors for the logical ordering of the hierarchy being known, if Crusoe, in a fit of compassion for historically oppressed natives in general, ignores the facts on the ground and insists that Friday take the lead in team decisions, then he is reducing the odds of his survival. If Crusoe is smart, he will ignore any factor in the determination of who should be higher in the hierarchy that is not directly related to survival. In this (granted, extreme) instance, Crusoe's desire to rule his world – or, more precisely, be responsible for the final decisions on the Island of Despair – is completely legitimate and valid. From a practical point of view, it makes absolutely no difference to Friday if Crusoe is an overly egotistical tyrant wannabe who would be inclined to attempt to rule over any environment or group he found himself, or if he was so humble that taking the mantle of leadership was the cause of grave internal misgivings. Crusoe's being higher in the social construct between them increases both of their chances for survival, and mutual survival is an attractive goal.

From Crusoe's point of view, then, as long as he is recognized as the most capable of delivering his and Friday's mutual objective in his role as leader, his hierarchical relationship with Friday is beneficial. It does, however, require Friday's acknowledgment, for if Friday becomes convinced that their standings should be reversed, and Friday should begin making the final decisions for the team, then their odds of survival have diminished, and their mutual goal has been pushed further away, if not rendered unattainable.

Why would Friday become convinced that a reversal of their standings was appropriate? Perhaps he had previously witnessed white Europeans make fatal errors in crucial survival situations, and believes Crusoe is similarly flawed. Maybe Friday, being a native to the area, perceives that his familiarity with the environment should be the determining factor in selecting the team's leader. Or, perhaps the reason is because Friday refuses to accept that having to be rescued from a gruesome death by a shipwrecked person who has, nevertheless, managed rather well in the exact circumstances where Friday finds himself is not ipso facto evidence that Crusoe is the better leader. Then there's the possibility that Friday is an overly egotistical tyrant wannabe who would be inclined to attempt to rule over any environment or group he found himself.

Whatever the motivations, it remains in our little stretched-to-the-limit analogy that efforts to cooperate within the hierarchy that includes Crusoe as the leader and Friday as the follower increase both castaways' chances of realizing their objective, whereas any attempt to undermine or overthrow that hierarchy, or even do away with it altogether, lessens those chances. Remember, both men have to cooperate in order for the hierarchy to remain in place. Should Friday become convinced that Crusoe is an overly egotistical tyrant wannabe who would be inclined to attempt to rule over any environment or group he found himself, and finds that prohibitively irksome, he could simply walk away, and attempt to realize his survival objectives on his own.

Once this hierarchy is established, and the team has begun to expend efforts to attain its goals, note that, should Crusoe become aware that Friday was contemplating either overthrow or exit, Crusoe would realize that the possibility that events will unfold in such a way as to threaten his survival has increased. In most humans, this recognition of a threat to survival would induce feelings of anxiety, fear, anger, or jealousy. Friday has not, in this branch of the analogy, actually done anything to overturn the rankings, nor prepare for disengagement. The mere awareness on the part of Crusoe that those events may unfold has introduced a level of conflict within their organization.

So, based on this analysis of the two-person social construct, a couple of assertions become plain, and will serve as a basis for much of the content going forward.

- First, a working definition of the word "politics" as it is used in the extra-governmental sense. This working definition is: *politics* refers to that set of behaviors undertaken by individuals within a social construct that benefits them personally, but is either neutral or even harmful to the pursuit of the goals of the organization to which they supposedly belong and support.
- Next, I believe that political acts so defined have two primary causes:
  1. The individual perceives, rightly or wrongly, that their placement within the organizational hierarchy is too low.
  2. Even in the absence of any relevant political activity amongst its members, organizations are vulnerable to the introduction of needless conflict due to lapses in communication, or other forms of misunderstanding.

Now, for a Larger Environment

While we've been focused on the dynamics of a two-person social construct, the implications for much larger organizations are apparent. Be it the two-person team, the group, the unit, a division, society, culture, nation, or globe, any coordinated interaction of humans will naturally tend towards a hierarchy, if its goals are to be pursued, effectively or otherwise.

Of course, as we begin to evaluate the larger networks, a myriad of other factors come into play. And yet one constant remains: as long as the predominate arbiter of assigned leadership is based on merit, the chances of the organization to realize its stated goals is maximized. In all instances where the meritocracy is abandoned, the chances that the macro organization will realize its stated goals are diminished.

And yet, even that distinction can be impossibly difficult to quantify, or define. In our previous analogy, let's say that the Island of Despair were to be hit with a hurricane. Fortunately, Crusoe's construction capabilities in upgrading caves to accommodate humans, combined with Friday's ability to convert coconut husks into water flasks, keeps them safe both during the storm and in the immediate aftermath. Which among them is more responsible for their survival? And, even if the answer to that question can be determined, by what precise measurement? Was Friday 54.3% responsible, while Crusoe was 45.7%? Does the Almighty enter into the equation, since, had the hurricane hit the island directly instead of tangentially, virtually the entire ecosystem would have been wiped out? And, if the Almighty enters into the equation at all, doesn't that mean that it is, by definition, unquantifiable?

So, it's impossible to know the precise measure of the organization's participants' comparative value. However, this value must be, somehow, grasped and used, no matter how imprecise; otherwise, there would be no rational basis for the establishment of the hierarchy, nor its members' placement within. This being the case, it's easy to see why, in larger organizations, people who have been involved in the macro organization's success will look at the way the past has unfolded, and come to the illogical conclusion that their role was larger than it actually was, which, in turn, serves as a faux indicator that they should assume the leadership mantle, and rightfully so.

Recall the angst our version of Crusoe would have felt had he become aware of Friday's contemplation of revolt or disengagement. Recall, also, that it would have made no difference if Crusoe had come by his role as leader legitimately, or through invalid means: the leadership mantle was his, and any deviation or challenge to that represented a reduction in the odds of his survival. Perhaps our larger, macro organization's goal is not for the day-to-day survival of its members. Maybe it's just to turn a profit, and keep the company viable in a free-market economy. By extension, though, this is a form of fighting for survival, even if it does not involve eating only hand to mouth, or evading belligerent cannibals. Losing a job can have severe career implications, and one's career is strongly associated with the ability to survive. Can there really be any mystery, then, why the members of the macro organization appear to be involved in a never-ending quest to attain higher and higher levels of leadership, and responsibility? Toss aside the associated perks of higher pay, nicer offices, etcetera; failure to assume one's appropriate role in the pursuit of the social construct's goals is not that dissimilar to life and death, and will often be approached that way.

To illustrate these tendencies, let's return to our Hollywood coffee shop, except this time we will examine the goings-on on the other side of the counter. The owner, Steve, has three employees:

- Doug is taking classes in business in his spare time, and is rather accomplished at ensuring that all of the shop's supplies are readily available when needed, while simultaneously keeping inventories remarkably low. This expertise saves the shop money, by minimizing both operating costs and tax liability.
- Dave is a master barista, also being a college student, and a chemistry major. Because of his expertise, the shop's coffee drinks are easily as good as the competition's, if not noticeably better.
- Lisa is not a college student yet, and hopes to be able to save enough to attend in the future. She's pretty, has a bright smile, and the regular customers really like her.

Unfortunately, the local economy has taken a downturn (you can only release so many movies like *Bruno* or *Brick Mansions* before the suffering becomes widespread in Movietown) and Steve is barely making payroll. He simply must let one of his employees go, but can't decide which one. In fact, Steve can't even devise a standard that would allow him to reach something approaching an objective, even-handed decision. With these problems before him, Steve decides to consult his accountant, Norbert.

"As you can see, Norbert," Steve begins, "I won't be able to make payroll next month unless something dramatically changes in the local economy. I'm thinking I'll need to let one of my employees go."

"Yeah, I see that," Norbert responds. "Who did you have in mind?"

"It's *whom*, and I haven't figured that out yet. That's why I called this meeting. Do you have an opinion?"

"In fact, I do. I think you should release Dave."

"But Dave is the best barista around – due to his expertise, my customers tell me that the shop's coffee and tea are the best in town."

"Well," Norbert continues, taking off his round, wire-framed eyeglasses, "if you're that high on Dave, then you should release Lisa."

"Lisa's personal charm is good for more than a few chance customers becoming regulars."

"You shouldn't release Doug," Norbert admonishes, "since he single-handedly saved you $750 on your last tax bill, by keeping the inventory so low without impacting operations."

"Norbert, Doug makes that much money every week. I appreciate his expertise, but I'm not convinced that $750 in yearly savings should be the determining factor."

"That's $750 more than either Lisa or Dave have saved you!" Norbert responds. Steve sighs, and stares out the window.

"Look," Norbert continues, "why are you in business in the first place?"

"I had a job as a barista when I was going through school, and I thought I saw some ways that shop could have done business better."

"Wrong!" Norbert storms. "You are in business to make a profit, and your decisions must be based on the analyses that provide the most objective, quantifiable data available. Doug saved you money on your taxes, and neither Dave nor Lisa can point to a similar impact on the profit-and-loss statement."

"That's because neither Dave's nor Lisa's contribution to the enterprise can be quantified empirically."

"Exactly."

"Exactly."

While our little exercise has reduced the evaluation criteria, in reality there are myriad data elements involved, including:

- how timely each employee is in reporting to work,
- how often they work their full shift, without getting sick or needing to attend to outside business during shop hours,
- how well they interact with each other, and with Steve,
- personal hygiene,
- work ethic,
- political views,
- what others within Steve's social network may say or know about them,
- how long they've worked at the shop,
- religious views,

- ... all the way down to things like how effective they are in disposing of sprung mouse traps, with hundreds (if not thousands) of criterion in-between.

Of course, Steve may only have first-hand knowledge of how, say, Dave deals with sprung mouse traps, rendering that particular data point somewhat unfair to even bring into the deliberations, since there's no basis of comparison to Lisa and Doug, unless Dave's response was to run shrieking from the shop upon observing the sprung mouse trap, and Steve could then reasonably deduce that the other employees would have handled the situation better.

Since all of the parameters involved in the decision can't be named, much less quantified, Steve's ultimate decision will have to involve his intuition, or gut feel. Should Steve's intuition lead him to select Doug as the person who should be terminated, Norbert would, no doubt, believe that real business sense had been trumped by politics, based on the colloquial definition of the term. Doug would almost assuredly come to the same conclusion, as he wasn't even aware of the extent of the efforts to quantify decision, as inadequate as those efforts were.

It's also worthy of note that any assumption by the non-Steve employees of the coffee shop that Steve had abandoned true business sense and made the decision to release Doug based on "politics" automatically carries with it the assumption that Steve is willing to compromise on the articulated goal or mission of the coffee shop. For, if by basing the decision on who to release was based on *anything* other than the most logically apparent strategies to realize the organization's goals, then it follows that something else is in play in the decision-making process. Like the perturbed orbit of Uranus pointing to the existence of a Neptune, the selection and implementation of a decision that impacts the organization or social construct that does not appear to be consistent with the most logical apparent one serves as an indication that either (a) the articulated goal is being compromised, or (b) there's another goal being pursued, but has not been made clear to the employees. These last two manifestations of the innate human tendency to attribute decisions within a social construct to non-reasonable motives can lead to a highly toxic development within the group, the emergence of treachery.

To examine this more closely, let's return to the Island of Despair. When Crusoe and Friday enter into the social construct under the ostensive terms of maximizing their odds of survival, they have, presumably, communicated that basis for their partnership. But, since Crusoe actually taught Friday how to speak in English, let's say that this communication is less than nuanced, and Friday enters into the agreement for the purposes of survival, but, beyond that, has no interest in advancing their mutual standard of living. It becomes, then, very possible for Crusoe to misunderstand, say, an incident where Friday was unwilling to help with crop-growing chores as a sign that Friday was beginning to renege on their mutual agreement when, in fact, Friday merely perceived that the two of them had more foodstuffs than could be consumed before they spoiled, and saw no reason to cultivate more. With (another) failure of communication introducing conflict into the relationship, Crusoe may be tempted to say or do something that would indicate his disappointment or distrust of Friday's motives. This, in turn, may lead Friday to come to the conclusion that Crusoe is seeking a higher standard of living rather than enhanced odds of basic survival, which would then lead Friday to believe that it was, in fact,

Crusoe as the member of the social construct engaged in the act of reneging of their agreement.

I contend that this happens all the time, across most (if not all) organizations. From the published mission statements of corporate giants to the unspoken goals of mutual support undertaken by a woman's bridge club, indications that the group's understood objectives have been compromised, or aren't really being pursued by certain members who are, instead, advancing their own personal agendas at the expense or under the guise of the social construct can easily lead to a cascading event, rendering whole organizations less effective, or even ruined. So, the takeaway from our little diversion back to the Island of Despair is that any perceived deviation from the pursuit of the generally acknowledged goals of the social construct will damage the integrity of the social construct, and potentially engender significant communication breakdowns.

Meanwhile, back at the Hollywood-based coffee shop, Dave, Lisa, and Doug are all vaguely aware that business is down, and some dramatic change is in the offing. However, each of them believes that they are not the logical layoff candidate, since they are superior baristas, possess charming smiles, or have saved the shop $750 in taxes, respectively. Indeed, each of them has expended considerable energy to avoid being seen as the most expendable person on the staff, energy that could easily be misinterpreted by the others as blind ambition. While each of the three may indeed be ambitious, none of them wants to be working in coffee shops the rest of their careers. Their drive to move up in the shop's hierarchy is not based on self-aggrandizement – they just want to help shore up their current (perceived) standing so as to avoid unemployment.

My Hippocampus Made Me Want to Rule the World

The hippocampus is a part of the brain located under the cerebral cortex, in the medial temporal lobe. While its precise function is the subject of some debate, most scientists believe it is responsible for processing memories into some form of structure. It processes short-term memories into long term, and is central to the creation of new memories and indexing them in such a way that when we encounter new or novel circumstances or events, we're not completely helpless in devising strategies to deal with them.

Almost all humans have a tendency to associate events that have happened to them into some form of a structure that includes the causes of those events, particularly if they occurred in sequential order. Friday can safely assume that his rescue was brought about because of the intervention of Crusoe. However, when the explanation for cold weather lingering into springtime is based on whether or not a specific groundhog from Punxsutawney, Pennsylvania emerges from his den on February 2 of a given year, this causal link might not be as solid.

We will examine the role of the hippocampus further in Chapter 3. For now, though, it's important to evaluate its most basic role, that of preparing us for new or novel events that the future holds in store. In a sense, it's basic human nature to evaluate what has happened to us in the past, and construct narratives consistent with the memories of those events that help explain the way our worlds work, or can be expected to work. We take these narratives – filled with the flaws of our memories, our understanding of causality, confirmation (as well as other) biases – and flip them forward, across the Time Now line, to give ourselves some notion of understanding how the future will unfold. Again, more on this in Chapter 3; for now, let's go back to the coffee shop.

Doug, Dave, and Lisa attend to their shifts, with each of their hippocampi humming. They know from experience that when business is brisk, they can retain a sense of confidence that their jobs are secure. But business has not been brisk. It has, in fact, been trending downward for some time, and the three have recently witnessed Steve going behind closed doors with Norbert. While each of them is reasonably sure the shop won't go bankrupt in the near future, they are also fairly certain that *some* change is in the offing, and that that change could easily involve at least one of them losing their jobs. Since none of them is in a position to lose their job without incurring some difficulty, they find themselves encountering each other with a keener sense of competition than had been there when business was booming.

A level of conflict has now been introduced into the coffee shop, and it can't help but to alter the relationship of each member of the staff. Whether they had previously recognized it or not, they are very much engaged in a hierarchical structure, with their precise placement within that structure now becoming an issue prominent in their ability to maintain peace of mind and lead happy and successful lives. They have never been in this particular situation before – it's entirely novel to them. Yet their hippocampi have indexed their memories in such a way as to make it easy to project future scenarios where they lose their jobs, can't afford college, and are therefore, long term, prevented from participating in high-paying careers in the future. Each of them feels this threat rather acutely – it is, in fact, singularly terrifying to them that their planned futures are now in the hazard.

Remember, though, that Steve hasn't released anybody – yet. Doug, Dave, and Lisa have merely projected these future scenarios based on little more than the two facts, that business is down and Steve is meeting in private with his accountant, and their other experiences as indexed and sorted by their hippocampi. And yet, the conflict within the hierarchy is real, and it is influencing their behavior.

Takeaways from Chapter 1

I entitled this chapter "Everybody Wants to Rule the World," loosely based on the Tears for Fears song, for a reason (and it is *not* because I'm an overly egotistical tyrant wannabe who is inclined to attempt to rule over any environment or group where I find myself). I believe it's human nature to believe, in those circumstances where we find ourselves involved in an organization where some sort of pecking order manifests itself and we find that our ranking is lower than we believe it ought to be, that such hierarchies are silly and artificial in the first place, and that the others involved are clawing their way to the top due to invalid motives. I hope, however, that our little mental exercises have demonstrated the following:

- All human interactions, or social constructs, are automatically overlaid with some sort of hierarchy.
- Such a hierarchy is not only natural, but actually beneficial in the abstract.

- Those in the social construct will almost always perceive their status to be higher than it truly is, or ought to be, in order for the organization to realize its stated goals.
- The organization's stated goals are virtually never all inclusive. There are always some other factors involved in the assigning of status of personnel within the construct.
- It's natural for everyone within the organization to attempt to advance their placement within the hierarchy, and in many cases such attempts have little or nothing to do with blind ambition,
- … even though that's the motive that others within the organization are most likely to impart to everyone else, particularly those successful at such advancement.

Another aspect, which we will explore in more depth later, has to do with the automatic and natural tendency to not only advance internally, within the given social construct, but to also advance the overall group. Friday and Crusoe have a wholesome, beneficial goal of seeing their two-person team succeed ahead of their rivals, the cannibals. It also goes without saying – but I'll say it, anyway – that our Hollywood coffee shop wouldn't have to let any of its employees go if it had more market share than its competitors. In short, the drive to move ahead within a given organization, while simultaneously pouring energy into having that organization succeed in relation to its competitors, is pretty automatic. And, being as automatic as it is, this drive can be observed, and quantified.

And managed.

Notes

1 "Discovery of Neptune," retrieved from *Wikipedia*, http://en.wikipedia.org/w/index.php?title=Discovery_of_Neptune&oldid=658114522, April 26, 2015.
2 Ibid.

Chapter 2

Where We're Coming From

Men rise from one ambition to another: first, they seek to secure themselves against attack, and then they attack others.

Niccolo Machiavelli[1]

Well, where *are* we coming from? In the attempt to analyze the tactics and strategies that manifest in the realm of organizational politics, some capturing of the motives and deeply rooted causes of our pursuing those strategies and tactics simply must come first. Three semesters of university-level psychology and reading the works of author/practitioners such as Marie Louise von Franz has led me to believe that much of the practice of psychology performed in the past was simply bad philosophy, and there can be little doubt that the theories from the psychological sciences are often as subjective and unverifiable as those in the management sciences. This is not a psychological treatise – I only wish to evaluate motives as far as necessary to establish the basis for the invoking of those strategies and tactics, to allow a sufficient analysis that can shed light on which maneuverings become attractive, and why.

In 1964, Eric Berne published *Games People Play: The Psychology of Human Relationships*, and it quickly became a best-seller.[2] Dr. Berne had two assertions that I would like to build on, specifically:

- We all maintain a script, or a narrative, in our minds, that helps us understand who we are, and why things happen the way they do.
- There are three parts of the persona, the Child, the Adult, and the Parent.

Berne modeled the Child, Adult, and Parent, as in Figure 2.1. The Child is entirely inwardly focused, and its needs and desires are primal in the extreme, similar to Freud's Id. In fact, the Parent-Adult-Child is similar to the Freudian construct of Superego-Ego-Id in many ways. The Id/Child part of the persona is primarily interested in obtaining sufficient food and sex, and is very much the stranger to the rules of logic or evidence.

The Adult is that part of the persona that deals with reality and the present moment, as they present themselves. As the Child is inwardly focused, the Adult is outwardly focused, but only to the extent that it seeks to satisfy the primal needs of the child as they can be, in the real world. The Adult represents that part of us that is reasonable and pragmatic, and is the near equivalent of Freud's Ego.

The Parent aspect of the persona desires the attainment of goals – spiritual, intellectual, professional, and others. The Parent reminds us of that to which we should aspire and, as such, is something of the natural adversary of the Child. The rough Freudian equivalent of Berne's Parent is the Superego.

Dr. Berne went on to hypothesize that conflict naturally arises in interactions among people when their lines of communication are crossed. Take a situation where two people are in proximity to each other.

In Figure 2.2, two people are interacting, sharing factual data or their observations about people, events, or, really, just about anything. Berne asserted that when different aspects of people's personas communicate, conflict naturally arises. For example, let's say the person mapped on the left of Figure 2.2 is Doug, and the individual mapped on the right is Lisa (from the coffee shop). Doug asks Lisa if she thinks she will need fewer than one dozen more of those little cylinders that go into the hissing espresso machine for the after-lunch crowd, and Lisa responds that she believes that an even dozen, when combined with the ones she has on hand, should be sufficient. In that communication, their mutual Adults have interacted, and no natural conflict is engendered from the exchange.

However, Lisa, mindful of the prospects of layoffs in the near term, attempts to gain status within the coffee shop's hierarchy by taking this opportunity to belittle Doug with a response like "While working your little supply issues might make you think you are management material, a real worker would have already known the

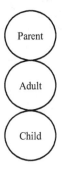

Figure 2.1 Berne Archetype Graphic, from Berne, *Games People Play*, used with permission

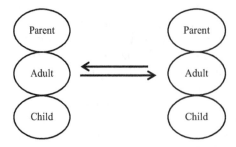

Figure 2.2 Sample Berne Archetype Interaction

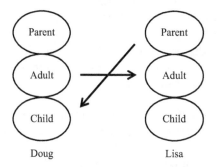

Figure 2.3 Misaligned Berne Archetype Interaction

answer to your question." Of course, Lisa's response is a non-sequitur, but it does redraw the interaction map, as in Figure 2.3.

Berne believed that much of these interactions, which he referred to as "transactions," revealed the true nature of interactional conflict. Indeed, his entire psychology was named "Transactional Analysis," and focused on the nature of the interactions more than the potential imbalances of the aspects of the personas of the participating individuals.

With the case of Doug and Lisa we see an aspect of the conflict that has been introduced in their uncertainty about their immediate futures manifest in a Bernesian cross-persona communication misalignment. While I'm sure Dr. Berne is right, and much conflict is created by such cross-personal communication misalignment, I'm also rather sure that there are many other sources of conflict, and that they are merely expressed through such malfunctioning transactions.

Meanwhile, back in the coffee shop, Doug does not take kindly to being spoken to in such a manner as Lisa has just engaged. He has several communication options open to him, including:

- Get his information without really addressing the conflict behind the bad transaction ("Can I just get a 'yes' or a 'no'?").
- Get his information while somewhat addressing the bad transaction ("Yeah, well, if you're so customer-focused, why don't you save everybody some time, and just give me a 'yes' or a 'no'?").
- Abandon the pursuit of the information altogether, and address the bad transaction directly ("Who do you think you're talking to, waitress?").

While Doug may be an insightful procurement agent, patience and understanding are not his long suits. However, just as he is about to exercise the third option – in a most dramatic fashion, of course – Steve's office door opens, and Steve and Norbert walk out.

Now the hierarchical dynamic has changed. Prior to the moment that Steve and Norbert emerged, Doug was in a position to choose his response to Lisa based on whether or not he wanted to engage in an attempt to shore up or overturn the informal hierarchy that exists among Lisa, Doug, and David. With Steve now observing the interaction, Doug really has no choice left to him but to respond in a way that's consistent with the *formal* hierarchy, as envisioned by Steve. If Doug wishes to affirm his allegiance to the stated, formal hierarchy, he will eschew any response other than the most direct, conflict-free communication that still retrieves the information originally sought. Otherwise, Steve will witness the conflict-laden response for what it is, an unnecessary injection of hostility into his business' work environment. Doug prudently selects the first option.

Some organizations will actually attempt to enforce rules of communication that seek, essentially, to eliminate instances of bad transaction analysis-type interactions. For example, colleges will often have speech codes designed to preclude the giving of "offense," as if "offense" can only be communicated through verbiage. While many companies have poorly articulated and rarely enforced rules on insubordination, most military forces have very clear standards for it, and enforce them rigorously. Depending on the organization type and structure of its hierarchy, these rules may or may not work, or may not even be advantageous to have in the first place. Colleges and universities ostensibly invite and welcome competing ideas and concepts in order to evaluate them. When they engage in labeling some ideas or concepts "offensive" or "hate speech," and seek to automatically exclude such ideas from evaluation or consideration, these efforts undermine their very raison d'être.

Meanwhile, back at the coffee shop, should any of the customers overhear the terse interaction between Doug and Lisa, they may decide that they would be better off getting their salted caramel mocha lights in an atmosphere without so much drama, and elect to buy their next cup from the coffee shop down the street. Of course, the whole reason that layoff fear has gripped Doug, Lisa, and David is because business is down: now, Lisa has acted in such a way as to further damage the coffee shop's ability to retain three employees.

Rather than directly assert that inter-organizational conflict has an impact on the team's ability to perform with respect to its competition based on just my example of the fictional Lisa's snarkyness, I believe I will appeal to the readers' common sense and personal experiences. Teams filled with members who do not trust each other, who perceive they are in competition for static (or even dwindling) resources, are not going to perform nearly as well – all else being equal – with that version of, say, the coffee shop team where Doug, Dave, and Lisa interact harmoniously. That is not to say that those teams that act with a sense of urgency won't outperform their calmer rivals; rather, if all of the other stress-causing parameters could be equalized (an impossibility, I know, but stay with me here) between two coffee shop teams, and team A's urgency stems from the internecine conflict caused by the uncertainty of their future employment, while team B's urgency is due to a sense that they must work better, harder, and more efficiently in order to gain market share during this difficult time, team B will win the vast majority of the time.

I actually worked for one chief executive officer who once said "Every employee should arrive at work every day a little bit scared." The quote was both intuitively obvious and undeniably creepy – a simultaneous acknowledgment that teams performing with a sense of urgency tend to do better than those without, and an admission that the attainment of the organization's goals are rightfully recognized as having a higher priority than the team's members' peace of mind. I will name any inclination from leadership to allow (or even inflict) a certain level of anxiousness to afflict the organization in order to illicit better performance "Executive Angst Tolerance."

Doug and Lisa clearly arrived at work that day (more than) a little bit scared. Recall the proffered definition of (non-electoral) politics from Chapter 1: *politics* refers to that set of behaviors undertaken by individuals within a social construct that benefits them personally, but is either neutral or even harmful to the pursuit of the goals of the organization to which they supposedly belong and support. So, let's see if Lisa and, to a lesser extent, Doug, have engaged in coffee shop politics.

- Are Lisa and Doug involved in a social construct? Yes – they work together in a coffee shop.
- Did Lisa's adversarial phrasing of her answer to Doug's question benefit her personally? It's hard to tell. Doug may have taken it as a put-down, and come away with a lowered sense of self-confidence that, in turn, *may* end up hurting him when Steve evaluates which employee to release, and which ones to retain. Or, it could have no impact on that evaluation whatsoever, and served to simply inject needless negativity into the workplace.
- Okay, well, did Lisa anticipate that her snark may end up benefiting her personally? Absolutely – otherwise, her perky self would have never made such a statement.
- Was Lisa's response either neutral or detrimental to the organization? Yes – a customer overheard her, and thought better of getting his salted caramel mocha light from our little coffee shop.

So, Lisa did engage in a bit of workplace maneuvering. Did Doug?

- Are Doug and Lisa involved in a social construct? Yes – they work together in a coffee shop.
- Did Doug's response to Lisa's question benefit him personally? No, not outside the execution of his nominal job duties.
- Was Doug's original question or response to Lisa detrimental to the coffee shop? No – Doug's Adult persona was engaged in each case. The customer who overheard the exchange decided on the low-drama option based entirely on Lisa's words.

Based on the definition offered in Chapter 1, Lisa has engaged in workplace politics, but Doug has not.

So, where *are* we coming from? From Chapter 1, we're all involved in hierarchical structures in almost all cases where we interact with others. When we interact with those others, is there a common motivating factor? I believe it's the desire to feel as if we're valuable and worthwhile to the others or, at the very least, ought not to be made to feel lesser in any given transaction. The acid test here is, in those situations where we have voluntarily interacted with others, but came away feeling worse about ourselves for reasons we view to be unfair, are we more or less likely to re-engage those people, under similar circumstances? Conversely, when we participate in groups that leave us feeling better about ourselves, are we not more likely to continue such participation?

I freely admit that "feeling better about ourselves," while intuitively true, is also hopelessly vague as a usable data point in assessing motives going forward. In the next chapters we'll take a closer look at *why* these interactions leave us feeling better or worse, and the tactics that are often employed in arriving at those outcomes.

Notes

1 Machiavelli, Niccolo, retrieved from *BrainyQuote*, http://www.brainyquote.com/quotes/quotes/n/niccolomac166592.html?src=t_ambition, July 12, 2015.
2 Berne, Eric, *Games People Play: The Basic Hand Book of Transactional Analysis*. New York: Ballantine Books, 1964.

Chapter 3

Where We've Been

Vanity and pride are different things, though the words are often used synonymously. A person may be proud without being vain. Pride relates more to our opinion of ourselves; vanity, to what we would have others think of us.

Jane Austen[1]

Another implication of Eric Berne's main assertions in *Games People Play* has to do with the creation of narratives, or scripts in our minds. These scripts tell us who we are to ourselves, and place a structure or order on our interpretation of our histories. The "games" Berne refers to have to do with a pattern of behaviors that have an anticipated outcome that has a special personal significance to the game player.

Consider a high-level manager who has been brought into a general contracting company. We'll call the manager Bob, and the company the Acme Corporation, which specializes in providing novel technology devices to the United States military, and the occasional southwest U.S.-based coyote that is attempting to capture a particular roadrunner (*Geococcyx californianus*). Prior to really getting to know his staff and the details of the projects within his portfolio, Bob immediately begins to make decisions that impact the way Acme does business. Is he playing "games"? Probably.

I believe that people play these games, or manipulate people and circumstances to replicate past events, in order to support their internal narratives. For those events that historically occurred where the person succeeded, it's easy to see why they would want to recreate – however artificially or analogously – those circumstances in the here and now. They were rewarded for the decisions they made under a similar situation, and seek to be so rewarded again. The constant here is their decision-making ability; therefore, the variables need to be aligned with those that brought success, in order for a successful outcome to be realized once again.

Alternately, they could simply be trying to relive past successes.

Then there are those times when the situation that's being re-created involved a failure. Let's say that Bob was hired off the street, having been laid off by a near competitor when their high-tech project lost its government funding, and Bob was among the dozens so released. This failure still weighs heavily on Bob's mind, and he is determined, should he ever have a similar management position, to take the steps to ensure it never happens again. Now, he finds himself with a new company, and in a position of some authority. He also has a clear vision of what he did wrong previously, and regrets not having made a very different decision than the one he made that (he believes) landed him in the unemployment line in the first place. Should he be placed in an entirely novel or new environment, his experience would count for little. He simply must re-create the circumstances that led to his previous failure, except, *this time*, he knows the "correct" decision, and can expect success to come his way for having made the correction.

Keep in mind that, in either circumstance, the decisions waiting to be made are highly formulaic. The game being played here involves aligning the people and circumstances in such a way that the decision waiting to be implemented has the desired impact. Of course, this turns the nominal approach most people have to solving problems on its head. Instead of taking in the facts and attempting to quantify the issues swirling around a problem to be solved, and employing logic (or, at least, some semblance of reason) to arrive at a solution, the game players already have their so-called solution in mind. It only remains to re-create the circumstances familiar to them, or at least interpret the situation presented in a way that's analogous to their familiar circumstances, so that they can impose their canned strategy.

It is this very practice of game playing that presents a key parameter to the person attempting to get a handle on the hierarchies that they encounter, and learning to get ahead within those structures. Assuming that the social structure under consideration has, as (at least) one of its purposes, the solving of problems, there are going to be two types of participants, evidenced by their approach to problem solving:

- The genuine participant will use the traditional method of problem solving. They will take in as much information about a given problem as they can, or deem relevant, process that data into usable information via some methodology (typically, logic, but other methods belong to other problems; we'll examine later), and make decisions based on that information.
- The game player has already arrived at their decision(s). These so-called insights (pre-selected canned strategies, really) invariably reinforce the game player's view of himself, however inflated. The only problem to such a one is in the ordering of the data points from the existing situation so as to create a script that can be plausibly used to not only justify the already ordained decision, but to make it look positively insightful.

In the former category, experience – where we've been – is an asset. Those genuinely seeking to advance the organization's goals are better situated when they have witnessed many analogous events, and are knowledgeable in those strategies that have a reasonable chance of success, and those strategies that are known to fail.

Conversely, the experience of the game player is actually a detriment to the group's ability to realize its goals. These people are not out to solve a problem, but to reinforce a rehearsed personal narrative. The cliché "if you're not part of the solution, you're part of the problem" is a colloquial way of capturing this divide. The tactic of carrying forward a canned strategy "solution" and attempting to employ it in situations that may not be highly analogous to the previous problem it solved I will entitle "Forcing History."

This is the situation where Bob, the new Acme manager, finds himself. Still smarting from his layoff experience, he perceives his new environment to be strongly analogous to his previous managerial experience – except, this time, he *knows* the "right" decisions. Confirmation bias – the tendency for people to accept and remember experiences or data that reinforce their ideas, theories, or (most importantly) internal narratives, and disregard experiences and data that tend to overturn them – kicks in. His new staff members, the ones attempting to get him to temper or reconsider his reflexive decisions, are not performing their jobs, in his book. Bob sees them as recalcitrant, defiant employees, who need to be put in their places if his agenda is to be successfully implemented.

None of the staff members that Bob has inherited has done anything to indicate that they are recalcitrant or defiant. On the contrary, Bob, being, at least on the surface, a likeable enough fellow, has earned their initial-opportunity goodwill. But since Bob has brought with him his canned strategies, ones that will help him realign his narrative away from the version that paints him as a loser, this initial goodwill is being squandered, as the staff realizes that Bob is not approaching the problems he faces as he should.

To analyze this phenomenon further, let's explore a couple of usable structures. Recall Berne's/Freud's nominal structure of the persona (Figure 3.1).

From Chapter 1, we've established that hierarchies are naturally and automatically present in virtually all human interactions. In Chapter 2 we explored those instances where, once such a structure is present, there is a tendency for people to seek a higher placement within that structure. Still working within the confines of the individual persona, the combination of these two ideas leads to the natural conclusion that each of us has some sort of handle on where we stand within a given social construct with respect to its other members. In other words, we think we know where we belong. Imagine a sort of ruler, stacked next to the Bernesian/Freudian map of the persona, as in Figure 3.2.

For any given social construct in which we are engaged, each of us has at least a vague sense of what our score, or ranking within that construct, is, or should be. Since every human tends to be in a host of social constructs, these rankings can become complex (Figure 3.3). According to this map, Bob thinks of himself as a pretty good husband, which has the Parent part of his persona (somewhat) satisfied. At the other end of his graded spectrum, he recognizes that he's not that great an athlete, even though he belongs to an organization (his local gymnasium) that

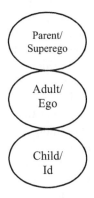

Figure 3.1 Berne/Freud Archetype Graphic

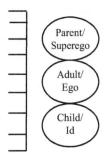

Figure 3.2 Graded Bernesian/Freudian Archetype

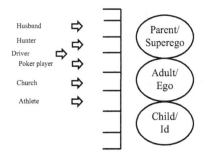

Figure 3.3 Ranking Ourselves

includes other members who are also pursuing a higher state of physical fitness. Bob bases his assessment of his quality as a spouse on his perceptions of the nature of his communications with his wife, compared with those occasions where he interacts with other couples and sees how they interrelate. He makes more money than Roger, spends more time with his children than Oscar, and knows for a fact that Pete is having an affair. Based on these comparisons, Bob is confident that he's an excellent husband, indeed.

On the other hand, at the gym Bob is constantly having to undo the bar clamps on the bench press bar in order to remove weights, reminding him that the person who went before him lifted significantly more than Bob intends to lift. There's also those confounded mirrors at the gym, serving as a persistent reminder that Bob could use a little more time pumping iron. But, since Bob is not a professional athlete and is, instead, a senior manager for Acme Corporation, being a sub-par athlete isn't that big a deal to him. It's far more important to his sense of well-being that he is (or at least believes himself to be) a superior husband, hunter, driver, and poker player than athlete that he's comfortable dividing his time and energies into those pursuits.

I drew the arrows in Figure 3.3 as hollow for a reason. These represent how Bob *perceives* himself to be ranked among the others in the constructs of his social circle of married couples, his hunting buddies, an automobile operator in traffic, among his poker-playing friends, other church-goers, and other members of his gym. These perceptions of how he is doing with respect to the other members of those hierarchies are extremely important to Bob. Should he recognize that being in better physical shape is more important to his quality of life than the ability to play poker, Bob will expend more energy at the gym, and less hosting poker parties for his friends. Ah, but here's the rub:

Bob's perceptions of his relative ranking are always inflated and, therefore, wrong.

This effect is commonly known as the Dunning-Kruger Effect, and represents a cognitive bias that results in illusory superiority.[2] Take his perception of his status as an excellent husband. While Bob outearns Roger, Roger is actually more attentive to his wife. Oscar doesn't spend as much time with his kids, but Oscar's kids are a little older, and perfectly okay with that. Pete is having an affair, yes, but he also donated a kidney to his wife's brother, saving his brother-in-law's life, even after learning that his wife had been unfaithful to him. Bob does not know any of these facts that would otherwise overturn or at least challenge his view of himself, nor, truth be told, does he want to know. He's perfectly happy believing that the placement of his hollow arrows on the personal gradient is quite justifiably above the median. To anyone other than the truly humble, this kind of disconnect is pervasive. The very idea that our real comparative value is lower than what we believe it to be is repulsive. For most, a mild delta between our perceived relative value in any grouping or social construct and our actual, verifiable value is ubiquitous, and does not rise to the level of life-disturbing pathology.

It's what keeps us sane.

What happens when Bob's scoring of himself comes up against harsh reality? It's the reason the word "harsh" seems to be so natural in front of the word "reality." The amount of confirmation bias, Childish/Id conceit, and selective memory access that goes into the construction of our narratives, and thence onto our self-scoring, is such that we can become absolutely delusional when it comes to the difference between our view of ourselves and our true, external value to the organizations to which we belong.

Almost nobody outside of genuine saints have an accurate view of themselves. When the delta between self-scoring and true value is mild, we tend to tolerate that in others. When it is blatant and profound, we go ahead and place the "delusional" label on the subject, though, in reality, we are all at least a little bit delusional. And that's okay – for the most part, these delusions are harmless. I enjoy believing that I'm the most attractive man my wife could have reasonably expected to marry, though the truth is probably very different. Such disconnects with reality allow us to function. I'm reminded of a quote, paraphrasing, that man teeters on the brink of disaster with every step he takes. I don't know who originally said it (neither does Google), but it does point to the idea that we are far, far more vulnerable than we like to allow ourselves to believe. The ability to make this disconnect helps shape the sense of proportion that, say, allows us to devote the necessary thought capacity to remembering to observe our wedding anniversaries, rather than be consumed with fears of being attacked by rocket pack-equipped coyotes.

But that disconnect also leads us to adopt pathologies of thought and belief that can blind us to the realities of the way our social constructs work, with harsh manifestations of those realities waiting to strike us when we least expect. Going back to Bob, let's add up his overall self-assessment score. On a scale of 1–9:

- he gives himself a 7.5 as a parent,
- 6.5 as a hunter,
- 6 as a driver,
- 5.5 as a poker player,
- 4.5 as a church-goer,
- and 3.5 as an athlete.

... which yields an average of 5.83. Of course, in reality Bob would have hundreds (if not thousands) of such scales, but we'll stick with the six articulated here.

Now, what would happen if harsh reality were to suddenly intrude into Bob's psyche, forcing him to confront the possibility that his self-ranking was improperly inflated? The updated map is shown in Figure 3.4.

Bob believes his overall ranking is around 5.8 (though, obviously, no such precise quantification would have taken place – he's just comfortable that he's sufficiently superior to the others in his various social constructs that he need not undertake extraordinary measures to improve himself) even though an objective assessment of his relative value would place him closer to 3.5, far lower than the score he has awarded himself and lower, even, than the median. Say Bob's wife, Jane, were to confront him with her perception that Bob was a rather poor spouse, compared to her expectations of him. Bob had given himself a 7.5 in the husband ranking, but now he is confronted with the inescapable assertion that he's actually sub-standard. Bob's response is to employ one or more ego-defense mechanisms, which include:

- denial
- displacement
- intellectualization
- projection
- rationalization
- reactive formation
- regression
- repression
- sublimation
- suppression.[3]

Figure 3.4 Self-Rank vs. True Rank

Jane, however, is relentless. She has a legitimate grievance against Bob, and actively interferes with his attempts to employ any of these mechanisms.

Next, Bob will attempt to escape an evaluation that would result in a lower overall internal score by placing increased emphasis on the relative significance of his other scores. Our assessment rather crudely took the average of his necessarily restricted set of gradients. If Bob's "husband" score of 7.5 is lowered to 3.25, then all that needs to happen in order for his overall score to remain at 5.8-something is for the importance of being a good husband to be reduced by 50%, and a couple of the other scores' emphasis to be relationally upgraded.

In this particular instance, however, these escapes have been denied Bob. Jane won't allow him to invoke an ego-defense mechanism, and being a good husband has long been integral to his self-esteem. What happens next is, only a little metaphorically, torture.

The realigning of the perceived ranking with its more objective – and almost invariably lower – counterpart is excruciatingly painful. Presented graphically, with the solid arrow depicting Bob's truly appropriate relative ranking and the hollow arrow indicating his perceived ranking, it is shown in Figure 3.5.

The pain that this realignment brings is difficult to overstate. Avoidance of this pain is the very reason that "ego defense mechanisms" exist in the first place. I'm convinced it's the proximate cause of more than a few suicides.

According to the Megan Meier Foundation, "(C)yberbullying was *strongly* related suicidal ideation in comparison with traditional bullying" (emphasis in the original).[4]

Now think about that: what, exactly, is it in cyberspace that could possibly induce a person to think about, let alone actually accomplish, killing themselves? Clearly it's confined to the realm of interpersonal communications – my bet is that these kids weren't suddenly motivated to pay an impromptu visit to the grim reaper after having read Kant, and realizing that existence was suddenly not worth tolerating. Certainly at least one other within their selected social construct had found a way to dramatically and inescapably drop the target's inner self-worth indicator to a level they could not forbear, and the pain was such that they sought a truly desperate solution.

I believe that the pain of having this internal score lowered due to external forces is so extreme that people will go to extraordinary lengths to avoid it. It is these extraordinary lengths, these outrageous strategies employed, that add an extreme dynamic to the way that organizations and social constructs are set up and function.

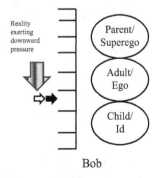

Bob

Figure 3.5 Forced Realignment of the Perceived and Actual Hierarchical Placements

Meanwhile, back at the Acme Corporation, Bob is returning to work, still smarting from the forced realignment of his inflated scoring of his self-worth handed to him by his wife, Jane, only to be confronted with another inflated score. When Acme's executives were going through the candidates for the job that would eventually go to Bob, they were very impressed with the level of education and talent possessed by the résumés that made the short list of those to be interviewed. They really had no idea whom among the candidates were being evaluated by other firms, potentially even Acme's direct competitors, but were anxious that they not overpay for the level of expertise they were hiring. In short, the hiring committee was hoping for a person whose assessment of himself on an economic scale was actually lower than their true value, so that Acme would be hiring a valuable contributor for the minimum amount of money needed to get him in the door. To that end, a significant part of the hiring process involved each of the candidates being presented with an overview of the company, featuring Acme's accomplishments, famous customers, shiny facilities, and happy employees. The sought-after effect was to impress upon potential hires that (a) the current employees were top-notch, leading to (b) the impression that any interviewee who might have had an inflated impression of their economic contribution score should consider lowering that score, so that (c) should an offer be made, and it was below the salary/compensation level the potential hire was expecting, the candidate would be disinclined to reject the offer out of hand.

The hiring committee accomplished all of this when they hired Bob. Bob had been unemployed at the time Acme hired him, and was prepared to accept offers even lower than Acme's, should it come to that. Bob was indeed impressed by Acme's accomplishments, famous customers, shiny facilities, and happy employees so that when Acme made him an acceptable offer, Bob's self-scoring arrow on his economic engine scale moved up. Bob's new managers didn't mind this self-worth inflation, even if they had noticed it. It meant fairly little to them in their day-to-day operations.

However, it meant a great deal to Bob's new team, the people at Acme who worked for him. Convinced that he had been hired because he had all the answers to the company's problems, and carrying with him the urge to correct the decisions that led to his earlier release, Bob saw little reason to take in the information he needed to fully understand the issues confronting Acme. Instead, he sought out circumstances and situations that were most analogous to the script (as he remembers it) that led to his previous failure, right up to the point that he made his erroneous decision. In this case, Bob's previous employer, Monolithic Corporation, had assigned him as a product manager for a line of gonculators due at a distributer by a date certain. As the due date approached, it appeared Bob's team would meet the deadline easily, when a key stamping machine on the assembly line malfunctioned. Only a few members of the product team even worked with or around this particular stamping machine, much less understood its function, so Bob arranged for them to either pick up ad-hoc work from the other product lines or else take leave for as long as it took to get the stamping machine repaired.

The stamping machine was finally repaired, and the product team reassembled, but by then it was too late. Despite heroic efforts on the part of the team, including excessive overtime, the deadline was missed, and a competitor's product made it to market sooner, eventually dominating said market. Even though Bob made what he felt were the best decisions at the time, in retrospect he regretted not taking more extraordinary measures to regain the production schedule.

This was the nature of the experiences Bob had had immediately prior to getting hired at Acme. So, when he met his product team for the first time, after the usual making of acquaintances, Bob asked to see the cost and schedule performance report on the existing product run. Speaking with Kim, Alan, and Larry (his team leads) while going over the cost and schedule reports, Bob began.

"This report is dated last week. Do we have anything more current?"

"No," replied Kim, "that particular report is issued every Wednesday, for every product line at this facility. You'll receive an updated one tomorrow."

"Then I'll have to work off of this one. It shows a schedule performance index of 0.93. Does anyone know the cause of that?"

"I do," offered Larry. "Some of the aluminum blanks were late in arriving, and a couple of my team members were out with the flu that was going around these parts last week. They're back now, so we should be good to go."

"Are everybody's teams available for overtime, say, this weekend?"

Larry, Kim, and Alan all look at Bob with expressions of surprise.

"We're only seven points back, Bob. That could be made up in an afternoon."

"The cost performance index is up by eight points – we have the resources to recover the schedule without changing anybody's hours," Larry adds.

"Besides," Kim interjects, "that may not even be the case right now. We'll have the updated cost and schedule reports tomorrow."

"But tomorrow may be too late to secure the facility's power and security functions if we do need to work this weekend," Bob replies, somewhat frustrated that he has to explain himself to his subordinates in the first place. "Prepare your teams for possible overtime work this weekend."

As Kim, Alan, and Larry leave the conference room, they begin to discuss the meeting among themselves, once they are confident that Bob can't hear them.

"Well, thank goodness we have Bob here to tell us how to do our jobs on his very first day!" Alan states ironically.

"Be fair, Alan," Kim responds. "Our previous super had us work overtime, too."

"Yeah, but only when it was necessary," Alan replies. "Half my team is already mad for having to pick up the slack when those two missed most of last week on sick leave. When I tell them to prepare for even more extra effort, they're going to regret their votes to not unionize."

"You would think that Bob would at least check the Wednesday reports before reaching that particular decision," adds Larry. "If I tell my team to clear their weekends, and then turn around and tell them no—never mind the next day, they will also be less than happy."

"I don't mind the overtime," Kim says, "but I am concerned that Bob didn't check to see if the current production run was for a critical deliverable, or for simple inventory replenishing. Since it's the latter, if we have to spend much money on labor and facility overtime, he's going to wipe out the margin, and the line will actually end up losing money. I'm not at all confident he's even looked into that. Besides," Kim continues, "I hate his cologne."

Here we have a series of communications that indicate that a certain amount of conflict has been introduced into Bob's new production team at Acme Corporation.

Using our crypto Berne/Freud interaction and value metric model, these interactions break down this way.

Bob, as a manager, is ranked in the Acme hierarchy over his direct reports, the team leads Kim, Alan, and Larry. Bob asks for a more current performance report, Kim replies one will not be available until the next day. So far, the lines of inter-persona elements' communication are Adult/Ego to Adult/Ego (Figure 3.6).

"Then I'll have to work off of this one." A tad condescending on Bob's part – just enough to come from that area where his Superego and Ego intersect. Larry offers up the cause of the negative schedule variance from the dated report, and Bob goes straight to everybody's weekend availability (Figure 3.7).

As the team leaders attempt to educate Bob, the crossed communication paths only multiply (Figure 3.8).

As the team leaders leave the conference room, note that the organizational conflict has already been introduced. The team leaders discuss a series of factors that they anticipate will affect their work, but had not apparently been considered by Bob, including:

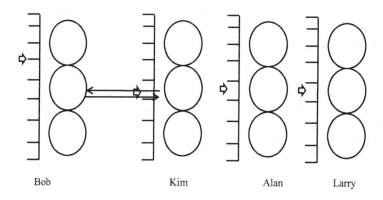

Figure 3.6 Mapping Bob's Interaction with Kim

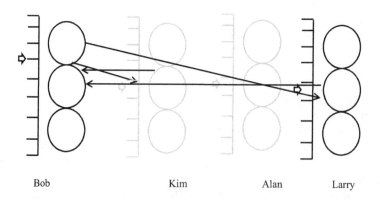

Figure 3.7 Mapping Bob's Interactions with His Team

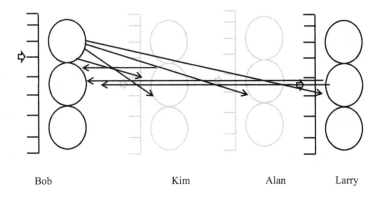

Bob   Kim   Alan   Larry

Figure 3.8 Mapping Multiple Team Communications

- Bob's early assertiveness.
- Whether or not the weekend overtime is appropriate.
- The morale of the team
- … and its impact on recent efforts to unionize the facility.
- Speculation on whether or not Bob has bothered to avail himself of the information needed to make the best overtime/no overtime decision.
- The anticipated impacts to the team should the overtime decision need to be reversed.
- Whether or not Bob is even aware of the fixed cost/variable cost/profit margin considerations.
- And Bob's taste in cologne.

These communications clearly deal with more than the one-dimensioned transactions posited by Berne. Kim's pointing out that an updated cost and schedule report would be available the next day – was that her Child/Id addressing Bob's Adult/Ego (because she wanted time to play over the weekend), or was it her Parent/Superego addressing Bob's Parent/Superego (since she wanted to have the facility operate as efficiently as possible, and recognized premature decisions of the type Bob was contemplating would work against that goal)? Even with the number of parameters reduced to a degree that borders on exploding the readers' willingness to suspend belief, the number of cross-transactions to be analyzed has become dizzyingly complex. Just imagine an attempt to analyze a truly complete and multi-participant group interaction using nothing but the Berne model. As insightful as this model was, it falls dramatically short when the attempt is made to go beyond just the two people interacting.

Like the previously discussed discovery of the planet Neptune, there are other things going on in this office politics dynamic than can be explained by this mono-dimensioned structure. It's almost as if a multi-dimensional structure was indicated.

The Nominal Structure Going Forward

There are nine aspects to the structure of the persona-generated narratives that influence or dictate our placement within the hierarchies we place upon ourselves and the social interactions in which we engage. I know nine sounds like a lot, but they are structured rather simply. We'll start with the Berne/Freud model, of the Child/Id, Adult/Ego, and Parent/Superego. Each of these three aspects of the personal generates its own script, its own contribution to the individual's overall narrative.

However – and this is crucial – when social constructs form, and the same participants interact regularly for some mutually accepted purpose, then that organization will begin to develop its own triad of scripts, also following the Child/Id, Adult/Ego, and Parent/Superego patterns. The nine aspects, then, assume the following structure:

1–3: The Child/Id, Adult/Ego, and Parent/Superego internal to the individual,
4–6: The Child/Id, Adult/Ego, and Parent/Superego that is external to the individual, but internal to the group, and
7–9: The Child/Id, Adult/ Ego, and Parent/Superego that is external to the group.

These nine nodes interact with each other, creating a network. While plumbing the inky depths of the human psyche is necessarily filled with speculation and conjecture, the behavior of networks is objectively observable. Patterns do emerge from the analysis of these behaviors, patterns that go a very long way indeed towards capturing the true nature of these organizations and their hierarchies, their values and real objectives, stated or not.

Let's take Bob's multi-dimensioned structure. He maintains one set of three narratives internal to himself, another set of three for how he interacts with the Acme organization, and a third triad of narratives for how he believes the Acme Corporation's interests are furthered in the world. A summary/compression of these is shown in Table 3.1.

Table 3.1 Bob's Multi-Dimensional Structure

Aspect/domain	Internal to Bob	External to Bob/internal to Acme	External to Acme
Parent/Superego	Bob's aspirations, economic, spiritual, physical, etc.	Seeks professional advancement within Acme	Seeks Acme's overall superior performance vs. competition
Adult/Ego	Tries to perform in such a way as to satisfy both aspirations and primal needs	Attempts to perform in such a way as to inspire confidence and performance in peers, underlings, superiors	Deals with customers in such a way as to advance Acme with respect to competition
Child/Id	Pretty much limited to sex and aggression	Just wants the paycheck	Wants Acme to stay competitive long enough for Bob to keep receiving paychecks until retirement

We could do similar tables for Kim, Alan, and Larry, but you get the point. The nominal Berne or Freudian structures are quite inadequate for an undertaking as large as the analysis of the dynamics of the transactions of participants in the hierarchies of macro-organizations. I do believe, however, that their structures can serve as an adequate starting point. When combined with an expansion module that stretches their approach to three dimensions, the ensuing structure can be used to identify and explain many of the behaviors that take place within these networks, and provide a rational, technical approach to dealing with them, and perhaps even succeeding within them.

Returning once again to the facilities of Acme Corporation, we see a level of frustration – conflict, really – among the team leaders and their new manager, Bob. Bob, of course, has his own difficulties, both at work and at home, as his various narratives are being forced into a rather painful realignment. His wife, Jane, is being singularly effective at overturning his personal narrative. Bob's interaction with his team leaders is challenging the script he wrote for himself when he accepted his new position, the script that addresses what the most appropriate manner for interacting with the people within Acme ought to be. Finally, the realization that his utility to the Acme Corporation may have been inflated by those who wanted him to accept the first offer sent his way is leading Bob to wonder if his placement in the marketplace beyond Acme's boundaries is as he has been led to believe.

Bob's team leaders have no grasp of any of these causal factors. All they know is that managerial decisions are being made that appear to be disconnected from practical business sense, as their various shared experiences inform them. Searching in vain for a coherent explanation that would align the data points coming their way in some sort of rational order, the three of them will eventually arrive at an all-too-familiar default explanation.

"It's all politics."

Notes

1 Austen, Jane, retrieved from *BrainyQuote*, http://www.brainyquote.com/quotes/quotes/j/janeausten139313.html?src=t_ourselves, July 11, 2015.
2 "Dunning-Kruger Effect," retrieved from *Wikipedia*, http://en.wikipedia.org/w/index.php?title=Dunning%E2%80%93Kruger_effect&oldid=663431183, May 25, 2015.
3 "Ego Defense Mechanisms," in *Psychology 101*, retrieved from *AllPsych*, http://Allpsych.com/psycology/101/defenses, September 18, 2014.
4 "Bullying, Cyberbullying, and Suicide Statistics," retrieved from *Megan Meier Foundation*, http://www.meganmeierfoundation.org/statistics.html, June 12, 2015.

Chapter 4

Why We're Headed There
It's All in the Game

Life's a game, and all you have to do, is to know how to play it.
Unknown

I'd like to begin with some takeaways from the previous chapters, namely:

* In virtually all human interactions, some form of a hierarchy will automatically be present.
* Such hierarchical structures are not necessarily bad; in fact, stemming as they do from early survival situations, they are usually highly beneficial.
* From Sigmund Freud and, later, Eric Berne, we learn that we tend to manifest three aspects of our personas: a base, primal aspect (Freud's Id, Berne's Child), one that deals with realities and circumstances as they unfold (Freud's Ego, Berne's Adult), and one that serves our higher purposes, or functions (Freud's Superego, Berne's Parent).
* In combining the reflexive introduction of interactional hierarchies with the Freud/Berne archetypes, the natural conclusion is that a form of a scale is present, one that determines what our rankings are in any of the multiple social constructs in which we engage.
* These scales are dynamic, and mirror the Freud/Berne triad structure.
* We tend to score ourselves higher on the scale than is probably warranted for the given hierarchy.
* Whenever our internally generated score is forced by "harsh" reality to realign with its more accurate, objective ranking, this realignment is extremely painful, and difficult for the person to endure, much less absorb or integrate.
* And people will tend to go through extraordinary means to avoid such pain.

Before we revisit Acme Corporation, and how Bob's doing with Alan, Kim, and Larry, let's go over some basic Game Theory. Game Theory is a way of reducing complex interactions among the participants in a given "game" to quantifiable, observable tactics and strategies. John Forbes Nash, the subject of the movie *A Beautiful Mind*, shared a Nobel Prize for his research in the area of Game Theory, and Game Theory has had a profound influence in the fields of macroeconomics, evolutionary biology, artificial intelligence – even traffic light timing. Game Theory can also bring some key insights into the analysis of why participants in a given group select the strategies that they do, and under what circumstances those unintuitive strategies may become appealing. Let's go over some of these "games," as well as the results from a couple of experiments, and take their insights into the discussion of the maneuverings within hierarchies.

The Prisoner's Dilemma

The Prisoner's Dilemma is considered to be one of the most informative games involving non-related biological units in a common environment. It was originally framed by Merrill Flood and Melvin Dresher working at RAND in 1950.[1] The basic premise is this: you are a prisoner, and your jailer comes to you with an offer. If you inform (i.e., "rat") on your cellmate, the jailer will reduce your sentence. The dilemma comes into play when you realize that your cellmate is going to get the same offer. There are, then, four possible alternatives (with some variability in the amount of time served, depending on which version of the game is being employed):

- If you betray your cellmate, and he does the same to you, you each serve two years.
- If you do not betray your cellmate, and he does not betray you, you each serve one year in prison.
- If you do not betray your cellmate, but he betrays you, then you serve three years, and he is set free. This alternative is nicknamed "the Sucker's Payoff."
- Conversely, if you rat out your cellmate, and he remains silent, you are set free, and he serves three years.

In the pre-computer era, conventional wisdom had held that you should *always* rat on your cellmate in the Prisoner's Dilemma, to ensure that you are never on the receiving end of the Sucker's Payoff.

Then, in 1984, Robert Axelrod set up a tournament of computer programs playing multiple (200) iterations of the Prisoner's Dilemma against each other. Some entrants, keeping with the conventional wisdom, ratted every time. Others would rat the first 50 times, and then cooperate the remaining iterations, or rat every other time, and so forth. One program designed by Anatol Rapoport won the competition – it was named Tit for Tat, and its deterministic strategy was this:

- Begin by cooperating (do not rat);
- thereafter, do whatever the other program did in the previous iteration.

After the tournament, analysts reviewed the programs' competitions, seeking the reasons behind Tit-for-Tat's success. They created variants, one that did not rat for the first five iterations, and then did the tit-for-tat deal, and another that ratted the first time, and then did the tit-for-tat tactic. In each case, the variants failed to outperform the original. The analysis on why Tit-for-Tat succeeded attributed it to three factors:

- It was originally "nice" (it did not rat).
- It retaliated immediately for defection.
- It forgave immediately and completely for cooperation.

Obviously a strong majority of the social hierarchies we encounter involve people to whom we are not related, and the most appropriate selection of strategies of cooperation or defection can be difficult to ascertain. The takeaways from the Prisoner's Dilemma going forward, then, include:

- Depending on the situation, winning may require defecting from the organization's stated goals.
- Structured, repeatable strategies (also known as "canned strategies") are useful, but only in the sense that they can respond to the selected strategies of the other players.
- Failing to respond to an act of defection from a planned participant or ally is a mistake,
- ... but then, so is holding a grudge for an improperly long period of time.
- For this particular game, the Tit-for-Tat strategy was a winner, even though it did not alter the behavior of the other programs, save for those selecting a similar strategy.

Hawk-Dove

The Hawk-Dove Game, as the name suggests, involves aggressive and passive birds, or neutral birds that can behave either aggressively or passively. Consider two birds in a set environment. If each of them forages about for food, and consumes or stores all it collects – i.e., acts as a dove – then their overall payoff is maximized. However, should one of them act aggressively, and rather than forage for food itself, seek to take the food that the passive bird has collected, then the sum total of food collected is lessened. This is key – in those environments where there is enough (or more than enough) food to sustain both birds, their overall well-being is maximized when they both select the dove strategy.

However, in those circumstances where there is not enough food in the birds' shared environment, if they continue to select the dove strategy, at least one of them will die. If one of them selects the hawk strategy, then that one will survive as long as there is sufficient food to sustain at least one bird. Many so-called foreign affairs analysts believe that, to the extent that Hawk-Dove is analogous to the world of international diplomacy, this necessitated selection of the hawk strategy explains the source of much of the warfare in the world.

Now consider a population of 100 birds. As in the two-bird version of the game, if they all forage for food, keeping what they collect for themselves, their overall payoff is maximized. This aspect is true even under those circumstances where there is not enough available food to support the entire population. But even in those circumstances where there is actually more than enough food for the entire population, the introduction of just one hawk into the population will result in the hawk behavior being adapted by others, until an equilibrium point is reached. This point is known as the Nash Equilibrium, named after the aforementioned John Nash. The Nash Equilibrium is a solution concept of a non-cooperative game involving two or more players, in which each player is assumed to know the equilibrium strategies of the other players, and no player has anything to gain by changing only their own strategy[2] (as opposed to communicating with others to coordinate a widespread adoption of different strategies). In the case of Hawk-Dove, the Nash Equilibrium works out to 25% hawk, 75% dove. Again, the overall population's payoff is maximized if all

100 birds select the dove strategy. The addition of just one hawk, though, will lead the population to quickly come to a Nash Equilibrium point of 25/75 hawk/dove.

The takeaways from Hawk-Dove, then, include:

- The entire group's payoff is maximized when they cooperate.
- The introduction of just one defector ("hawk"), however, will lead each member of the group to alter their strategy selection until strategy selection equilibrium point is reached.
- In environments where the group's population does not have access to sufficient resources to survive, the continued selection of the cooperative/passive strategy is fatal.
- In environments where there are enough resources for the population to survive, those selecting the hawk strategy will benefit disproportionally as long as the existing equilibrium rewards aggressive behavior. In other words, when it comes to attaining rank within the population of hawk/dove birds, the dove won't be in the upper echelons.

The Ultimatum Game

The Ultimatum Game involves three participants: one facilitator and two players, A and B. The facilitator addresses the players with the proposition that a sum of money (typically $100) will be divided among them if player A can propose a division of the funds that player B approves of *on the first attempt*. If B approves A's plan, the money is divided accordingly. If B disapproves of A's plan, neither of them receives anything.

Game theorists had postulated that player A's payoff is maximized if he proposes an A/B split of $99/$1, on the grounds that the alternatives left to B would be to either receive $1, or nothing at all. Naturally, player B would accept the $99/$1 split. Right?

A funny thing happened on player A's journey to deposit the $99, though. The 99/1 split was almost never accepted in actual instances of the Ultimatum Game. In fact, Players B almost always refused any offer that wasn't substantially better than 80/20. Some Asian cultures would even routinely reject the so-called "fair option," that of a 50/50 split.

These real-world experiments of the Ultimatum Game challenged not only the game theorists' calculations, but the notion of the very existence of John Stuart Mill's *Homo Economicus*, or economic man. The idea behind *Homo Economicus* is that humans can be expected to behave in their own economic self-interest, on a consistent basis. For example, when player B was offered a choice between receiving $1 or nothing at all, *Homo Economicus* would have near automatically accepted the offer. When the real-life players B rejected the 99/1 split, game theorists were quick to explain the observed results as having their roots in "cultural aspects." Of course, by throwing any potential scientific explanation away with the appeal to an entity as inchoate as "cultural aspects," the game theorists were essentially admitting that their theories were flat-out unable to be reconciled with the experimental data. Whether it was due to players B perceiving that players A were unworthy of such a disproportionate split of unearned income, or because participants from Asian cultures were anxious to avoid the perception of being indebted to strangers, the inescapable conclusion from actual occurrences of the Ultimatum Game is that *any* theory of economics that flows from the assumption of *Homo Economicus* must be considered suspect at best, and perhaps even invalid.

Takeaways from the Ultimatum Game include:

- Participants in an economic-based organization cannot be reliably predicted to select strategies that enlarge them personally.
- There are other factors in play in the strategy-selection behaviors of people that cannot be reliably captured and quantified.
- Modeling people's behavior, even in instances where the rules of the interaction (or game) are simple, is extremely difficult, and may even be impossible to do reliably.

Chicken

The game of Chicken is intended to test the physical courage of its participants. Since physical courage is a trait more highly prized by men than women and since older males don't become older without realizing the inherent idiocy of playing games like Chicken, participants tend to be exclusively younger males. The game was cinematically depicted in *Rebel without a Cause* (1955), where James Dean's character, Jim Stark, participates in a variant of the game where Jim and his antagonist drive stolen cars towards a cliff. The first person to abandon the car prior to its plunge over the cliff is considered to be a coward, or "chicken." The more common variant, though, is to drive two cars towards each other at high speed, the decision being to swerve or not. There are four possible outcomes:

- If both drivers swerve, they are both considered chicken.
- If neither driver swerves, they both die in a fiery crash.
- If driver A does not swerve, but driver B does, A is considered courageous, and B is considered cowardly.
- And, conversely, if A swerves while B does not, A is "chicken," and B is "cool."

Another way of analyzing the outcomes of the game of Chicken is to borrow the greater-than and lesser-than mathematical symbols (">" and "<") to mean "better than" and "worse than," so that:

Living > Dying
    and
Being Considered Brave > Being considered chicken

So that

Living brave > Living chicken > Dying brave > Dying chicken

Of course, unless something unexpected happens in the game of Chicken, one does not typically die after having swerved, meaning that the equation is essentially reduced to:

Living brave > Living chicken > Dying brave

But even here is some ambiguity, which brings into consideration the voyeurism factor. In most instances of the game of Chicken, the participants have an opportunity to communicate with each other (as they did in *Rebel without a Cause*). And, of course, if there are no other witnesses to the actual game being played, there's really no point, since the game is designed to establish within a given social construct whom among the males possesses more physical courage.

Typically, as dumb as repeat Chicken players must be, they have an idea of which strategy (swerve or don't swerve) they are likely to select prior to agreeing to participating in the game. It stands to reason that the pre-selection tends towards not swerving – otherwise, agreeing to play the game in the first place would accomplish nothing more than establishing the player as lacking in courage. Now, during this pre-game communication session, imagine our player A engages in communication with player B, who is also inclined to pre-select the no-swerve strategy. If player A can convince player B during this pre-game communication session that he (player A) is not only courageous, but recklessly so, to the point of being suicidal, then player A will have significantly improved his chances of selecting the no-swerve strategy and living to see the next morning. However, if player A's communication is not convincing of that message, his chances of living after having selected the no-swerve strategy have gone down. Add to this aspect of the pre-game communication that, should player B convince player A of his (player B's) enhanced courage/recklessness, leading to player A reconsidering his no-swerve strategy selection, then player B has enhanced his chances of not swerving and living to tell about it.

This pre-game communication event adds a dimension onto the game of Chicken. In analyzing each player's options, we see that they have the following:

1. Project that they will not swerve, and then don't swerve.
2. Project that they will not swerve, but actually swerve.
3. Project that they will swerve, and then don't swerve.
4. Project that they will swerve, and actually swerve.

Unless player A is deliberately trying to make player B look courageous in front of the in-crowd at Dawson High School, it's rather pointless to combine the communication/strategy selection as depicted in option 4. Player A might as well not participate at all.

Similarly, option 3 is somewhat suicidal, in that player A is deliberately increasing the chances of an outcome that would lead to his death. Still, I suppose it's possible. This leaves the only reasonable pre-game communication strategy as projecting a no-swerve intent, with the only remaining variable being how well that communication works.

You know what would really be helpful to player A in the minutes before he actually begins his run? An accurate history on the number of times B has played this game, how often he swerved, and a rendition of his pre-game communications prior to each of those games. Such knowledge would go a very long way towards leading A to select the strategy that accomplishes his goals, i.e., staying alive and appearing to be courageous. Who would have such knowledge? Player B, of course, but he's probably not talking. Who else?

The kids from Dawson High School who have indulged their voyeurism instincts and witnessed prior iterations have this knowledge. I will examine further the ways that voyeurism alters our placement in our organizations' hierarchies in the next chapter; for now, suffice to say that the nosey kids here have information that's of life-or-death import (literally) to player A – and they may or may not be inclined to disclose it.

Under what circumstances would the Dawson High School kids wish to inform player A of player B's previous pairings of pre-game communications and actual strategy selection? If they wish to see player A move up in the group's hierarchy. The game of Chicken is played, not in order to crash superfluous automobiles, but to establish or realign its players' placements within a hierarchy. The fact that the game of Chicken is played in real life is another indicator that those arrows pointing to our inwardly held rankings within a given social construct's hierarchy are so important to us as individuals that we humans are known to be fully capable of risking death in order to maintain or inflate them.

In this respect, the game of Chicken is not that dissimilar from Russian Roulette. Indeed, as idiotic as we tend to view players of Russian Roulette, the odds of a single iteration of this game actually has higher odds of survival than Chicken, assuming:

- Chicken has one of four outcomes resulting in death, but that outcome kills both participants.
- This particular version of Russian Roulette involves one bullet in the cylinder of a six-shooter revolver.

Of course, if the game of Russian Roulette continues past the single iteration, the odds go up significantly with each additional pull of the trigger – but the ultimate point of the game is the same (unless you are a prisoner of war being compelled to play as in the iconic scene from *The Deer Hunter*), which is to establish within a group your level of personal courage. Why is the establishment of a relative level of physical courage so important? Because it translates directly to the placement of the individual in the group's hierarchy – there's really no other reason in play here. The individual who has already established a high level of courage among those in the group has absolutely no need to engage in any life-threatening game; nor does the individual who either feels no compunction to establish/raise this particular perception, or else does not care about the opinions of those in the group witnessing the game.

This latter point illustrates another reason why the group of hip kids from Dawson High School is motivated to indulge their voyeuristic impulses. In addition to collecting potentially valuable information in the event that they find themselves behind the wheel of one of two cars speeding towards each other, the very act of playing Chicken (or Russian Roulette, for that matter) sends a strong, clear signal that the group witnessing (or even sponsoring) the game is so special, and membership in it so coveted, that avoiding exclusion from or a dishonorable placement within that group's hierarchy is worth risking death. For those already in the group whose hierarchical placement is comfortable and secure, witnessing others willing to risk their lives to become a part of the same organization is a thrill. While these non-player members of the social construct may maintain their specific ranking within the hierarchy, the illusion is that the entire group's ranking with respect to other groups is on the ascent.

Takeaways from the game of Chicken include:

- Within certain social constructs, humans are known to risk their very lives to establish a desired hierarchical ranking, or to avoid losing status within that hierarchy.
- Ranking perceptions can be (and often are) manipulated through a cycle of communications associated with the actual performance of the ranking-altering action(s).
- The voyeur instinct isn't just an idle indulgence. It is, in fact, a trait that can lead us to absorbing valuable information, information that can be expected to be of use in future analogous situations.
- The ranking the overall group gives itself (with respect to other, analogous ones) is buoyed by the efforts of those external to it who wish to join, as well as by the efforts of those already in the group to maintain or advance their rankings within the group's internal hierarchy.

Meanwhile, back at Acme...

Bob has some managerial strategies to select and execute. Without knowing the nuances of the Prisoner's Dilemma, he nevertheless has a certain expectation that as long as he is demonstrably pursuing Acme Corporation's economic objectives (i.e., cooperating), that his peers and superiors will support him and his decisions (reciprocal cooperation). However, as we saw in the Ultimatum Game, it is really quite impossible to reduce the relevant parameters of this sort of complex inter-action into something that can be quantified to the point of calculating the prob-able future. In other words, there's way more stuff going on among Bob and his project team than a simple cooperate/defect test can capture. Bob is nursing a fra-gile self-score in both his personal narrative and his hierarchical placement within Acme. He's also inclined to carry forward a series of canned strategies into situ-ations similar to the ones he has already encountered, like the Dawson High School newcomer having already arrived at a no-swerve strategy in the upcoming game of Chicken.

Like our Chicken player A, Bob has had an opportunity to communicate with his organization prior to the enactment of any of his planned strategies. Also simi-lar to player A, Bob used his communication opportunity to take a measure of his team, and the likely cooperate/defect strategies they may employ. Since each of them – Kim, Alan, and Larry – offered an initial objection to Bob's stated intent to have the entire production team work overtime the upcoming weekend, Bob came away from his Chapter 3 meeting not only convinced that his almost pre-selected strategy was appropriate, but that he could expect resistance (defection) from the team leaders as he implements his decisions.

For their part, Kim, Alan, and Larry came away from that same meeting with the impression that Bob was not pursuing the most efficient solution to a schedule delay problem that might not even be current. This team leader trio is professional enough to not dwell on the implications of Bob's communications and actions on their per-sonal view of themselves, but they are aware of the effect Bob's strategy selection has on Acme's hierarchy.

Acme's Child/Id, Adult/Ego, and Parent/Superego narrative, being the product of a group of individuals, works something like this:

- Acme's stated corporate goals (predictably enough) contain healthy doses of customer satisfaction, superior quality and service, competitive pricing, etc.
- Realistically, Acme must extract more value out of its resources – human resources included – than it pays out to them, but not by a wide margin. Employees who view their working conditions as unjustifiably difficult or harsh while their company makes a significant profit quickly become disillusioned, and will be inclined to generate less value.
- But the innermost desires of the owners are that profits be maximized, expenses be minimized, and the difference is deposited into their bank accounts (hence the widespread (but utterly invalid) notion that the point of all management is to "maximize shareholder wealth"). The pursuit of this not-so-secret objective is the source of macro-organizational behaviors that are unethical, or even illegal. I'll take this up in more detail in Chapter 8.

In Chapter 3 we analyzed the transactional maps depicting Bob's communications with Kim, Larry, and Alan, and saw where they quickly became overly complex. But just as there can be inter-tier conflict within the individual (the Superego wants the person to spend more time at church, while the Id wants more time spent in idleness (or worse)), there is also inter-tier conflict within the organization. Some of the 100-bird population game realize that their payoff is maximized if they all select the dove strategy, and oppose the birds selecting hawk. Some of the hip crowd from Dawson High School like both player A and player B, and do not wish for either of them to risk their lives in order to establish their levels of physical courage, and oppose those who wish for them to carry out the game of Chicken.

At Acme, Kim, Alan, and Larry are convinced that Bob's selected strategy is sub-optimal, and are nominally disposed to opposing it. As with most organizations, there is a strong taboo at Acme against team leaders taking their concerns to upper management, and bypassing middle management in seeking a decision that would override the one already in effect. As fate would have it, the executive who hired Bob, Paul, is actually Kim's uncle, and the weekend that Bob would like the project team to work overtime happens to be the same weekend that a family function had been planned. Towards the end of the work day on Tuesday, Kim and Paul happen across each other in the employee break room.

"What time are we due at your Mom's on Saturday?" Paul asks.

"Oooh – I don't know. I don't even know if I'll be able to make it," Kim responds.

"Why not?"

"That new manager, Bob, is talking about having our entire product team work this weekend."

"Why?"

"We're not exactly sure – he seems to be overreacting to last week's schedule performance report, that showed us a few points back."

"You want me to say something to him?" Paul offers.

"No, it will be okay. We'll see what tomorrow's cost/schedule report has to say."

As with the attempt to map the transactions among Bob and his team leads, any attempt to precisely quantify this simple interaction is doomed to irrelevance due to complexity. Consider:

- While Paul and Kim belong to the same economic social construct (Acme), they also belong to the same familial construct. The above conversation jumped between each set of constructs multiple times.
- Even within the same construct, the lines of communication were all over the place. Was Kim's personal Superego persona addressing Paul's corporate Ego, or vice-versa? To put it in a more direct way, in Paul's mind, who better represents Acme's interest with respect to the decision to work the upcoming weekend, Kim, or Bob?
- If we confine this interaction to an example of inter-tiered organizational communication, what are the implications for Bob? For example, if Paul came away from the exchange with a new-found concern about Bob's ability to take into account the misusing-the-staff implications of his managerial decisions, then Kim would have assumed a superior position to Bob in the informal hierarchy at Acme, even though Bob is, technically, Kim's superior.
- Although communications between team leaders and upper-level executives on matters managerial is discouraged, Kim just engaged in such a communication. The nuance here is that, since the communication was highly informal, Kim really can't be accused of going behind Bob's back in order to undermine his authority or decisions. But the same effect has been incurred – Paul even offered to intervene to enforce Kim's decision, had she so desired.

Now imagine what would happen if Kim takes Paul up on his offer. If Paul communicates a challenge to Bob's decision on how to handle the production schedule and the human resources assigned to him, Bob will probably become rather upset, ironically assuming that Paul lacked the information and perspective needed to arrive at the optimal solution that Bob had identified, and was trying to pursue. The irony would go further if, upon recognizing Bob's initial reaction to his intervention as resistance, Paul were to come to the conclusion that *his* decisions were being challenged by an underling.

In this swirl of personas, transactions, hierarchical placements, competing narratives and structures, we see that attempting to isolate the communications among just two of the participants and identifying those parts of the persona that come into play, as well as the implications of hierarchical placement, is futile. Even so, some usable constants do present themselves, including:

- Regardless of the hierarchical structure involved, participants will go to extraordinary lengths to avoid being downgraded in standing or rank.
- These rankings or standings are in perpetual competition in all but the most cohesive, simpatico of teams.
- These competitions manifest themselves in the transactions, or communications of the social constructs' participants.
- There are multiple ranking mechanisms in place at any one time, too many to quantify, though some insights may be gleaned from identifying and understanding them.

Prior to evaluating more complex human hierarchies, there is much to be gleaned from an analysis of the social hierarchies of some lesser creatures, the most notable of which is, beyond doubt, the wolf pack.

"Everybody's a Lobo, Woof Woof Woof!"

That's the slogan of the athletic teams from the University of New Mexico (UNM), in Albuquerque, where I did my undergraduate work. For those of you unfamiliar with the United States' National Collegiate Athletic Association's (NCAA's) Mountain West Conference, a lobo is a Mexican grey wolf, *Canis lupus baileyi*. While the slogan is intended to assert some sort of universal appeal of UNM's athletic teams, there is actually a kernel of truth to it. We *are* all lobos, at least in the sense that, as social animals, many of our maneuverings and machinations within the social constructs to which we belong parallel – or even mimic – the pack behavior of wolves.

In a given wolf pack, there is almost always a linear hierarchy, headed by a single leader known as the Alpha wolf. The Alpha wolf is typically the only one in the pack that mates, and has actual offspring. The Alpha also largely determines the status of the other members of the pack, with such hierarchical placement determining things such as which pack members eat, how much, and in what order they eat.

There is also a Beta wolf that serves as something of a second-in-command. The Beta wolf is subservient to the Alpha, but doesn't take much nonsense from him or her. As long as the Alpha wolf leads the pack appropriately, the Beta is supportive. But, should the Alpha falter or behave erratically, the Beta will typically challenge for the leadership.

At the bottom of the pack's society are the Omega wolves. These are usually smaller, or poorer hunters. They act goofy, or not as aggressive as the others in the pack. They eat last, if at all, and never mate, or even copulate. Interestingly enough, they are also known to be the most playful members of the pack, fulfilling the role of wolf comedian, if you will. Since they are largely ostracized from the pack without being actually banished, the Omega wolves are the most vulnerable to threats from outside the pack, and are usually the first to die off in times of famine.

In-between the Alpha/Beta and Omegas, we have a population of middle-mass wolves who do not appear to adopt specific roles within the pack. These middle ones may or may not have a more intricate hierarchical placing amongst themselves – researchers are generally hard-pressed to identify patterns that would allow such minute categorization (otherwise we would have Gamma through Psi wolves, I suppose).

While it's easy to focus on the attributes of being assigned or gaining a certain ranking within the pack, it's also important to note *why* the placement within the pack hierarchy occurs. It's there to help guarantee the survival of the pack as a whole, as they almost always live in highly hostile environments. According to the grey wolf fact sheet from PBS.org, grey wolves in the wild will live between 6–8 years, and "some can reach" 13 years.[3] By comparison, grey wolves living in captivity will live to 17 years, fully 100% longer than their wild cousins. Much like the Chapter 1 example of Crusoe and Friday determining who should be the leader, the harsh circumstances and environments inhabited by grey wolves pretty much determine that pack behavior that does not lend itself to improving life expectancy can and does have catastrophic repercussions *for every member of the pack*. Humans believe that compassion is an advanced, admirable trait, and indeed it is. But it must be acknowledged that, should some scientist find a way to spontaneously advance an animal's intelligence, *Flowers for Algernon*-style, and hit our little pack with this smart-ray to the point that the wolves begin to express compassion by socially promoting the Omegas, they wouldn't last long. Neighboring packs, less intelligent, not sympathetic, and carrying on time-tested pack behaviors would displace the miraculously made intelligent pack, either through direct aggression or by simply outperforming them in the competition for territory and food.

Now let's return to our normal, traditionally structured wolf pack. A pack wolf that is not an Alpha, but wants to eat more than the Alpha is currently allowing, has basically three choices:

1. It can improve its relationship with the Alpha, either by
    - demonstrating superior performance during the track/hunt/kill cycle, demonstrating its added value in attaining the goals of the pack,
    - or else by signaling its support of the Alpha (while also transmitting the acknowledgment that the Alpha ought to remain the Alpha), in the hope that the Alpha will allow it more food.

Either sub-choice has its hazards. If the former, the Alpha may perceive more aggressive hunting behavior to be a subtle challenge, somewhat similar to an employee bringing in more profits than her manager. On the other hand, by transmitting a signal of support for the Alpha, the transmitter is actually engaging in an act of submission, thereby also signaling a lower level of utility in accomplishing the pack's overall goals. And, of course, excessive submission will land the transmitting wolf to Omega status, which is the exact opposite of its intentions. Another manifestation of selecting a confirm-the-Alpha strategy has to do with playful behavior. Recall that the Omegas serve as the wolf pack's version of entertainment. It may very well be that the act of entertaining others in general, and in using humor in particular, is an act of submission within various social constructs. We'll examine this aspect more fully in Chapter 8.

2. It can challenge and then overcome the Alpha, and attempt to become the Alpha itself. Of course, if there are other wolves that believe that they couldn't take on the current Alpha, and a non-Alpha wolf that they believe can be defeated attempts to become the new Alpha, they may very well take the opportunity to improve *their* status within the pack and confront the erstwhile new Alpha.
3. Finally, it can disengage from the pack, and become the proverbial lone wolf.

The very reasons that wolf pack behaviors evolved the way they did are the same reasons that work against the survival odds of the lone wolf. Having disengaged from the pack, it can't attempt to occupy the same territory without inviting attack, and not just from its former pack's Alpha – from the entire group, which will now perceive the lone wolf to be in competition for the same resources that keep them alive. If the lone wolf encounters a mate, or one splinters off of the pack at the same time as our lone wolf does, then they can potentially create their own pack, meaning that they are in competition not only with their former pack(s), but with every other wolf they may encounter. In essence, ostracism from an organization devoted to enhancing odds of survival and/or life expectancy, either by a decision from the organization or an individual's selection of the disengagement strategy, is often fatal. I believe that this fact, that in survival circumstances ostracism can be fatal, becomes instinctive in social animals, and is carried forward into environments where survival is not necessarily at stake. No difference – among social animals, ostracism or voluntary disengagement is rarely an attractive strategy, even if it's the right one in a given circumstance, and even if the association is entirely voluntary.

"Hey, Hey, We're the Monkees"

Linear hierarchical societal structures are also present among primates, especially chimpanzees. Jane Goodall's work[4] has shown many similarities to wolf pack behavior, but also some notable differences. Like wolves, male chimps have an Alpha, but, unlike wolves, no apparent Omega, and males other than the Alpha can and do successfully mate.

Chimp society is at once more sophisticated and more barbaric. Placement within the group's hierarchy is established and reinforced through more subtle signals, rarely escalating to out-and-out confrontation. Even in confrontations, the males will often engage in threats, fist pumping, and vocalizations prior to actual combat. The Alpha male's main factor in establishing dominance is age: they are typically between 20 and 26 years of age. Other factors include:

- physical fitness,
- aggressiveness,
- skill at fighting,
- ability to form coalitions, and, interestingly enough,
- intelligence.

Interactions with outside groups is a different matter. Only pubescent females can move safely among groups or between territories. In one notable instance, Goodall documented a war, where one group of chimps killed *every other member* of a competing group.[5] As a point of reference, when wolf packs come into competition for some bit of territory, only the Alpha males tend to enter into combat – and, even then, the winning Alpha male virtually never kills the vanquished one.

Non-Alpha males in chimp groups can mate, but will usually engage in the tactic of luring away a specific female to cohabitate in an area on the periphery of the group's territory prior to her entering into estrous in order to do so. If a sexually popular female enters into estrous while living in the general population, the entire group of males will come together in a type of celebration, an "excited gathering." Chimps have been known to engage in infanticide, and one notable motivating factor is paternal ambiguity. While Alpha males will often engage in behavior to prevent other males from mating with sexually popular females, this behavior is not always completely successful, leading to this paternal ambiguity.

The takeaways from reviewing the societies of animals that naturally engage in linear hierarchical structures include:

- Because cooperation among individuals is a far more successful strategy than competition, cooperative social structures are hard-wired into the more intelligent species as a way of improving the odds of survival and increased life expectancy. In other words, linear hierarchies are pretty much automatic in virtually all social settings.

- The failure of the society to elevate the most competent towards leadership positions while delegating lesser individuals (if not out-and-out ostracizing them) to more menial roles is potentially fatal to the organization.
- Individuals involved in a social structure that are placed lower in the hierarchy than they believe they ought to be have a limited set of strategies from which to choose. They can challenge and overcome the principals in the existing structure; they can gain favor from their superiors in the current structure; or, they can disengage from the organization. The disengagement strategy is usually dangerous.
- Attempting to gain favor within the existing construct is also somewhat dangerous, in that the attempt to demonstrate the ambitious individual's higher-than-placed value to the community can be misinterpreted as a challenge to the existing leadership. Conversely, attempts to curry favor via transmitting signals that the current leadership has nothing to fear challenge-wise from the aspirant is consistent with Omega behavior, which can actually result in a diminishing of the aspirant's standing.
- The act of entertaining others within the social construct is, at its core, an act of submission. Alphas never engage in entertaining behavior, while Omegas often do.

The establishment of corporate narratives, then, somewhat parallels those of wolf packs or chimpanzee groups in that the corporations' participants, like the animals', are pursuing two primary objectives: survival (one economic, the other biological) as an organization, and the other pertaining to the well-being of the group's participants (again, one economic, the other biological).

As we continue to build on the observations and examples in the earlier chapters, we will start to bump up against that vast body of time-honored wisdom that has been distilled into small, pithy phrases known as clichés. The cliché that comes to mind here is "it's a jungle out there," usually applied to a specific industry within a free-market economy. Indeed, in a free-market economy, the list of industries where this phrase has not been invoked has to be miniscule compared to the ones where it's taken as a truism. The one who invokes this cliché is not talking about the presence of unrestrained plant growth, hanging vines, high temperatures and humidity, and the presence of dangerous, wild animals in the literal sense. They mean that the economic environment in which organizations compete is unforgiving of errors, particularly managerial or leadership ones – but it's simply easier (and quicker) to use the pat phrase.

Even the non-cliché terms used in competitive business parallel animal social order, or even warfare. The acquisition of a competitor's customers is to "acquire territory." Purchasing their stock in order to gain a majority share and sell their assets is a "hostile takeover." Companies do not introduce new products quickly, they "beat the competition to the market." As successful as the free marketplace has been in improving lives and advancing life expectations, it is this aspect of it that has the potential to terrify many of its most enriched beneficiaries.

Meanwhile, back at Acme...

Convinced that he has the insight to make the right decisions for his project team, Bob has arranged for them to work the upcoming weekend in order to regain the negative schedule variance he saw during his first project team meeting. Some of the additional expenses are variable – he can change his mind about the team coming in on the weekend, if need be – but other expenses are fixed. The security sub-contractor, staffed by union members, has already agreed to the overtime, as have the facility engineers who need to be there to ensure the plant's machines continue to function within approved operational parameters.

At that first project team meeting, Kim had suggested to Bob that he wait for the next cost and schedule performance report before deciding on the overtime assignments, but Bob, still smarting from his last job where a negative schedule variance manifested late and could not be overcome, decided to ignore her. Now, it's the second project team meeting Bob will have attended, and the updated cost and schedule reports are available. And wouldn't you just know it – the updated information shows that the gonculator production is now slightly ahead of schedule, but only 1% under budget. Being under budget at all is a good indicator, but at such a small level Bob doesn't have much leeway in his budget-oriented decisions. And he just committed some of his budget to paying for an overtime weekend his project does not need.

In attempting to secure a comfortable, or even acceptable hierarchical placement within Acme, Bob has access to a similar set of strategies available to the pack wolves or chimps. Practically, however, his choices are far more limited. Bob is in no position to challenge his Acme superiors with the option of displacing them, nor can he create a new company that produces the same types of products. He could disengage, but it took him some time to find his Acme managerial position, and he's reluctant to give it up.

This leaves him with the strategy to devote his energies towards shoring up or advancing his hierarchical placement at Acme. Since Acme's Superego/Parent narrative is one of delivering high-quality products to customers at an affordable price, if Bob can be perceived as successfully accomplishing this organizational goal, he can expect organizational recognition for it. However, in Acme's Ego/Adult narrative – how things get done in the real world (or, in this case, the shop floor) – a certain level of pragmatism is needed, and Bob has just made a rather non-practical decision. Had the gonculator line continued to be delayed, Bob's decision would have been appropriate and justified. Since that line is now *ahead* of schedule, the prepare-for-weekend-overtime call was the wrong one, and it will have repercussions, including:

- His team leaders have lost faith in Bob's ability to make the right decisions on an ongoing basis.
- The amount of non-recoverable budget that is to be spent on the weekend-overtime decision is more than the 1% pad Bob had in his performance reserve.
- Bob's team leads – Kim, Larry, and Alan – having experience of this type of project, all recommended to Bob that he at least wait on the overtime decision. Bob ignored them.
- Currently unbeknownst to Bob, Kim is niece to Vice President Paul. The fact that a person placed in a lower level of the hierarchy – Kim – recommended the right decision in this situation, while a higher-placed (and higher-paid) manager had the wrong one, is not going to be secret for long. Sooner or later, others – including Paul – will find out. When Paul does find out, he will not be able to help but wonder if the decision to hire Bob in the first place, and set him at the hierarchical level that they did, was the correct one (Figure 4.1).

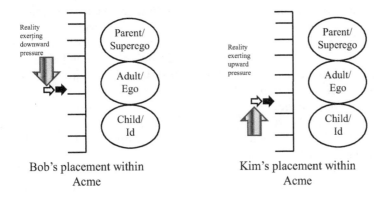

Figure 4.1 Bob's and Kim's Relative Placement at Acme

At this point, mapping out which part of Bob's or Kim's personal triad of personas were interacting with each other, and whether or not those lines of communication were parallel or crossed is irrelevant. The organization's – Acme's – trio of narratives overrides any perceived personal slight on behalf of either Bob or Kim. It's an important point, one that bears reiteration: when individuals join into a group or collective, their personal triads become subservient to those of the organization's. It's as if the narrative of the organization becomes dominant to the point of displacing the individual's ranking of himself.

Leaving Acme Momentarily...

Think about it – absent any observation of how wolves interact, would it not be rather impossible to identify the Alphas from the Omegas, much less the Betas? Indeed, the entire premise behind the television franchise *Undercover Boss* is that, once the owners or executive leaders of a given company change their clothes and other aspects of their appearance, and work with other entry-level employees of their own companies, they are utterly unrecognizable as their (truly) organizationally higher-placed selves. The organization's hierarchical placement, superficial as it may be, is designed to help ensure that the decision makers most likely to select the best strategies on behalf of the pack/group/company are put into positions to make such decisions. But, unless leader candidates are tested in identical fashion for such decisions, how can such placement decisions be made? Through analogous situations or tests. Wolf pups show aggression or submission from play, even at an early age. Chimps also indicate, through juvenile play, the traits (or lack thereof) of potential leadership, which, you may recall, include:

- physical fitness,
- aggressiveness,
- skill at fighting,
- ability to form coalitions, and
- intelligence.

Potential Acme Corporation executives signal their suitability for leadership roles in a variety of ways, but primarily by their performance in school, performance in similar organizations, or performance in lower-echelon roles within Acme. Bob's placement was based on an analogous position's performance, and Kim's upward pull is the result of her record of appropriate decisions in her lower-echelon position within Acme.

In addition to the pain (or, perhaps, adding to the pain) of a dropping hierarchical indicator, lower-ranked individuals experience less freedom of movement in wolf packs, chimpanzee groups, and corporations. Now that Paul is aware that Bob made a poor decision, and that, had Kim been in Bob's position, Kim would have made the correct decision, Paul is less willing to have faith in Bob's capabilities, and will tend to seek out information on his future choices. Again, Paul's lack of trust in Bob's actions is equivalent to an eroding of faith in the decision to place Bob in Acme's hierarchy at the level they did.

Depending on the degree of Paul's disapproval of Bob/approval of Kim, the weekend overtime decision may or may not have a lasting impact on Bob's career trajectory. Most reasonable executives – including Paul – will not make too big a deal out of one mild misstep, made very early in a manager's tenure at an organization. Unfortunately, the ranks of executives are filled with what we Americans know as "jerks" and, as in the case of differentiating between Alpha and Beta wolves on sight, being able to identify the reasonable execs from the jerks, sometimes even with extended interaction, can be difficult in the extreme. In Acme's case, while Paul does now have a heightened curiosity of Bob's managerial actions going forward, he is not yet prepared to second guess Bob's decisions, much less advise his fellow veeps that "something has to be done" about Bob.

Bob knows none of this about Paul. All Bob knows is that he is currently on the hook for paying out facility operations costs over a weekend he doesn't really need, and that eventually his error will be made known to his Acme superiors. Bob thinks he's down to two options, neither of which is very appealing:

- he can go ahead with the weekend overtime strategy, advancing the schedule performance even further, but incurring higher costs than what was budgeted, or
- he can cancel the project team's overtime, saving some money as he avoids the variable costs, but still incurring the fixed costs.

It should be noted that, had Bob been in possession of the highly relevant cost and schedule performance information in a more timely manner, he wouldn't be in his current fix. More on the epistemology of management information systems in Chapter 14, but, for now and for Bob, a sense of frustration is added to his other concerns.

Bob's focus is now on the interaction of Acme's narratives and his own placement within the company's hierarchy. From the narrative aspect, Bob has offered up an early data point: he made the wrong selection on the weekend overtime decision. Worse, his team leaders unanimously recommended that he not make the choice he did, and Bob ignored them. Communications networks are notoriously unmanageable, meaning that this event will become known to Bob's superiors, they who determine Bob's placement within the Acme hierarchy. If Bob's very next decision, the one he's working on now, is another wrong one, he could be in bigger trouble still.

Out-of-control narratives tend to take on a life of their own, as reflected in the Mark Twain quote that "A lie can travel halfway around the world while the truth is still putting on its shoes." Should the narrative that becomes associated with Bob become something along the lines of an incompetent manager who refuses to listen to his team leads, or even to common sense, and does not care about the quality of the lives of the personnel assigned to his teams, then Bob's tenure with Acme will become difficult indeed. Confirmation bias will kick in, where every appropriate (or even insightful) action Bob takes will be downplayed or ignored, while any action he undertakes that can be interpreted (or even misinterpreted) as being consistent with or supporting the uncaring incompetent script will be remembered, if not embellished. A sort of death spiral may be initiated, forcing a downward trajectory onto Bob's professional and economic path that could end very badly. Bob is very aware of these potential scenarios, and his worrying about them is only making things worse for his strategy-selection ability in the here and now.

It's now late in the day on Wednesday, and Bob needs to make his decision. Without a quantitative, formulaic standard to guide him (e.g., don't cancel variable costs of N if the ratio to fixed costs is above X), he must again rely on his instincts. As Bob struggles with the decision, another line's project manager, Eric, sticks his head in Bob's cubicle.

"Hey, Bob. I'm Eric – we met at your introductory meeting."

"Uh, yeah, I remember," Bob lies. "What's up?"

"I just called the security contractor. Are you paying for weekend ops this week?"

"I wish I wasn't, but it looks like I am," Bob answers ruefully.

"What do you mean?"

"I thought I needed the weekend to do some catch-up, but the Wednesday report showed I was okay. Now I'm committed, and don't have the budget."

"No worries," Eric says. "I'm having my team in this weekend, so just have the facilities and security guys charge to my code."

Waves of relief pass through Bob. Just moments prior, he had been torturing himself with visions of his error sending him straight back to the unemployment line, but now all that has been overcome.

"That's… that's great!" Bob stammers. "How can I pay you back?"

"Don't worry about it," Eric says with an easy casual quality. "You'd do the same for me."

Eric then takes a quick glance up and down the cubicle farm's hallway, leans in a bit farther, and says sotto voce,

"Listen, I heard about Kim talking to Paul about your little misunderstanding. You know she's Paul's niece, right?"

Bob, flummoxed yet again, barely responds, "No, I didn't."

"It's no big deal. I mean, Paul's a smart guy. But these shop floor team leads – they know everything in the universe, you know? They can get a little ahead of themselves, so, if you want my advice…"

At this point Eric could pretty much tell Bob about some available shares in a bridge, and Bob would listen.

"… don't give them any more ammunition than they have already – you know what I mean?"

"Yeah, sure," Bob responds, summoning his most canny-sounding voice.

"Thanks, Eric. I really appreciate this."

Eric smiles and nods, and then heads on down the hall.

If we were to map the interchange between Bob and Eric, there would be a lot of crossed lines of communication. Bob's Id/Child to Eric's Ego/Adult, Eric's Ego/Adult to Bob's, their Superego/Parents to each other, etc. However, despite the crossed lines of communication, no conflict was present. As insightful as Eric Berne was, his model was overly simple, his conclusions also. The existence of crossed lines of communication among interacting personas does not automatically lead to conflict, much as parallel lines of communication do not necessarily preclude it.

Besides, Eric has other purposes in mind. His archetype always does, as we will see in Chapter 8.

Notes

1 "Prisoner's Dilemma," retrieved from *Wikipedia*, http://en.wikipedia.org/w/index.php?title=Prisoner%27s_dilemma&oldid=626549973, September 25, 2014.
2 Osborne, Martin J. and Ariel Rubinstein, *A Course in Game Theory*. Cambridge, MA: MIT, 1994.
3 "Grey Wolf Fact Sheet," retrieved from *PBS*, http://www.pbs.org/now/shows/233/gray-wolf-facts.html, June 13, 2015.
4 "About Chimpanzees," retrieved from *Jane Goodall Institute of Canada*, http://www.janegoodall.ca/about-chimp-behaviour-social-organization.php, October 3, 2014.
5 Ibid.

Chapter 5

Instructional Voyeurism

It is hard to convince a high-school student that he will encounter a lot of problems more difficult than those of algebra and geometry.

Edgar Watson Howe[1]

Before we follow Bob back into the political labyrinth awaiting him at Acme, I would like to evaluate some of the strategies and maneuverings from perhaps the most intense crucible of human hierarchical establishment, destruction, placement, and upward and downward energies devoted to those placements, as well as their impacts to the personal, group, and institutional structures.

That's right: I'm talking about high school.

In most of the civilized world, people enter high school as pubescents (or even pre-pubescents) and leave as either functional adults, or near adulthood. The events that happen to these people, as well as the things that they engineer themselves, almost always have a profound, long-term effect on their personas. Indeed, in America there is a saying that you never really leave high school (which is kind of terrifying, at a certain level). Like the wolves and chimpanzees, these students can (and have been) observed and analyzed, which is what I intend to do here. However, I am not out to posit a theory on how they can become happier, more balanced (whatever that means) people into later adulthood. I'm interested in what their observable, more primal behaviors can tell us about how the establishment of social structures takes place, and how the members are assigned their places. Since high schoolers carry with them many of their attitudes and practices into academia and/or the workplace, these structures – which many may take to be inconsequential, or even trivial – can serve as the Rosetta Stone for understanding these hierarchies.

Consider the typical High School Freshman, in this case an adolescent male. In his previous group, interacting with females *at all* was considered a harbinger of weakness going forward. The very idea that the girls' toys, games, or conventions would have any appeal whatsoever to a boy, or especially an adolescent male, is repugnant to his peers and alarming to the lad's parents. Now, within a singularly short period of time, he will be expected to not only interact with the fair sex, but to arrange his affairs so that he is held in high esteem by them, all without impinging on his status within his particular pack (strikethrough) group (strikethrough) selected male-oriented social peerage.

As with our other hierarchies, there are several dynamic structures in play, and we'll analyze them one by one.

Internally...

Recall from Chapter 2 the combined Freud/Berne archetypes (Figure 5.1). As a natural part of maturing, our adolescent male's *actual* arrow placement should advance away from the more base Id/Child levels and towards the Ego/Adult. Where the downward push of our self-placed status within a given structure generates intense pain, the movement of the actual arrow creates confusion, on a similarly massive scale. The progression nominally involves inputs and experiences that instruct the individual on ways that the Ego/Adult persona interacts with the world around it in order to sate the demands of the Id/Child.

Then we have the Superego/Parent. At this stage... dang it! I can't keep calling him "an adolescent male."

His name is Scott.

At this stage, Scott's Superego/Parent persona is not very well developed. That role is largely shaped by his parents' expectations, with some input from his siblings and his pastor. Scott is aware of high achievers expending the necessary effort at an early age, and understands that, as he enters high school, much will be expected of him. But for right now, his thoughts are on basic survival. Do you think use of the term "survival" is a bit strong? There are over 4,400 high school-age suicides in the United States every year, and a study in the United Kingdom reveals that *at least* half of them are due to bullying.[2] And, as we shall see, what is commonly known as "bullying" is essentially just the creation and maintenance of the social constructs and the placement of its participants, a placement that is quite unavoidable (hence the book's title).

While Scott's older sister takes glee in pointing out every single ascertainable flaw in his character, the truth is that Scott, like almost everyone else in his age group, has some advanced talents in particular areas, is average in others, and is absolutely poor in yet others. Recall the observed basis for placement within chimpanzee society:

- physical fitness,
- aggressiveness,
- skill at fighting,

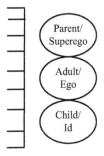

Figure 5.1 Combined Freud and Berne Personal Structures, with a Scale

- ability to form coalitions, and
- intelligence.

For now, this scale will suffice. Scott's scores, going in as a freshman and compared to other freshmen, and on a scale of 1–10, are:

- physical fitness = 4 (he could be an athlete if he put in the effort, but hasn't participated in team sports for over two years),
- aggressiveness = 3 (Scott's a pretty passive guy),
- skill at fighting = 7 (being passive, Scott has no idea, but has been blessed with better-than-average fast-twitch muscle mass. Essentially, he can throw a nearly unstoppable jab),
- ability to form coalitions = 3 (he's easy-going, but doesn't inspire confidence when the going gets tough),
- intelligence = 7 (Scott's intelligence quotient is 130).

Of course, the average man does not exist. However, on this grading scale, Scott, as much as his parents love him, is about average, perhaps a bit low, among his peers as he enters high school.

And below average as a freshman is a tough place to be.

Scott is unaware of any of this. He naturally overlooks his deficiencies, is confident in his strengths, and can't understand why everyone around him fails to recognize his value. It's been said that, if there was one characteristic shared by all humans, it is the tendency to believe that we are underappreciated, and that is certainly true of teenagers (why else would they be so ready to reflexively assume that they know more than their parents?).

Revisiting the Three-Tiered Hierarchy

Scott is about to enter into an extremely common, three-tiered hierarchical social structure. These tiers are:

- where he fits in the clique/group/pack within the high school,
- where that clique ranks among the other cliques within the high school, and
- where that high school ranks with respect to the other schools in the area.

In Scott's universe, the absolute highest he could attain would be the position of universally recognized leader of the coolest, richest, most attractive kids' group at the most prestigious private academy in his geographical area. At the opposite end of the scale, his nightmare scenario would be to be the equivalent of the Omega wolf of the poorest, ugliest group of students in what is widely recognized as the basest of schools. We have, in essence, three linear scales in action at any one time, as depicted in Figure 5.2.

The attractiveness of Scott's ideal, combined with the threat of realizing his nightmare scenario, generates an astonishing amount of energy that he will devote towards trying to move up in these structures. In order to do so, he must present and maintain a meme, a generally known and accepted script about who he is, and what his value is to any given pack or group. Like the three-tiered structure itself, this meme will

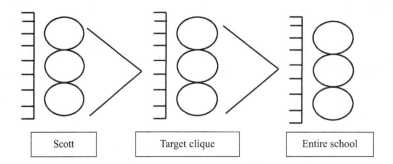

Figure 5.2 Three-Structure Model

have three different functions, combined into one overarching purpose – to help Scott advance within the hierarchies. An example comes from classic literature: in *Paradise Lost*, Milton's Satan claims:

> Here we may reign secure, and in my choice
> to reign is worth ambition though in Hell:
> Better to reign in Hell, than serve in Heaven.[3]

Adapted to our model, Satan is claiming that he prefers his personal arrow to be high within the lowest of organizations and in the worst place in the universe than to have his personal arrow low among the highest of organizations in the greatest place in the universe.

Recall the nature of voyeurism from Chapter 4, where we established its value well beyond the titillation angle. Voyeurism serves to inform the social construct how potential or current members are likely to respond to various scenarios, and if that will help or hurt the clique. There is also a myriad of other voyeurs, each with multiple purposes for their data gathering. However, these purposes tend to fall within relatively few general purposes, these having to do with the more primal linear social constructs. Scott should beware: part and parcel of the voyeur function is to ascertain exactly what Scott thinks of himself with respect to others, i.e., where he places his internal arrow on his own personal scale, his scale of the others in the group, and what he thinks of the group with relation to other groups.

The most immediate need that any of us has – survival – has as its most primal demand that of guaranteeing physical security. That this is tested regularly among high school males is blatantly obvious to even the most oblivious school administrator. Boys' first and most instinctive evaluation of others is whether or not they can prevail in a physical altercation with the other, and this evaluation will have much to do with the nature of any relationship they may have going forward (shorter version: "Can I beat him in a fight?").

The next most immediate survival needs are food and shelter. In human societies, this translates into an evaluation of how the individual being assessed is likely to perform as an economic engine. To reiterate Goodall's characteristics being evaluated in chimpanzee society, these include:

- physical fitness,
- aggressiveness,
- skill at fighting,
- ability to form coalitions, and
- intelligence.

Note that each of these capabilities has a direct bearing on the capacity of the individual to ensure both physical and economic security, both for himself, and...

Who's Watching? Pretty Much Everybody

To state some politically incorrect but fairly undeniable truths, women are, on average, smaller and weaker than men. When they become pregnant, their ability to fend for themselves is further diminished. Women's brains are hard-wired to seek out in potential spouses both an ability to guarantee physical security and economic well-being. So, as the boys in their own classrooms, classrooms across the hall, or across the township engage in these ritualistic challenges to each other's physical fitness, aggressiveness, skill at fighting, etc., it's rather inevitable that there will be a cadre of highly interested voyeurs. Not because the girls enjoy seeing bloodshed or humiliation, but because they have an innate need to be able to judge potential spouses for fit and meet.

Recall the pre-game communications from Chicken. At a certain level, the boys know that they are being watched by *their* potential spouses, and will behave accordingly. It's this pressure that leads to what outsiders view as bullying – the discovery and enforcement of a social hierarchy based on the first three of Goodall's chimp society rankings. If Scott meets another boy who is more physically fit, aggressive, and better at fighting, but these three are not manifestly obvious, the other can (and most certainly will) establish his ranking as being above Scott. This fellow – I'll call him Jeff – does not need to assail and batter Scott, at least not immediately. The establishment or reminders of rankings within a given social construct will take many forms, including (in order of escalation):

- eye contact
- angle the head is held
- standing proximity
- jokes
- teasing
- challenges
- criticisms
- mocks
- brow-beating
- physical contact in the form of physical teasing or mock combat
- other forms of physical competition, such as sports or ad-hoc challenges

   ... and potentially hundreds of other steps, leading to

- one-on-one combat, with the aim to humiliate,
- one-on-one combat, with the aim to disable or even kill,

- many-on-one combat, with the aim to humiliate, and finally
- many-on-many combat, with the aim to disable or kill.

Both Scott and Jeff find themselves in the same clique, having a mutual friend, Mitch, in the group already. This clique is composed of five core members – two male, three female – and around a dozen more casual members, also loosely evenly split male to female. Many of them have classes together, share an interest in a specific sport, attend the same church, or are otherwise connected in voluntary organizations or networks. Some of these associations, such as preference for a certain sport, are fairly easy to walk away from. Others, such as church membership, are a bit more difficult, and their attendance at their school is next to impossible to reverse. The observable preferences for those networks or associations that can be easily abandoned serve as indicators for fitness for inclusion in this (and, actually, virtually any other) group.

Because this clique is fairly easy to leave, there isn't (necessarily) the life-or-death gravity behind the establishment of the Alpha, Beta, muddling middle, and Omega roles. A poor group selection of who their male and female Alphas will be will result in little more than a loss of prestige within this clique with respect to the other packs of roving freshmen on campus. Of course, in more extreme environments this is not the case. In inner-city schools in America, for example, failing to gain the mutual support of other adolescent males – joining a gang – can quickly bring about fatal consequences as other aligned males come to realize that, as a non-aligned male, a vulnerable target exists within their brutal environment. At the other end of the scale, the ability to be readily accepted by the members of the more prestigious cliques in private prep schools can easily translate to increased odds of future success, both academically and professionally.

Scott is in neither of these extreme circumstances. For simplicity's sake, we'll say that on Scott's first day at Midtown High School, he is an average kid who views himself as typical, hanging around with a group of kids who are neither unnecessarily down on themselves nor entertain delusions of grandeur, at a run-of-the-mill high school that is not known for being violent nor academically advanced. Graphically, he maps out as in Figure 5.3.

The Black Arrows indicate that point in the respective hierarchies where Scott would be placed if his view of himself in a pure meritocracy could be quantified; same

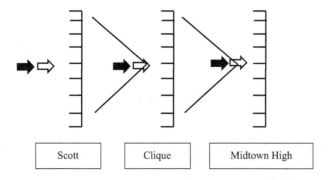

Figure 5.3 Three-Structure Model, with Scales

with his place within the clique, and the clique's place within Midtown. The White Arrows indicate Scott's view of himself inside his own skin, his idea of his placement within the clique, and the clique's concept of its comparative value among the other groups of kids at Midtown.

Already there are forces acting upon these arrows' placement. Scott's parents, for example, have no desire to raise an average child. Their expectation is that Scott's Black Arrow be moved higher, that his relative merit be advanced through studying, participating in physical activities such as team sports, or more attention to his spiritual journey. All of these take effort. Depending on Scott's inherent talents, some of these advancements may be relatively easy, others prohibitively difficult. If Scott is diligent, then his Black Arrow should move upwards; however, if he is lazy, it will move downward on the scale.

Similarly, within the clique, should they, as a group, accept an attitude that academic or physical excellence assumes a key role of rank amongst them, then the group as a whole will advance with respect to other cliques, who may be vulnerable to attracting slackers.

Finally, the school itself has its own way of ranking its students. Grades, obviously, reflect the views of this pack's principles, but the expansion of other awards or alternate ways of encouraging acceptable behavior are in play as well, and these can serve as powerful incentives. In the United States, virtually every high school will have a large trophy case, prominently displayed in or near either the administrative offices, or the school's main foyer. Academic awards – a listing of the school's valedictorians, or academic decathlon prize winners, for example – are occasionally included. The school's achievements in sports are usually emphasized, especially if that particular school happened to win in competitions with other, similarly situated schools. Championship trophies in football, basketball, soccer, or even tennis are guaranteed to not only be more gaudy in appearance, but will occupy superior shelf space in the trophy case than, say, championships in chess (I know this from first-hand experience).

And yet the members of the faculty of Midtown are also in a particularly weak position to impose the school's hierarchy on the students. Indeed, in particularly violent schools, the teachers' very survival may be in play. At a certain, widely accepted level, the students must be willing to embrace the norms associated with the school's hierarchical structure, which implies that the school's structure must be designed with some level of understanding of the way its subordinate cliques function, and why.

Similarly, the cliques will have some level of groupthink recognition of why any of its individual members might want to associate with it. Otherwise, unless participation is somehow compelled (as in, say, a prison gang), members would simply disengage, preferring to seek out other groups that are more amenable towards satisfying their needs or goals. If Scott were to, say, be inclined to join the speech and debate team because he was under the impression that such an association would look good on his curriculum vitae, but was then led to believe that successful participation in the chess team would be more appealing to the college he wishes to attend, he would depart the one for the other rather directly.

What we have is a two-way communication path, both up and down the three-tiered hierarchy. Each stop along the way has its needs and wants, even if they can't be communicated directly. From the individual upwards, we see:

- The individual seeks to have:
  - basic needs met,
  - an affirmation of the score given itself (that the individual's "White Arrow" has not been significantly misplaced),
  - to be free from the conflict that arises from having the true merit score ("Black Arrow") become noticeably divergent from the aforementioned self-score (White Arrow).
- The clique desires:
  - to be comprised of members widely accepted as being exemplary, or at least above average,
  - to be led by those members who are most likely to make decisions that advance the clique with respect to other groupings of kids,
  - to be free of the conflict involved whenever rival cliques compete for similar status in a given environment.
- The high school desires:
  - its students to be hard-working scholars,
  - who refrain from settling their conflicts violently,
  - while enjoying a rise in its standings with respect to other high schools.

In order to attain these objectives, each of these entities will attempt to enforce its will on the actors below, above, and around them, to wit:

- The individual will seek out others like himself, in order to form alliances, in order to make existence easier, if not to help ensure survival.
- The clique will impose its will on existing and potential members by common acceptance of the rankings awarded to members. Exemplary behavior is rewarded with a higher standing; poor performance will lead to the dreaded lowering of the hierarchical score, potentially all the way to Omega-wolf status.
- The faculty of the high school, in addition to the assignment of grades, will use other methods of, shall we say, encouraging the student body to behave better. In addition to the aforementioned awards and recognition, the school is in a position to punish unwanted behavior. In previous generations this power was far more significant than it is in the beginning of the twenty-first century (at least in the United States), and challenges to this power has led to a weakening in the school's ability to impose its will on its students.

A fascinating aspect of the differences between the ways that the individual will seek to impose his will vs. the strategies employed by the school (or any larger organization, for that matter) has to do with two major schools of psychoanalysis, the previously evaluated Freud/Berne model, and the assertions put forth by B. F. Skinner. In *Beyond Freedom and Dignity*, Skinner asserts that there is no free-thinking, autonomous man; instead, we are a collection of learned behaviors, inculcated via operant conditioning.[4] Scott's placement of his White Arrow has little to do with any punishment/reward cycle to which he subjects himself. It's subject entirely to the way he pieces together his experiences into an *internal* narrative. Conversely, Midtown High School's faculty really does not care what Scott thinks of himself. They will reward acceptable behaviors, and punish unacceptable ones. Scott can firmly believe that he is a descendant of the Romanov Dynasty, and it won't change his algebra quiz grades one iota. In a sense, the entire proposition of presenting a structure of how individuals interact and move within hierarchical social structures is an exercise in reconciling Freud/Berne and Skinner, as different as these two psychological schools may be. The individuals' behaviors are driven by the internal conflicts (and their potential resolutions), while the group's behaviors are far more behaviorist in execution. And yet, demonstrations of just such a reconciliation play out in millions of individual/group interactions every day, with high school being, perhaps, among the more dramatically observable venues.

How It All Looks to Scott

Revisiting Scott's Black and White Arrow placement, even though he may have walked into the school on his first day with the arrows more or less aligned, significant pressures are already acting on these arrows, in both directions, as he attempts to find and fit in with the clique best suited to helping him attain his goals. As the arrows separate, the difference between them is a way of capturing the concept of delusion. Graphically, this is shown in Figure 5.4.

To be fair to Scott, virtually all of us are deluded to some extent. Feeling good about ourselves, allowing the acceptance of the belief that we are better-than-average (if not exemplary) people in all or most of the relevant, important areas of human pursuit is a key component to happiness. The opposite, the pervasive sense that we are sub-standard in the things that matter, and that it is ether impossible or prohibitively difficult to change this ranking, is at the very heart of depression.

Based on this concept, there are four possible extreme combinations:

- An individual is low on merit, but views themselves as highly valuable (low Black Arrow, high White Arrow).
- An individual scores low on merit, and views himself appropriately (both White and Black Arrows are low on the relative value scale).

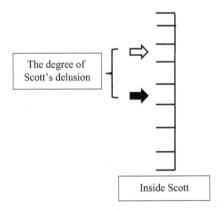

Figure 5.4 Scott's Rank Delta

- The person is highly meritorious, but views themselves as being of little consequence (high Black, low White).
- The person is highly meritorious, and knows it (both White and Black Arrows are high on the scale).

This structure parallels the ancient Arabic proverb:

> He who knows not, and knows not that he knows not, is a fool. Shun him.
>   He who knows not, and knows that he knows not, is simple. Teach him.
>   He who knows, and knows not that he knows, is asleep. Wake him.
>   He who knows, and knows that he knows, is wise. Follow him.

Converted, the parable references, in order,

- High White, low Black
- Low White, low Black
- Low White, high Black
- High White, high Black

Consider also the parable about the student of philosophy who had sought out and finally discovered a renowned wise man. The wise man invited the student into his hovel, and offered him tea. As the tea was brewing, the student talked excitedly about his desire to learn from the ancient, and discussed his ideas on the significance of the wise man's writings to the field of philosophy. Once the kettle whistled, the wise man began to pour the hot water into the student's cup, and kept pouring even as the cup overflowed.

"Can't you see that the cup is overflowing?" asked the student.

"Yes, I can," replied the wise man. "Can you not see that I can teach you nothing if your mind is already so full?"

In the structure I am proposing, another way the wise man could have made his point would have been to say "Your White Arrow is too far above your Black Arrow to be taught anything. In order for that to change, you are going to have to lower your estimation of your relative value, painful as that may be."

As Scott presents himself to the series of cliques at Midtown, he does not want to appear as if his White Arrow is significantly above his Black Arrow, but he would very much like his Black Arrow to not be perceived lower than it is to the hundreds of voyeur eyes that are upon him. Walter E. Williams' mom may have said "It's a sad dog that won't wag its own tail," but the fact is that braggadocio may as easily be rooted in a legitimate desire to not be underrated as it could be a signal that the subject doing the bragging is a high White/low Black Arrow (or, in the Arabic proverb, a "fool"). It is for this reason that advanced but hidden, unadvertised talents, of almost any practical value at all, have their maximum potential to change others' perceptions (and, therefore, estimation/ranking) of the hidden-talent holder if the talent is revealed accidentally, as a matter of course. This is especially true when the hidden talent being revealed is something the hierarchy truly craves at that time.

Scott recognizes two old friends of his from junior high, Mitch and Jim, with whom he had played soccer for a couple of seasons. Mitch and Jim, in turn, spend much of their time with a group of other kids, and invite Scott to join them during recesses and lunch periods, and Scott accepts. After his first four classes of his first day, Scott makes his way to the cafeteria, hoping to spot Mitch and Jim. He does, and they're sitting at a table with some other kids, some of whom Scott recognizes from his earlier classes. Scott gets his tray of food, and makes his way over to the table, hoping to get there before the last seat at that table is taken by another student.

As Scott arrives, he sees that Mitch's books are stacked on that part of the bench that Scott had assumed was a vacant seat. As Mitch sees Scott approach, he calls over, and removes his books. Mitch has just signaled to the rest of the clique the belief that Scott would be an acceptable addition to the group, and has emphasized it by not only inviting Scott over, but by saving him a place at the table. It's easy for those not caught up in the dynamic of this early clique forming to ascribe trivial or even unsubstantial significance to such behaviors as the saving of a certain seat in a high school cafeteria, but to those in the middle of it they can be of immense, even life-changing consequence.

As Scott sits the entire clique scrutinizes every readily apparent aspect of him, from the cut of his hair, selection of clothes, any books he may be carrying, the foods he has selected – basically, everything. Oh, they don't have mental checklists or anything like that (at least most of them don't). They are simply getting the proverbial first impression; or, using our adopted vernacular, performing the initial placement of the Black Arrow. Of course, a (relatively) reliable initial Black Arrow placement can't be performed simply on looks (once again accessing that library of pithy insight, the clichés, "Never judge a book by its cover"), so members of the clique will introduce themselves and engage in the practice of extracting the key talents and virtues that may be brought to the group, should they let him in, known as "small talk."

Within the clique is a not-so-subtle line of distinction between the sexes. This is due to the primary role of the high school clique, the ascertainment of its members' fitness as potential spouses. This particular clique's girls include (in no particular order):

- Lori, a pretty blonde,
- Phyllis, with black hair and a pleasant smile,
- Tammy, who initially comes across as fairly non-descript,
- Celeste, who could pass as a librarian,
- Nancy, tall with long red hair and a sunny disposition, and
- Audra, who appears to be the most retiring and shy, and has taken the nickname "Sam."

The list of males includes:

- Jeff, tall and muscular, but with harsh features,
- Mitch, as tall but not as fit as Jeff, plays baseball and soccer,
- Jim, slight of build and intellectual,
- Chris is also an intellectual, but is no stranger to athletics and has a calm, cheery demeanor,
- Marcus appears to be nervous about something, and
- Eike (pronounced *EYE-kuh*), an exchange student from Germany.

There are many dynamics occurring all at once within the first moments after Scott has taken his seat. Should Scott eventually gain admittance to the clique, for example, the boys would outnumber the girls. Even though the notion that each of the males will align in their pecking order with the clique's similarly ranked females as they marry is patently absurd, group dynamics will often unfold as if this is an unstated but self-evident truth. It's a conceit similar to the notion that, once admitted, any member of the pack can't simply leave without enduring difficult circumstances, as in the creation of lone wolves. Unfortunately for Scott, the accidental implication that's attached to him, *even before he has taken his seat*, is that should he (a) be accepted into the group, and (b) assume any role other than that of Omega Wolf, that at least one of the current male members of the clique will not mate. As absurd as that may sound, I can assure you it is a subliminal part of virtually any voluntary grouping of high school-age *Homo Sapiens Sapiens*.

Recall one of the lessons brought forward from Game Theory, specifically the Hawk-Dove game. Just as the population's payout is maximized if each of them adopts the Dove strategy, so, too, would Midtown's student body benefit if such maneuverings were not taking place. However, with the introduction of just one Hawk into the bird population, the Nash Equilibrium quickly moves to 25%/75% Hawk-Dove strategy selection. Similarly, within this clique the kids would have a much better chance of achieving their academic (and other significant) goals if they were not engaged in this sort of hierarchical competition. But, with the introduction of just one Jeff…

Meanwhile, back at Midtown's cafeteria, the girls are also involved in some hierarchical maneuverings. Just as Scott's dream hierarchical position throughout high school would be the accepted and acknowledged leader of the coolest group of kids at the best available private prep school, the girls' goals are very similar. Though the girls may not have an equally intense drive to assume a leadership position, they do have a highly acceptable, if not maniacally sought-after, alternative: to be the presumptive mate of the male who is the most attractive, best able to guarantee economic and physical security, and most likely to form an emotional attachment so intense that the selected male would sacrifice everything to be their consort. For all the talk of so-called "trophy wives" in American culture, the truth is that, generally speaking, adult males are far less likely to change their opinions of other males based on the sexual attractiveness of their mates than women are to change their estimation of each other based on the hierarchical placement of those women's spouses, primarily economically.

Imagine a time traveler coming back from 30 years in the future, and addressing the clique's girls alone. Without revealing specifics about their future biographies (that whole changing-the-future business, you know), this time traveler can reveal:

- of the six girls, five of them will marry at least once,
- two of them will marry twice,
- one of them will be relatively poor, one relatively well-off,
- three of them will encounter some sort of medical condition that strains their marital relations, their economic status, or both, and
- all of these outcomes will be at least partly influenced by their decisions and behaviors in high school.

And yet, these revelations should not come as a shock to these girls. In fact, it's pretty much what they would expect, the ego self-defense mechanism being that each of them believes that they will be the one to be economically well-off, married once, and not facing any serious medical conditions. To get to that place, though, they have to be spot-on with their choice of mates in addition to any other academic achievements expected of them, and the ability to make the best choice will depend on their ability to collect the most clues about potential mates. Here's where both Game Theory and voyeurism play key roles.

A potential clique inductee's status in other associations will provide clues as to the appropriateness of allowing them into the circle of friends, as well as their standing should they be accepted. If Scott had arrived at his invited seat wearing expensive clothes and shoes, and discussed his internship at his father's investment company, both his admittance and high initial ranking within this particular clique would be virtually guaranteed. Conversely, if his clothes and appearance are disheveled, and he sports a marginally obscene tattoo on his lower arm, his rejection becomes a foregone conclusion. While there are outside chances that disheveled tattooed freshmen will eventually become captains of industry while wealthy, expertly trained ones are destined to lives of marginal existence, the voyeuristic girls are usually going to be unwilling to expend the time nor energy to collect additional clues, and will come to their conclusions about the fit and meet of extreme presenters fairly instantaneously.

Scott presents as neither extreme as he sits down for lunch. Mitch begins.

"Hey, everybody, this is Scott. Jim and I have been playing soccer with him for the past couple of years."

Everybody: "Hi, Scott."

"Where are you from?" asks Jeff.

"I live down off of Uptown Boulevard, across from the strip mall at Jefferson."

"Isn't that outside Midtown's boundaries?" Jeff continues, with a sneer.

"No, actually, the boundaries were adjusted this past summer."

"It just seems weird," Jeff continues, addressing the other kids in the group more so than Scott, "that a kid who lives on *Uptown* should go to *Midtown* High School."

"Remember that one game against Highland? Where you had that gnarly hit against that one dude… that reminds me – how's your knee, Scott? Did it ever completely heal?" Jim asks.

"Not one-hundred percent," Scott replies.

"Well, at least you're not limping," Mitch adds.

"Yeah, I can get around on it, but I'm not so sure about trying out for the soccer team."

"What happened?" Nancy asks. Mitch jumps in.

"Oh, you should have seen it. The score's tied, with minutes left, the ball's on our side of the field, right in front of the goal, and Highland has this one dude that had been playing nasty all day. It looks like he's going to score the winning goal when, out of nowhere, Scott comes flying at the ball. This dude sees Scott, and squares up against him like he's going to try and take him out. Then there's this collision, the ball goes flying off, and both Scott and this guy aren't getting up."

"You guys are talking soccer?" Jeff interjects.

"Yeah."

"Huh," grunts Jeff.

"What's your sport, Jeff?" Scott asks.

"Wrestling."

"You trying out?"

"Don't have to. The coach knows my dad, and has invited me on the team. I'm going to be first in my weight class."

"What weight class is that, gorilla, or orangutan?" asks Tammy.

Jeff looks over at her with his rapidly-becoming-familiar sneer.

"Silverback."

"Scott, are you coming to the bonfire?" Nancy asks.

"Oh, uh, I'm not sure. When is it?"

"This Friday night."

Both Mitch and Jim look over at Scott, and Mitch gives him an ever-so-slight nod.

"Sounds great."

The school bell rings, and Scott looks at his tray.

He hasn't eaten a bite.

* * * *

Several interactive dynamics that will have a direct bearing on Scott's acceptance and ranking within the clique have taken place, so we'll take a moment to analyze some of them. Let's begin with the assertion that to map out the individual-to-individual interactions among the triple aspects of the kids' personas reveals very little, if for no other reason than the interactions involved most of the members of the clique. The communications threw off so many clues in different directions, and to different consumers/voyeurs, that isolating them to just the speaker/speaker's target would return misleading clues. Besides, even if we were to map these interactions out in a manner similar to the analysis technique in *Games People Play*, they would quickly assume the opaque density of an old-style telephone exchange switchboard circuit map, as happened in the far fewer participant analysis from Bob and his team leaders from Acme, in Chapter 3.

As complex as it was, however, several clues were offered up, including:

- Jeff views himself as the Alpha male. Advertising a membership in a high school wrestling team is prima facie evidence that the one doing the advertising is almost certainly capable of overcoming most adversaries in a fist fight, in American high schools, anyway.
- Mitch, Jim, and Nancy have all signaled that they are okay with Scott joining their circle of friends, at least initially. Jeff, on the other hand, is signaling opposition. Whether this means Jeff prefers exclusion, or inclusion as long as Scott acknowledges Jeff's "superiority," is still an open question.
- Tammy recognizes that Jeff views himself as superior, but that supposition is backed up by an implicit threat of force, something that Tammy dislikes in the group dynamic. Knowing that Jeff can't harm her physically (or even threaten to do so) without immediately losing any ranking within the group leaves her free to challenge him with impunity, as long as it's not seen as capricious or mean-spirited; hence, the cloak of humor.
- Jeff's one-word reply to Tammy, while consistent with the level of humor Tammy was employing, also reinforced both his view of his standing, and served to reinforce the implicit threat of demonstrated physical superiority.

- While it was Mitch who made the initial overtures to bring Scott into the group, Jim is okay with it, and went out of his way to let Scott's story of sportsman-like courage be told to the clique without Scott having to appear like a braggart. Whereas Mitch's motives in bringing in Scott may have been apparent, Jim's motives are more complex, and will become more apparent later.
- Nancy engaged Scott in communication, which is, all by itself, remarkable. Girls will only rarely initiate non-essential conversation with a male of her own age without signaling some level of spousal interest, if only at the curiosity level. Once initiated, though, the rules of this game are all in the female's favor. Should Scott's unrevealed Black Arrow prove to be highly placed according to the standards of the clique, Nancy's early overtures, as innocent and innocuous as they were, could return huge benefits. Scott is clearly in a vulnerable position, and Nancy provided a level of solace, however miniscule. If Scott proves to be a winner, Nancy can leverage her early emotional gambit into something more substantial. Should Scott prove a loser, she can claim nothing more than common courtesy, and discretely disengage.

Lori, Phyllis, Celeste, Audra, Chris, Marcus, and Eike haven't said a word. They were only too happy to eat their lunches and listen, and watch the events as they unfolded. The extent to which they took in the interactional dynamics listed in the above bullets may or may not influence their behaviors going forward. For the time being, though, the interactions they just witnessed do provide, at some level of cognizance, information on:

- Whether or not they will support Scott's acceptance.
- How comfortable they are with Jeff's continued efforts to assert his group supremacy.
- Whom among the females is most willing to abandon the available pool of males (Nancy).
- The nature of the narrative of the clique as a whole. As previously mentioned, an obviously base, poorly dressed individual would not have even been introduced to the group, while the introduction of a well-bred, wealthy overachiever would have been automatically accepted (even by Jeff). The willingness – or lack thereof – of the clique to accept the in-betweens is a type of barometer of the clique's value vis-à-vis the other groups of kids at Midtown.

Our clique is experiencing the "new kid in town" effect. What's happening is that, with the introduction of an unknown (or barely known) potential inductee into the pack, nobody really knows where this person's Black Arrow is placed. By engaging in conversation or other social interactions (sports, behavior at a cafeteria table, participation (or lack thereof) in a school bonfire) with the newcomer, some clues can be gleaned, primarily about where the newbie's White Arrow is placed. From there, it's a short hop over to being able to gauge the difference between the White and Black Arrows, to arrive at a usable ranking of the individual, both with respect to their position as clique member and, ultimately, as potential spouse.

The ever present, inescapable zeitgeist here is the fact that there are many eyes on the myriad goings-on in the lunch room at Midtown High School. These voyeurs seek clues, to be instructed, if you will, on the parameters of the game that they will all enter into, the outcome of which will have a profound impact on the academic, romantic, and professional trajectories they will most likely take for the rest of their lives.

Think I'm exaggerating? In a subsequent chapter I will go over Metcalf's Law, also known as the Butterfly Effect. Briefly, Metcalf's Law states that even very small variations in a limited number of nodes in an extended network can (and, often, will) cascade into cataclysmic events to nodes on the other end of the network. It's nicknamed the Butterfly Effect after the speculative question "If a butterfly flaps its wings in Brazil, does that cause a hurricane in Texas?" Several movies (*Mr. Destiny*, *The Butterfly Effect*, *Back to the Future*) deal with the idea that relatively small and (considered at the time) events of low consequence did, indeed, have life-altering consequences. I'm not using these fictional settings as evidence to buttress the idea that Scott's performance in the cafeteria on his first day of high school will have long-lasting consequences – the evidence for the validity of Metcalf's Law does not need this manner of support. What I am asserting is that there is much voyeurism present in the creation, realignment, and possible destruction of all social constructs, and that this voyeurism isn't idle, nor (necessarily) malignant.

It is, however, on several levels, highly instructional.

Notes

1 Howe, Edgar Watson, retrieved from *Desktop Quotes*, http://www.desktop-quotes.com/high-school-friendship-quotes.html, July 5, 2015.
2 Retrieved from *Bullying Statistics*, http://www.bullyingstatistics.org/content/bullying-and-suicide.html, June 14, 2015.
3 Milton, John, *Paradise Lost*, Book 1, lines 258–63, retrieved from https://en.wikiquote.org/wiki/Paradise_Lost, February 10, 2016.
4 Skinner, Burhus Frederic, *Beyond Freedom and Dignity*. Indianapolis, IN: Hackett Publishing Company, 2002.

Chapter 6

The Unavoidable Hierarchy

Shame may restrain what law does not prohibit.
Lucius Annaeus Seneca[1]

The American music band *Creedence Clearwater Revival* (CCR) sold 26 million records in the United States alone.[2] Its four members – brothers John and Tom Fogerty, with Stu Cook and Doug Clifford, were inducted into the Rock and Roll Hall of Fame in 1993. *CCR* was active from 1968 to 1972, when they abruptly split.

The American music band *The Monkees* sold over 75 million records worldwide, and had the 12th-highest selling album of all time (*More of the Monkees*).[3] Appearing in a television program of the same name from 1966–8, the band would abruptly split in 1971 (though sporadic reunions continue to the present day).

The English music band *The Beatles* formed in 1960, dissolved in 1970, and, in-between, became what is largely regarded as the most influential music group of the generation (if not beyond). They are the best-selling band in history, selling more than 600 million records.[4] The band abruptly split in the early 1970s.

The American football club *The Dallas Cowboys* have been to more Super Bowls than any other team. In the late 1980s, they were purchased by an oil executive, Jerry Jones, who, in turn, hired his (then) friend Jimmy Johnson as head coach. In the years they worked together, the Cowboys returned to championship form, winning back-to-back championships 1992–3. Following the 1993 season, Jimmy Johnson abruptly resigned.

What do all of these packs (strikethrough) groups of people have in common?

There's a certain fascination on the reasons behind the sudden, dramatic dissolution of voluntarily enjoined organizations that experience next to unfathomable success. In each of the instances cited above, at least one of the principals perceived that he was not receiving sufficient credit for the overall group's success, and was in a position to prove the assertion by voluntarily disengaging from the group.

Tom Fogerty was reportedly put off by his younger brother taking charge of the artistic and business aspects of *CCR*. He left the group in 1972, and died in 1990, with his brother John at his bedside. His last words were an insult to John, intended to convey that they could never be reconciled – all over the management of (and credit for) the music they had made together with *CCR*.[5] Prior to their success as artists, members of *CCR* worked at a car wash.

The three founding members of the Beatles came from humble beginnings as well, working some of the rougher venues in Liverpool and Hamburg. Once their successful trajectory began, though, it became such a phenomenon that it spawned its own terminology: "Beatlemania." Other music groups from the United Kingdom that found success in American markets were considered to be part of the "British Invasion."

In the January 1981 issue of *Playboy* magazine, Lennon said the following:

> PLAYBOY: "That was the one that contributed to the 'Paul McCartney is dead' uproar because of the lyric 'The walrus is Paul.'"
> LENNON: "Yeah. That line was a joke, you know. That line was put in partly because I was feeling guilty because I was with Yoko, and I knew I was finally high and dry. In a perverse way, I was sort of saying to Paul, 'Here, have this crumb, have this illusion, have this stroke... because I'm leaving you.'[6]

At a meeting in January 1967, producer Don Kirschner presented the members of The Monkees – Davy Jones, Michael Nesmith, Peter Tork, and Mickey Dolenz – royalty checks of $250,000 each (£155,000), the equivalent of $1,800,000 (£1,120,000) in 2014 funds, for their work through their second album. However, Michal Nesmith got into a heated argument with Kirschner over management issues, particularly the group's latitude in selecting which songs to record, the use of their own material, and the right to play their own instruments on the recordings rather than studio musicians.[7] The argument became so intense that Nesmith punched a hole in a wall, and told Kirschner "That could have been your face!" Kirschner would soon leave the franchise, the television series lasted only two seasons, and the band would break up in 1971 after a five-year initial run.

The Dallas Cowboys football club is the most valuable franchise in America's National Football League. The team maintains several records – longest winning streak (20 seasons), longest home sellout streak, longest road game sellout streak, most number of NFC championships, among others. However, starting in 1986, the team's fortunes began to decline, culminating with a disastrous 3–13 record in 1988. Its then owner was forced by his economic circumstances to sell the team by the Federal Savings and Loan Insurance Corporation, when it was purchased by Jerry Jones.

Jerry Jones set out to turn the team into a champion again. He hired his friend and ex-Arkansas Razorback football team mate and then University of Miami head coach Jimmy Johnson, and between them changed the moribund team into a Super Bowl winner. However, after an NFL owner's meeting held in March 1994, after a long day of meetings, Jerry Jones walked into a lounge where Jimmy Johnson and several other coaches from the Cowboys' successful 1992–3 seasons were convened. According to Skip Bayless' account of the incident, Jones proposed a toast to the Cowboys, and Johnson simply glared at him.[8] After years of difficulties with Johnson, Jones had had enough, and Johnson was sent packing (although, at the press conference announcing his departure, Johnson would refer to it as a mutual decision).

In each of these four instances the sudden and – to fans, anyway – disappointing breakup of wildly successful entertainment packs (strikethrough) associations had their roots in the conflict engendered when key participating members could not agree on the amount of credit owed them for the group's overall success. This tends to happen a lot in entertainment venues, but not so much in, say, international chess competitions. Have you ever wondered why?

Typical chess associations, such as the United States Chess Federation, assign newcomers a certain number of points. From that starting position, points are awarded or deducted from your score based on your chess-playing performance. Wins against higher-ranked opponents bring in more points than wins against lower-ranked opponents, and losses against higher-ranked opponents are not as big a hit on the score as losses against lower-ranked opponents.

The game of chess also has a unique quality to it, not shared with virtually any other competitive endeavor. If you win, it's because you are probably the better player. If you lose, you were the poorer player. Period. Oh, masters and grandmasters can certainly have their off-days, like anybody else, which is why World Championships are never awarded off of just one (or even a few) games. But there can really be no doubt about it: a pattern of winning in chess is due to the talent and expertise of the player doing the winning, and nothing else. Having your value to, say, the United States chess team be so definitively and exactly quantified precludes any ambiguity about the level of your contribution. The tactic of disengaging from a chess team, or threatening to disengage, in order to be accredited with more value to the team than the member believes he is receiving is a pointless maneuver.

But when the subject turns to music groups, or even athletic teams, the proximate cause of the subject group's success becomes much, much more subjective. As with other pursuits within the macro economy, there are simply far too many parameters to evaluate, even if those parameters could be definitively quantified (which, except in extremely rare circumstances, they can't). All of which brings us to a trio of truisms:

- In purely voluntary-associated groups – ones where the members could walk away with little or no perceived negative consequences – disengagement is the ultimate arbiter of individual value.
- Even here, though, an accurate assessment of an individual's contribution to a group is quite impossible, as the group is invariably more than the sum of its individual contributors.
- In groups where association is mostly or completely involuntary – school, or prison, say – the ultimate arbiter of individual value is success in violent confrontation.

What's a Pack to Do?

The key to understanding group behavior, then, is to embrace the idea that the group itself will develop and manifest a personality, defined as observable patterns of behaviors. These behaviors present themselves to three targets:

- individuals, or how the group treats its own or potential members;
- externals, with whom the group interacts;
- external hierarchies with which the group competes, or must comply.

For example, borrowing from *Romeo and Juliet*, the first category pertains to how the Montagues and Capulets treat the members of their own clans, and other, non-aligned individuals. The second aspect of the group's (actually, in this example, family's) character would be the behaviors exhibited when interacting with their rival clans, in this case, incessant brawling. Finally, the Montagues and Capulets manifest a third facet of the group personality when interacting with the character of the prince, who represents the hierarchical structure that both families – actually, all families in Verona – must obey.

In case the reader has not noticed, these are loosely aligned with the combined Berne/Freud model, of the three aspects of the persona, the Id/Child, Ego/Adult, and Superego/Parent, respectively, and we'll look at them in that order.

The individuals who are already in the group will often sort themselves into a linear hierarchy not unlike that of wolves, chimpanzees, or a host of other social animal groupings. In doing so, they take on roles within the clan that lead them to behave in ways they would not otherwise act. The social construct begins to take on a life, a personality of its own, which is why the expression "If you want me to tell you the quality of the man, show me his friends" rings true. The individual chooses (to some extent) the groups to which he belongs, but the groups also exert a type of selection process that allows or disallows new members.

The voluntary social construct, then, behaves almost as its own entity. This entity, generally speaking, has access to a series of tactics, including the following:

- rejecting a potential member
- accepting the potential member
- threatening to reject a current member
- actually rejecting a current member, which has two variants:
  - reducing them in status, down to and including Omega wolf role
    - a quick caveat: removing an Alpha, or sometimes even a Beta, usually means complete removal. It's rare that an individual, having once been in the upper levels of group rank and then removed from there, will continue on in that particular group in the muddling middle.
  - banishing them from the group altogether
- raising the rank of an existing member.

In order for the group as a whole to be considered to have implemented any of these tactics, a preponderance of the more important members must have reached the decision to do so individually. It is something of a paradox that the overall group's decisions are comprised of a consistency among the participating individuals, but that this is so is evident in the strategy employed by those who seek to change the character of a group. There are two ways of making a social construct's character adhere to a specific vision: start one yourself, that adheres to your vision, and, as it grows, ensure the group's character does not diverge; or, infiltrate a group that is somewhat similar to your vision, and persuade key influencers within that group to change things in the direction you seek.

Packs of wolves exist in a wilderness environment, pods of killer whales exist in the sea, and social constructs of humans form in response to their environments, as well. Just as the wolfpack that abandons the tactics that lead to the most capable wolf assuming the alpha role, the second-most capable assuming the beta role, etc., will eventually become extinct, so, too, do the social constructs humans enter into eventually fail if the individuals who assume leadership or influential roles turn out to be lacking in the talents that benefit the association overall. The kids in the clique evaluating Scott may resent the feeling of being placed too low in the group's hierarchy, but the ironic fact is that, if some hard, recognized, and accepted evaluation system were to deliver the wrong leaders, then that clique would very quickly become unattractive. The first board of Midtown High School's chess team should verifiably be the best chess player at the school who is also willing to play competitive tournaments. Alas, the most appropriate leaders or influencers for virtually every other social construct are not as easily identified, due to the exceptionally subjective nature of evaluating value brought by the members of the social construct.

While all of this consideration simmers beneath the group's surface, the group has a need to show to the outside world (or the other cliques at Midtown, anyway) an image of tranquil attractiveness. High-achieving, cool high schoolers will not wish to join a clique that they perceive is contentious or adversarial. Further, should enough kids decide that a certain clique is decidedly uncool, then that clique can and will be quickly reduced to simply a quasi-consistent gathering of a handful of friends – hardly a factor, or even a presence, in a typical high school's social structure. Conversely, should a clique become so attractive that dozens of kids wish to join, all while some form of a social filter fails to exclude low-performing, unattractive (for whatever reason so deemed) kids, then the organization, even with a relatively large population, will lose standing with respect to the other voluntary associations available to the students of Midtown.

For example, the population of varsity cheerleaders is typically limited to five to twelve attractive, at least somewhat athletic girls, and for this reason (among others) membership in this association tends to be highly valued. Contrast this with, say, the aforementioned varsity chess team, which is made up of the best seven players of a board game then in attendance at the school. Of course, the ability to play chess well often points to advanced intelligence, but little else associated with the realm of demonstrating potential fit and meet for a future spouse.

Still, the members of the chess team do enjoy a certain aura of intelligence and, therefore, implied potential future success in professional or economic competition, one that cheerleaders typically do not experience. Indeed, the popularity of cheerleaders in high school is often shadowed by a brutal truth, one that tends to be kept in the background for the four years that the students attend classes. And that truth is: the moment that each of them walks across the stage and receives their diploma, *all* of the rankings of *all* of the social constructs that have been built up, maintained, and meant so much to the happiness of so many, in an instant, disappear.

This truth is evident elsewhere. The moment that Credence Clearwater Revival split, Tom Fogerty never played on a number one song. Nor did Michael Nesmith when the Monkees split. John Lennon's solo career was far less successful than his time with the Beatles (and significantly less successful than the solo careers of Paul McCartney or George Harrison) and, after leaving Dallas, Jimmy Johnson only won one more playoff game.

So, in addition to the characteristics that the social construct takes on that lead it to resemble its own entity, they also tend to have a lifespan. From the organization's point of view (remember – it is its own entity) the longest possible lifespan is preferable, since those who join it voluntarily are receiving some form of benefit, sometimes even a substantial one. A harmonious relationship among the group's members is far more conducive to group longevity than contentiousness, which is why fans of an association of entertainers – music groups, television show casts, sports teams – are usually very interested in any news of a breakdown in such relationships.

But, again, some level of internecine conflict is going to be automatically present, since organizations that fail to enforce the optimal rules for assigning rank or value will trend towards becoming less competitive with similar groups, and those that fail to enforce any rules at all will quickly cease being effective social constructs of any kind. What we see here is a never-ending dynamic: individuals within the group seek higher and higher rank, while the group itself can't provide such positive reinforcement on an ongoing basis without becoming irrelevant, and then onto extinction. All organizations have a lifespan and, when that time is up, *all* of the energy, all of the time, all of the conniving and maneuvering and manipulations that went into supporting the high rankings of the groups' leaders, it all comes to naught.

Some years back the New York Metropolitan Museum of Modern Art had a display that was trash. I'm not engaging in hyperbole here – it was literally litter, framed. One prescient art critic pointed out that, if everything is to be considered art, then nothing is really art. The aesthetically mundane, when raised in rank to the equivalent of the aesthetically rare and coveted, displaces the rare and coveted rather than makes the mundane attractive. So it is with social hierarchies. A particular grouping may deliberately elevate a non-virtuous member to a ranking that would normally require some display of talent or virtue (with politics being the most obvious such venue), but that does not make such an individual talented or virtuous. Indeed, such a tactic serves as a black mark against the organization that employs it. An institution predicated on that which must be one of the most subjective of predicates – what is and what is not "art" – has more latitude to indulge in such misapplied ranking assignments, since those who disagree that framed litter is an appropriate attraction simply can't damage those responsible for the decision to do so. However, other hierarchies – like high school cliques – are more vulnerable to foolish or indulgent behaviors.

The third tier of hierarchical interaction with which the group must deal is with its competitors and structured superiors. The rock band must behave a certain way with the captains of the music industry, the professional (American) football team must comply with the edicts of the front offices of the National Football League, and the kids' cliques at Midtown High School must agreeably interact with the faculty and administration of the school, or else face the consequences.

This third tier, for its part, has its own problems. Even the most heavy-handed hierarchical control of a non-voluntary association, the administration of a prison, can't be overly arbitrary or capricious. As bad as prison conditions tend to be, if they drop below a certain point over a long enough period of time then the inmates will expose themselves to danger and depravity in order to overthrow the existing regime. I once attended a talk given by a psychologist who had spent time as a counselor in a penitentiary, and was asked by an incredulous attendee why hardened criminals should have access to television programs, law libraries, or even conjugal visits. The answer was that, even though these reprobates were in prison, they could still riot, and the threat of a prison riot was sufficient to persuade the guards, managers, and administrative staff of the penitentiary to introduce into the inmates' environment items that kept them entertained, distracted, or otherwise disincentivized to plot or carry out revolutionary strategies.

Another way of putting it would be to say that, even in those instances where the rankings of the members of a group are appropriately and inescapably placed low (their Black Arrows are resting on the lowest rung of the scale), forcing their White Arrows at or below that level will invariably result in an attempt at reordering the hierarchy and, in non-voluntary associations, that means violent confrontation.

High schools, of course, are a bit different, but there can be no question that resolution of many an intractable conflict occurs through either forced disengagement (expulsion) or through violence, though the violent resolutions almost always occur outside of the reach of the faculty or administration of a school. Midtown High School may grant official recognition to the chess team, and even sponsor its events, while banning the white supremacists from organizing a club that meets on campus. This "banning" comes with the implicit threat that, should the skinheads arrange to meet in a certain part of the school anyway, that each member will be expelled should they be caught doing so. Ultimately, should the skinheads meet anyway, get caught and expelled, and still insist on meeting on campus, the police will be called in. Should the white supremacists *still* resist, then the police will employ violent tactics to remove the group's threat to non-white minority students (who are being opposed as members of a group, even if such a grouping is not entered into by those targeted students, voluntarily or otherwise).

From the point of view of Midtown's principal, the optimal goal of the organizations on campus would be for the attainment of academic or athletic excellence, with each member of the entire school's student body affiliated with at least one of them. Such organizations would gladly employ "Midtown" in their names, and the school itself would encourage these groups' formation and performance. As their combined and focused energies come to fruition, as evidenced by higher test scores, championships in competitive endeavors (especially academic ones, such as academic decathlon, speech and debate, and the aforementioned chess team), and consistently proffered scholarships to higher-level universities, attendance at Midtown would become more and more coveted, and the payout for everyone involved would be maximized.

Wow – remember that phrase, "payout maximized," from earlier in the book? I made reference to it while discussing basic Game Theory, specifically the Hawk-Dove game. In that chapter I pointed out that, in said Hawk-Dove game, the 100-bird version, that when all of the birds consistently select the Dove strategy, the entire population's payout is maximized. However, with the introduction of just one Hawk strategy-selecting bird, the Nash Equilibrium quickly reverts to 25% Hawk, 75% Dove. Since the groups themselves become something of an entity, they will begin to behave in certain ways that fall into patterns – in other words, the members of the group will select strategies at a rate that will resist change unless a change benefits the group as a whole. The cliques will find their own versions of the Nash Equilibrium within the game's environment, in this case, Midtown High School.

At the opposite end of the spectrum, Midtown's principal's nightmare scenario would be that few or none of the students joined or participated in the officially recognized and sponsored organizations, and the students who did would expose themselves to ridicule and rejection from the groups that did come into existence outside of the administration's influence. These groups would have as their goals the discovery and exploitation of the loopholes or gaps in the school's official rules that would allow minimal (or even no) participation or effort in the attainment of just-good-enough-to-get-by performance. With all of that extra energy diverted from Midtown-approved objectives, the kids would be far more inclined to engage in immoral or illegal activities, leading to plummeting scores on standardized tests and a consummate erosion of Midtown's reputation as an establishment of learning. Such a downward spiral is not only possible, it actually happens on a frightening scale, and with terrifying consistency. Faculties of schools caught in such a trajectory can rail all they want about the overall population's payout being maximized if everyone cooperates with the macro organization's stated purpose (especially if they engage Game Theory-type verbiage), and it probably will do exactly nothing.

Much like the first-tier individual and the second-tier organization (clique within the school), the third-tier organization has its Id/Child, Ego/Adult, and SuperEgo/Parent aspects of its persona. In this case, Midtown's three tiers contain the following characteristics:

- Its Id/Child seeks to survive, and minimize pain or other forms of distress. This aspect of the school's persona is stress-free when there are no violent confrontations among the students or faculty, or other forms of conflict that occur inside the school's walls.
- The Ego/Adult seeks to survive in the environment in which it finds itself. These goals include good relations with the teachers' unions and having a budget that is sufficient to cover all expected costs.
- The SuperEgo/Parent's goals are oriented towards excellence, especially in comparison to the other high schools in the area – the aforementioned scholastic and athletic excellence, high standardized test scores, a widespread reputation, etc.

In order to achieve these goals, Midtown – like virtually any other construct – has a series of rules. Some of them are formal and articulated, if not published; others, however, are never articulated, but still have energy behind them. But the rules that the SuperEgo/Parent aspect of the organization often run contrary to what is actually the normal functioning of the student body. Consider the examples in Table 6.1.

But even as the faculty enforces, however unevenly, the official, articulated rules, we see yet another conflict dynamic, since the teachers are themselves subject to their Id/Ego/SuperEgo demands. At one end of the spectrum, they would love to be widely accepted as brilliant instructors, uniquely qualified to connect with a wide variety of students in ways that facilitate their learning and lead to those high standardized test scores. On the other end of the scale, they have their limitations, in both time and energy, with their own careers and households to manage. Unless they are, indeed, uniquely talented as scholars and communicators, the chances are that attaining the ideal would require more (scarce) time and energy than they are willing to invest. Again, as with the Hawk-Dove game, if all of Midtown's teachers were to invest the amount of time and energy needed to supply a first-rate curriculum, then the odds of attaining that goal suddenly move upwards. But let just one of them come to the realization that much of the macro organization's success in attaining its goals depends on factors beyond their control (such as parental participation, willingness of the students to do the work, inherent intelligence of the students, etc.) and, despairing, select the just-get-by strategy in instruction, and a Nash Equilibrium will quickly set in, leading to mediocrity at best, with utter failure as a definite and ubiquitous possibility.

Table 6.1 Midtown: Rules vs. Practical Application

Official rule	Practical application
All bullying is prohibited.	It's impossible to stop all bullying, and overly zealous attempts to do so often result in more grossly unfair punishments handed down than are warranted. That being the case, the teachers observing the "bullying" will make a judgment call, a judgment call based on their own (extremely subjective) point of view.
No scholastic cheating is tolerated.	The kids are aware of whom they want to help and whom they wish to see fail academically, and for a variety of reasons. "Help" with homework, insight into which teacher's favor can be attained through which tactic, and so forth happen all the time.
No athletic cheating is allowed.	Depending of the value of the team's athletic programs, this rule can be anything from a truism to out-and-out joke. In order for their athletes to maintain the minimum grade point average, the University of North Carolina was accused of allowing a whole series of fake classes, where student athletes who were struggling academically could receive passing grades without ever actually attending class.[11]
The faculty is expected to behave in a fashion consistent with the well-being or advancement of the students.	If that's the case, then the teachers' unions would not be so adamantly opposed to the school choice movement in the United States, which has consistently shown to be of significant benefit to the individual students.
No running in the hallways.	The picayune makes an appearance! Rules like these are almost always unevenly applied, to students who, for whatever reason, have been singled out by the faculty for poor treatment.
For the purpose of reserving certain parts of the facility, it's first-come, first-served.	All well and good if the academic decathlon team wants to hold a fundraiser in the school's cafeteria on the same Saturday that the speech and debate team does. But, let the varsity cheerleading squad make their entreaty moments after academic decathlon does, and see who wins this one.
All parts of the school are open to the students during operating hours.	But the chess team probably should avoid walking down that part of the sidewalk where the varsity athletes congregate. No strict enforcement of the no-bullying rule there!
Detention is meted out only for disciplinary purposes, against verified transgressions of the stated rules.	Actually, no. I have known teachers to recognize, accept, and even help implement the social rankings of the cliques among the students by misusing the formal mechanisms of school discipline, including the meting out of detention.

Back to the Black and White Arrows

Just as an individual can believe of himself a higher deserved ranking within the organization than is deserved, so, too, are organizations themselves susceptible to believing of themselves a higher value than is justified by the facts. And, just like individuals, organizations can (and do) suffer from the gap between their actual value arrow (Black) and perceived, self-awarded arrow (White). When this gap is experienced by individuals, they will engage in the previously discussed ego defense mechanisms. By now, I am sure the reader knows where I'm going with this: groups, displaying, as they do, behavior consistent with being their own entity, will also adopt ego-defense mechanisms in order to accomplish the exact same purposes: that of keeping the White Arrow high on the scale, and defensibly so.

These are the titles of the ego defense mechanisms, as represented from Allpsych. com:[9]

- denial
- displacement
- intellectualization
- projection
- rationalization
- reaction formation
- regression
- repression
- sublimation
- suppression.

A common American expression when dealing with a government organization is "you can't fight city hall." It is similarly difficult to get an individual to recognize the difference between where their White and Black Arrows are placed in their internal hierarchy, for the same reasons (extreme pain) covered in Chapter 3. Each of these ten tactics can be useful; taken together, they can be insurmountable, and here's the kicker: the organizational entity has them, just as surely as does the individual.

Before we follow Scott back into this rat's nest of interacting, overlapping, parallel and opposed inter-relationships amongst this network's nodes, a quick reminder of a couple of theories is in order.

Berne's mapping of the communication channels between two individuals, while remarkably insightful, becomes inadequate as soon as we factor in the aspects of the personae of not only the two individuals then-communicating, but of other individuals within the immediate social construct, the individuals within the extended social construct, the groups within the overarching social construct, and so on, and so on. The simple map of three stacked circles with lines or arrows indicating the specific personae interacting quickly becomes a snarl not unlike the proverbial Gordian Knot (which, ironically, was also overcome by a violent solution).

We have also set the stage for demonstrations of Metcalf's Law. Again, also known as the "Butterfly Effect," it is the theory that, in large networks, relatively minor variations among relatively incidental nodes can cascade until they have cataclysmic impacts on many other nodes on the other end of the network map. Such occurrences are impossible to quantify, much less manage, as we shall see in Scott's adventures at Midtown High.

Meanwhile, Back at the Bonfire...

Scott actually lives within walking distance of Midtown, and arrives after the sun has set and the bonfire has been lit. There's a festive mood about, with enthused kids and wary faculty assuming various positions around the fire. Scott eventually finds Jeff, Mitch, Eike, Celeste, Tammy, and Nancy standing together, and approaches them.

"Hi, Scott!" Nancy exclaims.

Completely innocuous? Hardly. Nancy is transmitting several things:

- She believes Scott should be accepted by the clique.
- If he is accepted, Nancy has first dibs on whether or not a romantic relationship ought to be pursued.
- Preliminary analysis leads Nancy to believe Scott to potentially be a superior future spouse than any of the other available males already in the clique.
- And any opposition to Scott's acceptance in the clique increases the odds of Nancy's voluntary disengagement.

"Hi, um, Nancy," Scott answers. Two and one-half words, combined with Scott immediately assuming a position closest to Nancy, and the following is evident to the observant:

- Scott is relieved that at least one person in the clique other than Mitch appears willing to accept him.
- Scott doesn't know Nancy's standing in the clique's hierarchy, and so, while relieved, has yet to determine the value of an implied Nancy approval.
- Nancy, being pretty, will almost certainly be the first person that Scott is paired with on a trial basis for dating.

"Didn't see you pull up," Jeff sneers.
"I walked."
"Beats having your parents drop you off, I guess."
In an instant, Tammy knows she's being slighted, having been dropped off at the bonfire by her parents. Since the earlier-evaluated lunch period, Jeff has been waiting for an opportunity to casually but indirectly insult Tammy, for her remarks about Jeff's having been invited to join the wrestling team. Tammy's first impulse is to fire back, but her famous wit fails her. Not willing to appear overly willing to engage in a trite tit-for-tat with a person she considers her intellectual inferior, she says nothing, but inwardly seethes.
"Guess that depends on the walk," Scott offers, innocently.
Hierarchical alignment chaos ensues. Scott hasn't challenged Jeff as much as dissipated the power of his sleight, and has done so indirectly, as indirectly as Jeff has insulted Tammy. Jeff, assuming the role of Alpha, has the usual choices available to him with respect to his reply, ranging from no response, all the way to physically attacking Scott. But there's another dynamic in play – Alphas can't arbitrarily oppress the other members of the pack, not without the threat of losing status, or even being rejected. Also, Scott's challenge was not direct, meaning that Jeff's position as Alpha wasn't being contested, only his thinly veiled slight against Tammy.
At the same time, Tammy realizes she has (at least) a potential ally against Jeff, and Nancy is confirmed in her belief that Scott is no Omega. An Omega would have not responded to a quasi-insult from a clearly superior physical specimen, but Scott did not keep quiet, and Nancy took note.
And so did Mitch, Eike, and Celeste. Even prior to the instant-messaging age, the other members of the clique are quickly informed, and a consensus forms: Scott is in.
Part of the elements assisting Scott's quick acceptance into the clique has to do with his early standing: he can disengage, quickly and easily, with little or no long-term negative consequences.

And so it is with any group. Any potential member whose inclusion presents as attractive to others in the group will have a certain amount of energy behind them if they are in a position to quickly and without consequences disengage from the pack. When the group, and its own persona, perceives that it is enriched by the inclusion of an additional individual, it will behave in such a way as to make itself attractive to the candidate. Organizations that are confident that inclusion is highly desired will create barriers to entry, compelling potential members to overcome hardship to prove their "worth." Scott's new clique likes to believe of itself that membership is coveted, but the fact of the matter is that kids who can at least maintain an appearance of being better than average, while demonstrating an ability to assimilate the important portions of the group narrative embraced by a majority can expect quick acceptance.

Note how we haven't even touched on the perceptions of Celeste, Lori, Phyllis, or Audra, all of whom have a stake in the inclusion of Scott in the clique. If nothing else, the potential matching of Nancy with Scott will influence – if not out-and-out determine – the hierarchical ranking of the girls in the clique. Lori is Jeff's romantic interest, even though she makes it a point to keep the exact nature of their relationship ambiguous. Should their particular clique become prominent among the ones at Midtown, and should Jeff be widely recognized as its Alpha, of course Lori would want to be associated with Jeff. Conversely, should the clique begin to unravel, or should Jeff manifest behaviors that indicate possible lack of fitness as a future spouse, then the clique's lifespan will have come to an abrupt end, with all of the efforts expended in hierarchy climbing immediately put to waste. Lori will manipulate circumstances and people to the end of maintaining her maximum amount of latitude in delaying any kind of commitment with respect to clarifying the nature of her relationship with Jeff, at least until it's to her benefit to stake a claim, one way or the other.

Now imagine mapping all of this out in the Berne models. It would quickly become indecipherable – and we're only analyzing two – *two* – interactions, the latter being reduced to three sentences.

And yet, as haywire as all of this gets, there are some indicators of group rank that are more objective than others, economic status being one of the more obvious. While there are many examples of people becoming fantastically wealthy from extremely humble beginnings, the odds are far better for an individual to achieve and maintain an economically comfortable existence if they start from at least the middle of the pack. From my previous anger-the-feminists discussion in Chapter 5, pubescent females on the lookout for potential spouses are fully aware of this, as well as a host of other indicators that may point to a superior candidate for mating. The overall structure is in Figure 6.1.

In this case the evaluating female – Nancy – is not sure about Scott's fitness as a potential future spouse. One of the ways that she can quickly and effectively evaluate this fitness is through the group dynamic. Scott's Black Arrow – his actual value relative to his peers – is a mystery, hence the question mark arrow in Figure 5.2. As the clique goes through its acceptance/rejection strategy selection ritual, Scott's eventual score is being narrowed. He has shown no signs of cowering before Jeff, the putative Alpha, so the bottom end of the funnel has an upward trajectory, indicating that an Omega ranking is probably not in Scott's future. However, Scott is obviously not the physical specimen that Jeff is, nor is he as aggressive; hence, the Alpha role is ruled out. While a Beta role may be in the offing, it's not likely, so the upper line of the

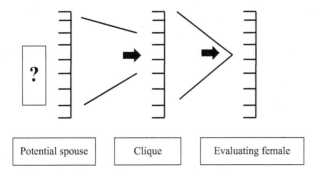

| Potential spouse | Clique | Evaluating female |

Figure 6.1 Individual Evaluation via Group Dynamic

clique's funnel is on a mild downward trajectory. Somewhere in the 4–7 range of a nine-point scale is Scott's current trajectory for his initial ranking in this particular clique, which is still within Nancy's acceptable range though she would prefer a 7, may tolerate a 6, and, should Scott ever be evaluated at 5 or below, she will abandon any emotional investment she may have had in him. Of course, none of these clique members quantify their feelings and attitudes in this manner and, since these rankings aren't quantified or captured, they can (and do) change in a most capricious and arbitrary manner. This malleability leads to another truism, on the differences between objectively and subjectively assigned ranks. The objectively assigned ones – military rank, chess club points – do not need defending on a subjective basis. They are what they are, irrespective of others' opinions of them. However, the subjectively defined ranks, like Scott's placement within this clique, *do* need defending, and this defense can usually only be accomplished by taking command of the group's narrative, or at least influencing it. For once a particular aspect of the clique's narrative, such as Scott's attractiveness as a potential member, takes on a critical mass (or reaches a tipping point) where the majority of the members accepts it, then the impact that the now-accepted part of the narrative has on Scott's standing becomes nearly permanent.

For example, during the lunch room introductory conversation, Jeff revealed (again) that his preferred sport is wrestling, and that he is so good at it that Midtown's coaches have invited him to be on the team. The thinly veiled threat that accompanies this oft-evoked revelation is that Jeff is highly likely to win any one-on-one physical or violent confrontation, since that is what happens in wrestling competitions. Scott, on the other hand, is revealed to prefer soccer over other sports, and soccer is not generally known as a contact sport. However, Mitch made it a point to talk about a severe injury Scott had endured while in competitive play, the implication being that soccer isn't such a sissy sport after all. On a scale of the implications of these facts, there are two extremes. Either:

- soccer is a sport for non-aggressive pseudo-athletes, and Scott couldn't escape injury even in this relatively safe competitive environment, or
- despite appearances, soccer can be an extremely violent sport, as indicated by Scott's injury, and Scott performed courageously and athletically in this highly competitive environment.

As an aside, virtually all narratives that retain some level of subjectivity in their creation and perpetration have this sort of scale, with an extremely negative and highly positive version on each end. The ability to manipulate this narrative towards the end that best suits the social-climbing individual has far more to do with their eventual placement than any other factor. We'll discuss this further in the chapters to come.

If Jeff were insecure in his ranking as Alpha, or if he simply wanted to drop Scott down a few points in rank, or even make a case for Scott's rejection from the group altogether, he might have taken the extra time and effort to push the former narrative, with its consequent lowering of the odds of Scott's being accepted into the group, or, having been accepted, lowering his preliminary rank. Conversely, if Jeff were to signal acceptance of Scott, he might make a positive comment about soccer in general or players in particular. In the event, though, Jeff made no such remark. Jeff doesn't think much of soccer, but heard Mitch praise Scott's performance. Not wishing to unnecessarily antagonize the clique's Beta, Jeff simply let it go, leaving his take on Scott's fitness for acceptance in the group ambiguous, at least for the time being.

However, it is worth noting that a consistently reliable way of assessing whether or not another member of a given social construct is a friend, foe, or neutral is to employ the following five-step exercise/test:

- Assess, as objectively as you can, where you believe your Black Arrow to be within the particular hierarchy.
- Do the same for the person with whom you are interacting.
- Learn to recognize when lines of conversation are doubling as exercises in reinforcing or challenging the group's rankings, and tease out the underlying narrative being reinforced or challenged.
- Does the version of the script being discussed show you in a good light, bad manner, or is it neutral? And, finally,
- Does the person with whom you are interacting support, refute, or show neutrality towards the narrative?

Naturally, this should never be used as a one-off test. It's not litmus paper. But if a pattern of a certain person consistently reinforcing a narrative that represents a negative view – in Scott's case, that soccer is not a manly sport – while challenging the script that represents a positive view – that Scott's previous display of athletic aggression is consistent with expectations of pack leadership – then that person is probably not an ally.

Recall the factors in chimpanzee social ranking, from Chapter 4:

- age,
- physical fitness,
- aggressiveness,
- skill at fighting,
- ability to form coalitions, and
- intelligence.

From the (human) female voyeur's point of view, the relative capability of a prospective mate in these categories points to a score in two areas: the potential spouse's ability to provide for her economic security, and the ability to provide for her physical security.

That this is so is readily demonstrated by a little mental exercise. In our Midtown motif, imagine the impact to Nancy's view of Scott's desirability if it were to be suddenly revealed that Scott's parents had recently come into vast wealth. A similar effect would occur if, say, Jeff had insulted Scott openly, and Scott, having had enough, beat the stuffing out of Jeff. If either of these were to occur, Scott's rank within the clique would soar. On the other hand, should it be revealed that Scott's parents were, in fact, bankrupt, or should Jeff humiliate Scott with impunity, then Scott's rank would plummet, since these types of incidents would represent direct evidence of Scott's inability to provide physical or economic security going forward into adult life. And, if either (or both) of these types of incidents were to be shown to be recurring, not only would Scott's chances of attracting a coveted potential future wife be severely imperiled, Scott would probably be led to feel...

Ashamed.

The Vital Role of Shame

According to Merriam-Webster online, shame is

1 *a*: a painful emotion caused by consciousness of guilt, shortcoming, or impropriety
  b: the susceptibility to such emotion <have you no *shame*?>

... which is a bit general. For our discussion, a little more detailed structure is called for. I would like to proceed with this discussion using a definition of *shame* that takes into account the hierarchical ranks we have been using, leading to a definition of shame so:

> Shame is the emotional consequence of having one's view of self-worth (the White Arrow) be realigned downwards, towards a more humble ranking.

This definition carries with it some implications, including:

- The energy of the shame – the amount of force pushing down on that White Arrow – is entirely contingent on the norms of the particular hierarchy. If Scott were determined to become a clergyman, and attend seminary immediately upon graduating from Midtown, whether or not his athletic performance could be considered shameful by the other members of the subject clique would become utterly irrelevant.
- Shame is not necessarily based on whether or not the person experiencing it deserves it. If the chess club miscalculates a member's score too low, and that member is unaware of the invalid nature of the new score, he or she may still feel ashamed.
- Since the actual placement of the Black Arrow does not necessarily serve as a lower-limit backstop (bottomstop?) to a White Arrow being driven downwards through shame, it's entirely possible (and probably even common) for a person

experiencing shame to think less of himself than is warranted. In other words, the White Arrow can be pushed below the Black one on the hierarchical scale.

Recall the discussion surrounding manager Bob's placement of his White Arrow. The composite White Arrow was placed where it was due to having been derived from a whole series of specific rankings – Bob as manager, Bob as athlete, Bob as husband/father, etc. A more detailed analysis of the previously mentioned ego defense mechanisms would certainly indicate that, in those instances where significant downward pressure is being brought to bear on the White Arrow, they essentially become shame deflection devices.

A further, common defense against the effects of shame exerting downward pressure on the White Arrow is to challenge the basis for the diminished reranking. Jeff may feel ashamed if it turns out that he does not make the Midtown High School wrestling team, but Scott wouldn't. Even though both Scott and Jeff belong to the same clique, wrestling is just not Scott's thing. It's a personal preference. For Jeff, much of his persona, his views of himself, the placement of his White *and* Black Arrows, are tied up in earning a spot in this other hierarchy. As an example, in the wider world it is common for those engaged in a pattern of immoral behavior to reject religion wholesale, since most of the world's major religions specify that committing sin represents a lowering of the Black Arrow (my terms, obviously, not theirs) in terms of one's relationship with the Almighty.

Which all brings us to the use of shame by the group itself. Recall that groups of people can and do take on the three aspects of the Berne/Freud persona, and that they will behave in such a way as to survive, if not advance with respect to other groups. If the Midtown clique we've been discussing should suddenly adopt a practice of shaming all green-eyed people, then they would have revealed a flawed model in the way group rankings are assigned. Green-eyed people would avoid this clique, obviously, but so would anyone who recognizes that eye color is a very poor indicator of individual merit or talent. This was the essence of Martin Luther King's message, that he dreamed of a day that people would be judged, not on the color of their skin, but on the content of their character. Who was doing this judging? American society of pre-1964, writ large. As a social construct, the principals of that society had adopted invalid criteria for the placement of its members' rank. This was a social construct where voluntary disengagement was not a viable long-term, complete answer, since economic concerns (at the very least) dictated *some* level of group-level interaction. That's not to say that disengagement, both forced and voluntary, wasn't tried; but in practice segregation would cause more problems than it solved, and had to be abandoned.

Much like the wolf pack that adopts poor hierarchical ranking practices is soon rendered extinct, so, too, do societies that misapply shame to members undeserving of forcible arrow dropping become dysfunctional, and cease functioning (or even existing) if some self-correction method is unavailable.

Shame, then, is the primary tool available to the group for realigning inflated White Arrows. Within this context there are four possibilities (Table 6.2). An example of an invalid ranking system, effectively enforced, would be the aforementioned United States up to and including the Civil Rights era. A society ordered based on skin color was clearly unworkable, even with the apparatus of a police state enforcing its

Table 6.2 Enforcement/Structure Payoff Grid

	Bad structure	Valid structure
Effective enforcement	Invalid ranking structure, effectively enforced	Valid ranking structure, effectively enforced
Ineffective enforcement	Invalid ranking structure, ineffectively enforced	Valid ranking structure, ineffectively enforced

norms. As with other invalid systems, it could lead to only one of two eventual outcomes: change to eliminate the dysfunctional basis, or else collapse.

Ironically, the ineffective implementation of an invalid hierarchy has a better chance at survival than does its effectively enforced cousin. The lack of an effective enforcement strategy, such as shaming, means that participation is largely voluntary. For example, while there may be pockets of racism in the United States (I reject whole-heartedly that it is an inherently racist country), those who cling to that opinion are not in a position to affect the minority community at large. These types are at liberty to continue to cling to their invalid assumptions, much as minority communities are at liberty to believe what they want about the majority race, or other minorities, for that matter. But most benefits that would ordinarily be accessible from forming a social construct would elude them.

The effects of a removal of an effective enforcement mechanism from a valid structure can be – and usually is – devastating. Exhibit A has to be the descent into chaos and misery experienced once drug cartels became more powerful than the constabulary in the nation of Mexico (though, to be fair, many other examples are available. Mexico just happens to be among the richest and most prominent nations to suffer in this manner). This leaves us with the only combination that maximizes the chances for long-term beneficial survival: a valid structure, effectively enforced.

The so-called validity of the structure is highly malleable in voluntary organizations. Your typical high school clique can embrace things that are "cool" and reject cultural artifacts that are not, with relative ease, without a preference for, say, rap music over hip-hop representing an existential threat to its longevity. Conversely, non-voluntary associations, such as nation-states, must articulate their governing structures formally, and enforce them effectively. A robust society can survive fluctuations in the validity and enforcement variables, while weaker ones will not. A quasi-Darwinian effect comes into play and, as it is in nature, it is merciless among competitors. Societies great and small rise and fall in consistent patterns, almost as if they were their own personas, with a set lifespan, apart from their individual members.

All of which brings us back to shame. Consider the phrase "you ought to be ashamed of yourself." Based on our model, I would paraphrase that to "you should have already recognized that your White Arrow is placed inappropriately high above your (now evident) Black Arrow's placement." However, I seriously doubt that anyone could have said "pudet debes" ("you ought to feel ashamed") to Nero, or Tiberius, or Caligua, or any of the other destructive brand of Caesars who led the Roman Empire, even as their "leadership" was clearly headed towards Roman diminishment, if not ruin. Or, if such a brave, prescient one did say it, they didn't tend to survive very long afterwards.

Once Julius Caesar crossed the Rubicon, and the Roman Republic started down the path that ended with the Roman Empire, shame as a tool to modify the behavior of Rome's Alpha males became highly problematic, as evidenced by what happened to Cicero. It simply wouldn't work. Previously, shameful behavior on behalf of its leaders may have influenced voters and, by extension, the makeup of the Senate (or not, if you believe Will and Ariel Durant). But once absolute power was taken by military force, maintained that way, and transferred (loosely) through lineage, shame became less relevant than the success of the agricultural season, or the narrative of martial conquest and success.

As Rome's structure moved from valid to invalid, and with self-correction methods rendered ineffective, all the effective enforcement in the universe could not have reversed her decline and fall. And among those self-correction methods rendered moot, shame must certainly have a place of prominence.

What Shames Us?

Warranted or not, what drives that White Arrow downward, along with its consummate internal pain? The cliché "no one can make you feel bad without your consent" is true, since the placement of the White Arrow is contingent on how we view ourselves *internally*. However, should someone perform an objectively evil act, and feel no remorse, that person is either delusional or a sociopath. A person with a properly functioning method of evaluating themselves will experience pain upon the realization they have done something they ought not to have.

Psychiatrist Stephen Rittenberg wrote:

> We are drowning in a therapeutic culture, saturated by a fantasy version of human nature in stark contradiction to the original psychoanalytic view, a view much closer to the stoics and St. Augustine than to Deepak Chopra. Unfortunately for the adherents of the therapeutic culture, conflict can never be "resolved", and they are doomed to disappointment. Never mind, there will be another self help guru next week.
> *The human mind, however, is in conflict as long as it is alive.*
> Conflict between wishes, fears, moral prohibitions, and demands of reality never go away. The ways of handling conflict can change, with very hard and prolonged work, but that is a far more modest and realistic goal than the utopian one of transforming human nature implicit in the notion that mental conflict can be resolved.[10]

With respect to how this never-ending conflict expresses itself in our rankings within the social structures we select, this conflict energy expresses itself in two ways:

- Recognition (from the SuperEgo/Parent aspect of the persona) that our externally driven true value – the Black Arrow – is too low, and energy needs to be expended into making us better persons.

- Energy driving our internally placed White Arrow (from the Id/Child) upwards is in automatic conflict with the external factors, such as where the selected social structure would place us.

In short, as we blaze our lives' paths through unfolding time, many things are inevitable, among them that we will engage with others in social constructs, and that these associations will bring with them automatic conflict.

Some Takeaways from Chapter 6

This chapter has been the longest thus far, fitting, I suppose, for the chapter that shares the title of the book. We've covered a lot of ground, so I'd like to revisit some of the points I intend to build upon in future chapters.

- Even in extremely successful groups, conflict is ever present.
- For as long as this conflict remains at a manageable level, voluntarily-entered-into social constructs will continue to function.
- Once the conflict level becomes unmanageable, members will begin to exercise the disengage option, often leading to the end of the particular grouping.
- Much of this conflict originates in the ambiguity of the true value of the individual members' contribution, especially when contrasted with their self-perceived value.
- This difference is captured graphically with our Black Arrow (true value) and White Arrow (self-ranked value), and the distance between them on a nominal scale.
- The group itself will often act as a person, with its own Black Arrow vs. White Arrow issues.
- Rankings derived from subjective data, based as it is on the quality of popularly accepted narratives, need to be continually reinforced.
- Objective ones, well, don't.
- The ego defense mechanisms that individuals employ in dealing with their Black Arrow vs. White Arrow issues can also be used by the group persona.
- The group as persona has a lifespan, often with a predictable beginning–ascendency–climactic performance–descent–dissolution arc.
- The group has at its disposal a variety of strategies it uses to enforce its preferred hierarchical structure.
- Attempts at mapping or otherwise quantifying the interactions of the group's members, or its employment of enforcing rank on its members, quickly become hopelessly convoluted, and probably cannot be logically navigated (per Metcalf's Law).
- However, how members of the social construct manipulate or spin the narratives that go into group ranking will illustrate whether they are friends, foes, or neutrals.
- Shame can be an extremely valuable tool for enforcing group norms and rankings.
- Just as the individual can use ego defense mechanisms to avoid feeling shame, so, too, can the group persona.
- Placing the effectiveness of the enforcement tactics available to the group and the validity of the group's purposes into a Game Theory-style payoff grid shows that

only those (voluntarily-entered-into) groups with both a valid objective/structure *and* effective rank enforcement mechanisms will maximize their payout, or maximize their lifespans.

- And, finally, according to Stephen Rittenberg, the human mind is in conflict as long as it is alive, and much of this conflict, I believe, originates in the inevitability of people entering into hierarchical social constructs, and struggling for rank within those constructs.

Notes

1 "Seneca," retrieved from *BrainyQuote*, http://www.brainyquote.com/quotes/keywords/shame_3.html, June 14, 2015.
2 "Creedence Clearwater Revival," retrieved from *Wikipedia*, http://en.wikipedia.org/w/index.php?title=Creedence_Clearwater_Revival&oldid=630747612, October 25, 2014.
3 "The Monkees," retrieved from *Wikipedia*, http://en.wikipedia.org/w/index.php?title=The_Monkees&oldid=630762851, October 25, 2014.
4 "The Beatles," retrieved from *Wikipedia*, http://en.wikipedia.org/w/index.php?title=The_Beatles&oldid=629786795, October 25, 2014.
5 Lello, Michael, "John Fogerty, Former Creedence Clearwater Revival Bandmates, Trade Barbs, Take Legal Action," retrieved from *HNGN*, http://www.hngn.com/articles/52513/20141211/john-fogerty-former-creedence-clearwater-revival-bandmates-trade-barbs-take-legal-action.htm, June 14, 2015.
6 "The Beatles Ultimate Experience," retrieved from *The Beatles Interviews Database*, http://www.beatlesinterviews.org/db1980.jlpb.beatles.html, October 25, 2014.
7 "The Monkees," retrieved from *Wikipedia*, http://en.wikipedia.org/w/index.php?title=The_Monkees&oldid=630762851, October 26, 2014.
8 Bayless, Skip, "Jones Is Right about Johnson," retrieved from *ESPN*, http://espn.go.com/nfl/story/_/id/11465560/bayless-jerry-jones-jimmy-johnson-dallas-cowboys, June 14, 2014.
9 Retrieved from *AllPsych*, http://allpsych.com/psychology101/defenses.html, February 10, 2016.
10 Rittenberg, Stephen M. D., "Courage, Cowardice, and the Wordsmiths," retrieved from *American Thinker*, http://www.americanthinker.com/articles/2007/08/courage_cowardice_and_the_word_1.html, August 24, 2007.
11 Ganim, Sarah and Devon Sayers, "UNC Report Finds 18 Years of Academic Fraud to Keep Athletes Playing," retrieved from *CNN*, http://edition.cnn.com/2014/10/22/us/unc-report-academic-fraud/, June 14, 2015.

Chapter 7

On Organizational Narratives

The Stories We Know, the Secrets We Keep

> If you want to make enemies, try to change something.
> Woodrow Wilson[1]

In 1962, Thomas S. Kuhn published *The Structure of Scientific Revolutions*, in which he noted a distinct pattern in the advancement of science through tested and testable theories. This pattern tended to follow (however loosely) the following steps:

- A given theory is tested with available experimental or predictive data, and consistently shown to be valid.
- Certain anomalies are observed, which cannot be readily explained through the existing theory.
- The existing theory is modified to account for the anomalous observations.
- A rival theory is introduced, one that accounts for the new, anomalous data, and, to a certain extent, the previous body of experimental findings.
- The rival theory is opposed and, often, its originator(s) and supporters vilified.
- More and more data that appears to contradict the existing theory is made available.
- As the new, rival theory is fine-tuned, it is shown to be consistently more reliable in explaining existing experimental data and predictive capability than the existing theory.
- Practitioners in the field begin to abandon the former theory, and the newer, rival one becomes the current "existing" theory.

We humans tend to look back at the advancement of science and technology as something of a smooth trajectory upward. Kuhn showed that this is not the case, that such advancement tends to happen in fits and starts, as well as being accompanied by substantial conflict.

Conflict? About science? Yeah.

Historical examples abound. Kuhn himself used the Copernican Revolution as one. At the time Copernicus introduced the idea that the Earth revolved around the Sun (1543), the Ptolemaic Model, based on the idea that the Sun revolved around the Earth, was widely accepted by the cosmologists of the era. Scholars hold that 60 years after the publication of *The Revolutions* there were few astronomers espousing Copernicanism in all of Europe. But, with the invention of the telescope around

1608, more and more observations were published that appeared to challenge the Ptolemaic Model. Ptolemaic Theory used cycles and epicycles to explain observed phenomena and to predict future ones, such as eclipses, or the observable position of Mars. As more data was collected that appeared to contradict Ptolemaic Theory, more epicycles were posited that "explained" the new data. Indeed, in the Ptolemaic Model, the planet Mars did not have a circular or even ecliptic orbit. It was thought to have a period where it performed a little loop within the circle of its nominal trajectory. As implausible as this aspect of the Ptolemaic Model strikes a twenty-first-century audience, it wasn't until around 1700 that a sizable faction of astronomers were prepared to accept the Copernican Theory. In the interim, a significant amount of resistance to the new theory – conflict – was experienced by the foremost scientists of the age.

The late Michael Crichton noted more examples in his speech "Aliens Cause Global Warming."[2] One such example was that of Alexander Gordon (1752–99), who came to the realization that women who died from childbirth may have been exposed to infection. In his Treatise on Epidemic Puerperal Fever (1795), he stated:

> The observations which I have to offer are of the utmost importance to society, and I am only diffident of my ability to express them in the manner they deserve. I have, however, made an attempt which I hope will meet with a favourable reception from the public; especially as I have advanced no opinion that is not an obvious conclusion immediately resulting from the facts, and as all the facts may be depended on… that the cause of the epidemic puerperal fever under consideration was not owing to a noxious constitution of the atmosphere, I had sufficient evidence; for if it had been owing to that cause, it would have seized women in a more promiscuous and indiscriminate manner. But this disease seized such women only as were visited, or delivered, by a practitioner or taken care of by a nurse who had previously attended patients affected with the disease. In short, I had evident proofs of its infectious nature, and that the infection was as readily communicated as that of the small-pox or measles, and operated more speedily than any other infection with which I am acquainted.[3]

Gordon may have hoped for "a favourable reception from the public"[4] to a great extent, but the medical community would not accept the infectious nature of puerperal fever on a widespread basis until after 1920. That's 125 years, ladies and gentlemen (mostly ladies), of mothers dying from "complications of childbirth" because, generally speaking, scientists, in this case medical doctors, were unwilling to accept a new theory of disease propagation, despite the evidence that was being widely published.

Nicolas Tesla developed the concept of alternating current, at a time when his rival and former boss, Thomas Edison, was advocating electrical transmission via direct current. Edison would end up with 1,093 patents, Tesla with fewer than 300.[5] Indeed, to this day, people outside the professions of electronics or academics may have never heard of Tesla, while Edison is virtually universally recognized. However, in the realm of the best way to transmit electricity, world-renowned Edison had it wrong, and Tesla had it right.

The atom was discovered in 1897. Three years later, Lord William Thomson Kelvin—after whom the Kelvin temperature scale was named – actually said "There is nothing new to be discovered in physics now. All that remains is more and more precise measurement."[6] I'm sure Robert Oppenheimer, Hans Bethe, Neils Bohr, and dozens of other Manhattan Project scientists would have disagreed. And particle physics is just one example – Kuhn's observations on how existing theories are challenged and ultimately overcome by newer hypotheses, which then turn into theories of their own, only to be challenged by yet more hypotheses repeats itself over and over in the hard sciences.

But what about the social sciences?

It's been said that, while the understanding of the so-called hard sciences will always advance, human nature never will. What Kuhn was actually describing in *The Nature of Scientific Revolution* was not so much the nature of scientific revolution as much as the reaction of the researchers and established experts in those particular fields to the unfolding advancement of science, through the prism of scientific "revolution." The science changes; the human reactions to it, generally speaking, do not.

Consider that social constructs were created – or grew spontaneously, whichever – around these theories. Established scientific theories are supposed to gain quick and widespread acceptance, with the next advance built upon what has gone before – in a perfect world. But what we see over and over in our imperfect world, even in the academic cocoon of the laboratories' hard sciences, are ideas with empirically tested validity being ignored, stifled, resisted, tolerated, grudgingly acknowledged, and marginally recognized all prior to actual mainstream acceptance. Clearly there are other forces in play here, outside of the collection of repeatable experimental results that either support or refute a given hypothesis, forces that are far more subjective in nature.

Those forces belong to a category: human nature.

All of this analysis raises a question: why is it consistently observed human nature to tamper with, or even actively resist, scientific or technological advancement? Isn't it advancement in these two areas that extends lifespans and improves quality of life for all of mankind?

Let's take a quick look at the opposite extreme, the aforementioned Manhattan Project, the United States' effort to build a deployable nuclear bomb. At the time of Albert Einstein's famous letter to Roosevelt (August 2, 1939) describing the possibility of a nuclear weapon, both Germany and Japan had launched atomic bomb projects, meaning that, unless the United States (and her principal ally, Great Britain) followed suit, any subsequent war with the powers that possessed such a weapon would be impossible to win. That subsequent war began 30 days later, when Germany and the Soviet Union invaded Poland, and Great Britain and France declared war on Germany. It wasn't until two years later, however, after Japan attacked the U.S. naval installation at Pearl Harbor, that the Manhattan Project officially began. While it started out with its scope and personnel scattered throughout universities across the country, its main research would soon be concentrated in remote northern New Mexico. Of course, one of the primary reasons for selecting an out-of-the-way location and moving all of the principal researchers there had to do with security – the farther away the work was from curious eyes, the better the chances were that the technology being discovered could be kept under wraps. But another key component may have been that, in a technological competition with the award for first place being the attainment of superpower status at stake, secluding the primary researchers would isolate them from the tamping-down effects of the acceptance/rejection cycle Kuhn had observed being so prevalent in the hard sciences.

For whatever motivational mix was in play in the decision to isolate the scientists working on the Manhattan Project in northern New Mexico, there can be no doubt to its effectiveness. The project's scientists were the first to develop not one, but two different working designs, the deployment of which certainly shortened the war and reduced the number of deaths stemming from that conflict. The genius inherent in the project's setup was, at least partially, in the idea of encouraging the development of hypotheses that would have to endure scorn and ridicule elsewhere in the academic world, but just might be valid and usable in the world of weapons development. The renowned genius Neils Bohr actually once told a young physicist "Your theory is crazy, but it's not crazy enough to be true."

Keep in mind that, when we're discussing automatically, spontaneously created hierarchies, a remote facility of the greatest minds could not be further away from Midtown High School's machinations, of where Scott and Tammy, Jeff and the rest of the clique scramble and claw for status. And yet, the view from these two extremes reveals some fascinating aspects of human nature, especially as it comes into play in hierarchies.

For example, scientists and organizations of scientists adhere (supposedly) to the scientific method. Put briefly, it is a method for discovering valid, usable theories by testing hypotheses empirically. If the predictions stemming from a given hypothesis are (a) observable and (b) repeatable in a laboratory or experimental setting, the hypothesis is considered to be a valid theory. If an entire category of professionals are devoted to this method, then what in the world was Kuhn observing? Why would whole organizations of scientists behave in the ways they provably did, resisting scientific advances, and targeting the challengers for ridicule? I believe there are two reasons, and they have to do with the rankings of individuals within a given hierarchy, and the behavior of the group with respect to its competition.

First, the Individual within the Group

Consider the plight of a sixteenth-century cosmologist. For this example, I'll borrow from Shakespeare's *Henry IV, Part II* characters to name him – his name is Aumerle, and he has been educated in the finest universities of the time. In order to gain any level of acceptance into the cosmology community of the period, he must proceed from the premise that all observable celestial bodies orbit the Earth. Should Aumerle make an observation that challenges, or even threatens to overturn the Ptolemaic structure, he should expect to have his data collection methods challenged, his education, even his sanity called into question. To advance within this particular group – based on the scientific method, mind you – Aumerle simply must reinforce what the other members of the community have accepted as true. And why is that?

Because, much like Aumerle, the peers within this scientific community have spent considerable amounts of time, energy, and money in advancing human knowledge, based on Ptolemy's theory. Should that theory be proved false, *everyone* within this community would see that time, energy, and money be seen as largely wasted, their lives' pursuits reduced to near pointlessness. Accountants' training usually includes an admonishment to never advance an argument based on the sunk-cost assertion. The way my accounting professor explained it to me was in the form of a story of the construction of the Golden Gate Bridge. The bridge cost $35 million (USD). If, however, a perfectly usable alternative (my professor used a *Star Trek*-style transporter device) should be made available just prior to bridge completion, at a cost below the remaining budget, the logical choice would be to abandon the almost-complete structure, and invest in the alternative. My professor readily admitted that, in the real world, that would never happen: politicians would never tolerate a nearly complete Golden Gate bridge standing as a monument to their having selected the wrong theory. But, from a purely practical point of view, such an abandonment is the logical thing to do.

Not so from the participants in this particular scientific community's standing. There's an old Turkish saying, "It's never too late to turn back from the wrong path." This is consistent with the avoidance of the sunk-cost argument. But these sixteenth-century scientists – including Aumerle – have their entire lives invested in the Ptolemaic structure. All of their observations, predictions, and, most importantly, *the placement of their White and Black Arrows* depends on the validity of that structure. Assuming these scientists' White Arrows are in some proximity of their Black Arrows, their usefulness to the society of cosmologists, as well as the scientific community at large, is entirely predicated on the validity and usefulness of the theory they have been espousing. Should that theory be proved false, not only would their Black Arrows take a hit, their (inflated) White Arrows would be forced lower. Recall that the forced lowering of anyone's White Arrow is excruciatingly painful, and that people have been known to engage in extreme behavior in order to avoid it. So, when Aumerle is confronted with a heliocentric view of the cosmos, one that actually helps explain some of his own observations better than the Ptolemaic structure, his choices are fairly simple, and very different from those that we, his future judge and jury, would expect. It's very easy for we twenty-first-century dwellers to presume that, *of course*, he would reject the old theory outright, and embrace a heliocentric view. But doing so would be very painful for Aumerle, who has spent considerable time building up his ranking as a serious cosmologist. After publicly embracing the heliocentric model, in a flash his ranking would fall dramatically, perhaps even ruining his standing and career. Universities would ignore him, and any other vestige of scientific inquiry would not engage him. Copernicus died the same *day* that he was presented with the printed pages of *De revolutionibus orbium coelestium*, saving him from having to endure the typical blowback from the community of cosmologists who had staked their careers on the Ptolemy model. Our fictional cosmologist, Aumerle, has no such escape as part of his deliberations.

As an alternative, Aumerle could continue to support the Ptolemaic Model and, when confronted with data that appears to directly challenge it, be expected to employ one of the aforementioned ego defense mechanisms. After all, should the Ptolemy model prove to be invalid, Aumerle's ego would take a significant beating. Consider how easy it would be to employ one of those mechanisms at any time, e.g.,

- denial
- displacement
- intellectualization
- projection
- rationalization

- reaction formation
- regression
- repression
- sublimation
- suppression

Further, if Aumerle can employ these mechanisms to protect his ego with little chance of being (a) found out for acting outside of the scientific method and entirely within the confines of maintaining rank within a community of like-minded individuals, or (b) having to pay a price for such actions, what does that say about the strategies most likely to be employed by such a community?

Now, the Group

English astronomer Thomas Digges is credited with popularizing the Copernican model in 1576, 33 years after Copernicus died. The intervening years are known as the "Copernican Revolution," and represent a metaphor for the concepts of modernity. Note that the period is referred to as a "revolution" – nobody uses the term "Copernican Smooth Transition." Why is that?

As explored previously, the social construct/group takes on a personality of its own. The association of astronomers and cosmologists had made widely known its conclusions. Imagine the (again, extremely painful) adjustment to the members of this group's perceived rank, or standings within the scientific community if they, as a whole, had been found to be largely incorrect. In an era where medical doctors were applying leaches and bleeding patients as treatment for a variety of ills, medicine would have been considered positively advanced in comparison.

Let's morph all of these astronomers and cosmologists into a wolf pack. Their territory isn't geographical, but in the arena of ideas. This "pack" had survived for hundreds of years using a particular set of group strategies that ensured that the most appropriate member of the pack would assume the role of Alpha, Beta, muddled middle, and Omega, and that set of rules had led to the pack's success over a significant period of time. It's only natural that, whenever a member of the pack challenges that basis for existence, the pack deals with it as it would any perceived invalid challenge. During these centuries, of course, it wasn't just the valid challengers rising up – there were many theories about the origination and nature of the universe, many of them completely and utterly unscientific. Some native tribes in North America of the time believed the universe to be situated on the back of an immense turtle, for example. The notion that these theories should be quickly and completely accepted by the community of astronomers at the time would have struck those practitioners as only marginally more absurd than the instantaneous acceptance of the heliocentric theory.

As colloquially observed before, human nature never changes, and yet how it will impact the future is nearly impossible to predict. In Isaac Asimov's novel series *Foundation, Foundation and Empire* and *Second Foundation*, a human civilization that spans the Milky Way represents a population with a predictable future, calculated through "psychohistory," a way of mathematically projecting sociological behavior. A basic part of the premise of psychohistory is the idea that, while the behavior of a single atom of a given gas is impossible to predict, a container with many such atoms does exhibit predictable behavior. Once the galaxy is home to billions and billions of humans, the sample size begins to exhibit similarly predictable behavior. The novels' main protagonist and discoverer/inventor of psychohistory, Hari Seldon, sets up an independent community of scientists who map out the future of the civilized galaxy, in somewhat general terms, of course. The emergence of a character known as "The Mule" upends this calculated future trajectory. The Mule is a mutant and, as such, could not have been predicted through psychohistory. This character comes very close to galactic domination before being thwarted, and the galaxy returns to some semblance of where it should have been, according to the calculations.[7]

As best I could glean from the novels, psychohistory is a kluge of statistics, game theory, network theory, with allusions to psychology and sociology. However, its treatment of network theory, let alone Metcalf's Law, is lacking, which is part of the reason why the notion of a calculable unfolding of future events can successfully serve as the theoretical underpinnings of such a popular science fiction mainstay.

And yet, while Asimov could not have possibly been accurate in predicting how technology would influence mankind's future, there is a certain constant that can be relied upon to remain far into the future: human nature. Kelvin might have been comically incorrect in looking back at advances in physics and, projecting forward, concluded that nothing new awaited on the horizon. But Kuhn was onto something, in that he could observe the behaviors of the sub-groups within the scientific community when new theories were advanced, and the manner in which they were initially rejected, grudgingly acknowledged, marginally accommodated, and, eventually, embraced, and reach the entirely reasonable (and, in my opinion, completely valid) conclusion that those patterns would consistently repeat themselves into the future.

This is how groups *behave*. And, if it is so in the social constructs that are erected around something as objective as the scientific method, it is certainly prescient in predicting the behavior of groups that are not nearly as closely connected to the verifiable.

So, what do we know about how the group – any group – behaves with respect to (a) its members, (b) the environment where it seeks to survive, or even thrive, and (c) its competition? There are some overarching ideas in play, which impact each of these specific aspects, to wit:

• Whether or not the group is aware of it, it has a limited lifespan.
• The group will take on a personality of its own.
• It will execute decisions based on this personality.
• Those decisions will either lead to prolonging its existence, or to its demise.

In each of these domains, there are strategies that the group has available to it. Let's look at them, one at a time.

With respect to its members the group will seek to attract those individuals who will help it attain its nominal objectives, or reasons for being in existence in the first place, while dissuading those who would otherwise hinder (or even thwart) those objectives. This is why groups predicated on a given idea, or theory, will tend to embrace those whose efforts support the idea/theory on which the organization is based, while rejecting those who challenge it. Early cosmologists may have advertised the reason for their association as being the collection of facts about the nature of the universe, but their *real* reason for existing was to promote the well-being of those who adhered to the Ptolemy model. Had Copernicus lived to see the evaluations of his theories, he almost certainly would have been ostracized by those in the cosmology community, since his theories would overturn their raison d'être. Similarly, should Scott present himself as challenging Jeff's Alpha status, he would also be rejected from that particular Midtown High School clique he wishes to join.

But, of course, the existing members of the group have their own agendas, bound up in their view of themselves (White Arrow) as well as their genuine contribution value (Black Arrow). Chess teams (and similar groups) have a true advantage here, since there are no subjective factors in play when it comes to evaluating individual members. As stated before, one's US Chess Federation (or FIDE (World Chess Federation)) rankings are indisputable. Highly ranked individuals are more valuable than lower-ranked ones, period. Absent such an objective basis for assigning ranks, however, highly subjective human nature kicks in. Kuhn's theories and observable patterns may manifest in the hard sciences, but begin to lose efficacy as the social constructs under evaluation go further and further away from any objective basis for assigning ranks, until we get, at last, to the cliques at Midtown High School. Here, past any background desire for the clique to present itself as desirable to join when compared to others, the ranking is almost entirely subjective, and vulnerable to any narrative or script that can be furthered with respect to its members' value. If Copernicus had embraced a particular clothing fashion trend, it is lost to history, and has no bearing on the assessment of his ideas. Conversely, should Scott, who happens to be undergoing the growth spurt so common to adolescent males of his age, show up to class with pants that are clearly too short, he would almost automatically be rejected by any clique seeking widespread acceptance within the community of students at Midtown.

However, should Scott (or Copernicus, for that matter) establish *a priori* his value to the clique as very high, and showed up to class in the exact same too-short pants, the others within the clique would probably choose to either not notice, or else even emulate the new "trend." How the group treats its individual members is highly predicated on the perceived value of the Black Arrow. In certain groups, this value can be objectively ascertained. In others, it can be reasonably gauged. In the most subjective of groups, it can only be guessed at, and is highly susceptible to the narratives proffered, and adapted.

In the environment where the group seeks to survive, or thrive, the available strategies take on a different aspect. Even in those circumstances where the group itself might reject an individual member, signs of antagonism coming from outside the social construct can be reliably predicted to meet with a collective resistance, or push-back. A highly cohesive group, say, a street gang, may treat its Omega member mercilessly; but let a competitor gang attack the Omega, and a collective response defending the Omega is fairly automatic.

In competition with other groups, cohesion becomes a significant factor. Just as the group is motivated to discourage the perceived low performers from entering and encourage high performers to join, so, too, is the social construct best served when its already admitted high performers are influenced to stay, and already admitted failures encouraged to leave, or rejected outright. One indicator of the true value of competing groups (macro Black Arrow) can be gleaned from another game theory

Table 7.1 Group Cohesion/Group Coercion Payoff Grid

	Compelled/coerced membership (Column A)	Purely voluntary membership (Column B)
Low group cohesion (Row 1)	Hopelessness/despair (Situation 1A)	Individual contributors (Situation 1B)
High group cohesion (Row 2)	Survival/elimination (Situation 2A)	Highly attractive (Situation 2B)

payout grid, comparing organizations where membership is completely voluntary vs. compelled, compared to groups that enjoy high levels of cohesion vs. those that do not (Table 7.1).

Situation 1A is the least desirable group structure formulation. Its members do not want to belong to it, but either cannot leave, or face perceived added difficulties if they try to disengage. Prisons, reform schools, and men drafted into the infantry during wartime are extreme examples of this genre, but more common versions abound. In the film *Jersey Boys*, the character Tommy DeVito shares a detail of life in the neighborhood where they live, that there are only three ways out: by joining the military (where you might be killed), by joining the mob (where you might also be killed), or to become famous. Obviously, "only three ways out" is hyperbole: a person born into virtually any neighborhood could always scrape together enough money for a one-way bus ticket to another locale, and begin anew there. If desperate enough, they could even hitch-hike. A more accurate way of expressing Tommy DeVito's insight would have been to say that the social structure of the neighborhood in question was such that economic progression that was free of that social construct's available anti-disengagement strategies was virtually non-existent.

The essence of low-adhesion groups populated by unwilling members is that, if members can overcome the barriers keeping them in the group, they will disengage (unless some form of Stockholm syndrome kicks in, which is outside the scope of this book). It's why it's a crime to desert the military or escape from prison. At the other end of the spectrum, but still within type, it's also why some people will automatically quit their jobs when they win the lottery. The coercive factor – pulling in a paycheck – is overcome in such circumstances, and such lucky ones are free to disengage – which they promptly do.

Situation 2A, where there is high group cohesion despite the coercive nature of its assembly, is common to high-performing military units or other organizations where survival is an issue. A new infantryman may be less than thrilled to have been conscripted, but if he wants to maximize his odds of surviving he had better learn (a) how to fight effectively, and (b) how to interact with his associates at an advanced level. Paradoxically, the same issues are present in potential recruits to organized crime, the second of Tommy DeVito's neighborhood exit strategies. Membership in any organized crime group, from street gangs to the Mafia, depends heavily on members' reliable refusal to elect the disengagement strategy. For most such organizations, the penalty for electing to leave after having been a contributing member is death. For this reason category 2A groups take on behaviors that enforce a never-leave aspect. Whereas the wolfpack is largely uninterested in members breaking off and becoming lone wolves, organized crime has no such luxury. The wolfpack will likely survive (or even thrive) if middle-range members who, frustrated at not being higher placed, seek to disengage rather than continue in hierarchical maneuverings. But former organized crime members are in a position to bring their former organization to an abrupt end, and therefore need to either be reliably retained within the group's ranks, or eliminated altogether.

Of course, these groups will never come out and articulate to its members that it is due to the *group*'s adopting behaviors to ensure its ongoing livelihood that individual members must never leave: it's almost always represented as an aspect of personal virtue, specifically, loyalty. To illustrate, imagine an organized crime family, headed by a character similar to the actor Joe Pesci, with his main lieutenant being the character from *Star Trek*, Commander Spock. (For those unfamiliar with *Star Trek*, the Spock character is from the planet Vulcan. Vulcans do not experience emotion, as we humans do, and their motivations and decision-making processes are entirely based on logic.) Now, imagine that Jeff from Midtown High, having graduated but not retained marketable skills, has decided to join this particular organized crime family. After having experienced the crime and bloodletting involved, Jeff has come before Pesci and Spock to tell them he wants out.

Spock: "The ability for this organization to continue to function in a profitable manner is predicated on each and every admitted member reliable avoiding a disengagement strategy. In short, it's harmful to every other member for you to elect that strategy, or even consider it."

Pesci: "Why you disloyal piece of ^%$^! I've got your 'exit strategy' right here!" Upon which the Pesci-like character produces a gun, and kills Jeff.

(Don't worry – Jeff will be okay when we revisit him at Midtown High School's clique environment. Besides, Spock would never join the Mafia.)

As potentially painful as bringing this up may be, situation 1A is also applicable to marriages where the love has clearly evaporated (if it was ever present in the first place), but which trudges on because of any of the several external restrictions against separation. Again, situation 1A is the least desirable configuration, and people trapped within such a marriage should maintain little hope of relationship bliss. A tradeoff is in effect, essentially bartering away emotional well-being and peace of mind in return for economic or religious benefits. Don't misunderstand – I'm not saying that in every case such a tradeoff is ill-advised, or even not attractive. But such a tradeoff does exist, and it is a manifestation of rank within the available-spouse hierarchy.

Situation 1B, low group cohesion on an entirely voluntary basis, includes our oft-mentioned chess team. Even when chess players are formed into teams, their competitions are still individual. And, with the exception of the truly bizarre-world chess teams, there are few repercussions to quitting a chess team. The remaining team members have some incentive to retain members, since the team's existence is based on its ability to successfully compete against other chess teams. Appeals to personal integrity (specifically, loyalty) will probably not work in organizations that are purely voluntary and yet display low cohesion, which is why situation 1B organizations will typically allude to some other, overarching structure in order to claim some semblance of cohesion. The chess team from Midtown High School will point to the need for Midtown to outperform other high schools as the reason why the chess team's members should engender team unity, for example. In fact, in almost any situation where it's clear that some essentially irrelevant structure is being invoked as a reason for group unity, it's a rather obvious indication that association with said group *is* entirely voluntary, even while cohesion is a desired aspect. A perfect example: political parties.

A more detailed analysis of how people successfully maneuver within political parties and manipulate their rankings will be covered in Chapter 8. For now, it's sufficient to describe political party affiliation with a situation 1B structure. In free societies, switching political parties carries few negative consequences, past the potential rejection of family members made vocal at holiday get-togethers. It's more a reflection of the individual's preferences and grasp of the social-economic world around him. So, in order to implement a form of group cohesion, political parties will invariably allude to standards of morality, patriotism, economic acumen, common sense, or any number of other narrative-building strategies, which leads us to…

Situation 2B, high group cohesion with purely voluntary participation. The most obvious example of this is the highly profitable company. Supposedly, Microsoft Corporation has made over 10,000 millionaires (people who have earned more than $1 million USD, a nominal threshold of wealth). This organization can be expected to enjoy a very high level of cohesion, even though all of its members are perfectly free to disengage at any time. From the organization's point of view, they elevated (or joined) Bill Gates to the Alpha, or leader, role, and his ideas of how software companies ought to be structured, managed, and operated turned out to be optimal. The comparatively new territory of computer software had much to offer the packs who could successfully occupy it; many others, such as Apple, Oracle… heck, even Blizzard Entertainment enjoyed success that would have made turn-of-the-century railroad barons green with envy.

Indeed, the major threat to such high-performing, highly cohesive organizations is that they will allow in sub-par performers to share in the organization's successes while not devoting much energy into its progress against competitive orgs. Consider the following names:

- Derek Taylor
- Neil Aspinall
- Dick James
- Pete Best
- Stuart Sutcliffe
- Jimmie Nicol
- Tony Sheridan

The reader can be forgiven for not having recognized any of these names. They are the individuals who were, at various times, referred to as "the Fifth Beatle," a reference to unaccredited contributors to the success of The Beatles.

From the situation 2B group, the most coveted, to the situation 1A organization, the one where members can be counted on to escape at their earliest opportunity, several group behaviors remain constant. These include:

- A desire to prevent members from joining if they represent a degradation of the organization's ability to compete.
- Once it is realized that sub-par members have already joined, the invocation of strategies that either reduce the unattractive member to Omega status, or eliminate them altogether.

- Advance in rank those members who are perceived to be able to further the group's objectives, both stated (the nominal objective) and unstated (to advance the power and/or comfort of those already advanced in rank).
- Defend accepted members from attack from competing organizations, regardless of rank.
- Portray the pursuit of the group's objectives as being extensions of the individuals' merit (e.g., loyalty to an organized crime gang isn't about the absolute necessity of gang members never electing to voluntarily leave – it's about the members' "virtue" in displaying the necessary level of loyalty).
- Put into positions of macro influence the most capable.
- Reduce in rank (or even eliminate) those in positions of high rank who make decisions detrimental to the group as a whole, or a significant part of its population.

Like the individual, the group, taking on as it does its own personality, will experience pain if its White Arrow is forced downwards. Because of this, it will, like its individual members, often invoke one or more ego defense mechanisms to avoid having to endure a self-perceived lowering of rank. However, should a genuine and valid reason for the group to endure such a lowering of comparative rank (as in those instances where a group is supposedly dedicated to the advancement of science, but clings to an obsolete theory) be staved off by successfully invoking an ego defense mechanism that delays the pain of such a lowering of rank, then the odds are that that group's lifespan will have become shortened. Remember, all social constructs have lifespans. Like the wolfpack that promotes an inept member into the Alpha role, organizations invoking ego defense mechanisms to avoid the pain of stark reality will shorten their existence. Human nature, being, as it is, virtually unchanging, makes such analyses and predictions fairly easy. That organizations will behave in a fashion that simultaneously benefits its members – particularly its high-ranking members – while sowing the seeds of its own demise is not only predictable.

It's inevitable.

Notes

1 Retrieved from *Simplicable*, http://management.simplicable.com/management/new/60-tho ught-provoking-change-management-quotes, July 5, 2015.
2 Crighton, Michael, "Aliens Cause Global Warming," retrieved from *SEPP*, http://stephensch neider.stanford.edu/Publications/PDF_Papers/Crichton2003.pdf, May 3, 2015.
3 Retrieved from *BMJ*, http://fn.bmj.com/content/78/3/F232.full, May 3, 2015, used with permission.
4 Ibid.
5 Retrieved from *Livescience*, http://www.livescience.com/46739-tesla-vs-edison-comparison. html, November 25, 2014.
6 Retrieved from *ScienceWorld*, http://scienceworld.wolfram.com/biography/Kelvin.html, November 22, 2014.
7 "Foundation Series," retrieved from *Wikipedia*, http://en.wikipedia.org/w/index.php?title= Foundation_series&oldid=656393857, May 4, 2015.

Chapter 8

Preparing to Play the Ranking Game

The deepest problems of modern life derive from the claim of the individual to preserve the autonomy and individuality of his existence in the face of overwhelming social forces, of historical heritage, of external culture, and of the technique of life.

Georg Simmel[1]

Part I: Who Are the Players?

As we've discussed earlier, modern game theory is predicated on the idea that, for any given situation or circumstance, there are (usually multiple) analogous situations or circumstances that have taken place in a competitive environment. As such, the strategies that succeeded in the analogous competitive situation may be adapted to the present situation, even if that situation doesn't appear to be game-like in the least.

And yet much of the premise of this book is that *some* level of insight may be gleaned by observing how people who participate in hierarchical structures (hint: that's everybody) select and implement observable strategies with the intent to alter (almost always advance) their ranking, and how well those strategies actually work from organization type to organization type.

When I first introduced the idea of evaluating competing strategies of people seeking to advance their rankings within social structures to the members of my immediate family, they were, as my older son put it, "skeptical hippos." The arguments they submitted against the notion were basically along the lines of the impossibility of quantifying the boundary parameters that would be required to perform any such comparison. My counter-argument was, essentially, that it wasn't necessary to know all of the parameters of all of the possible hierarchies that my readers might encounter. Rather, by articulating the strategies that are recognizable in their patterns and redundancy, it *is* possible to gauge their effectiveness across a variety of types of organizations. The strategy of murdering one's rivals, for example, might have worked somewhat effectively in Ancient Rome or the Nazi Party; it's probably not going to work very well in, say, the Royal Navy. In other words, the effectiveness of the strategies employed to advance within a given hierarchy serve as a reflection of two images: the character of the person selecting the strategies in question, and the environment in which they seek advancement. First, we'll address a structure that will allow for an evaluation of the players in our massive game; then, we'll analyze what the nature of the game(s) says about the organizations playing it.

But First, a Quick Addition to Our Analytical Tool...

Recall from Chapter 3 the use of the ranking meter, with its graphic placement of the Black Arrow (the value of the individual's actual contribution to the group) and the White Arrow (the value of what the individual believes is his contribution). In case you've slept since that discussion, the graphic is shown in Figure 8.1.

The new notion I want to introduce has to do with the value that others within the group place upon the target individual. Since I've already used black and white, and I'm guessing printing this in color is not in the cards, I'll use grey. So, for the purposes of our evaluating the players in the hierarchies being analyzed, the Grey Arrow will represent the *perceived value* of the individuals within the hierarchy. In those instances where all three ranks are relevant, the model/graphic will now look like Figure 8.2.

Invoking that tried-and-true tool of game theorists everywhere, the payoff matrix (or grid) reveals eight possible combinations. In *The Gamesman,*[2] Michael Maccoby had his four categories:

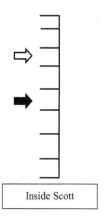

Figure 8.1 Nominal Value Ranks (for Scott, from Chapter 5)

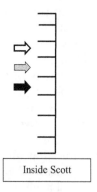

Figure 8.2 Scott's Grey Arrow Placement

- Craftsman, who does not care so much about his organization but is invested in the quality of his output;
- Company Man, who tends to assume the persona of the organization around him;
- Jungle Fighter, who will engage dishonest or disruptive tactics to get ahead; and
- The Gamesman (after whom Maccoby's book is named).

Similarly, Richard Bartle[3] had his four categories of people, named after suits of playing cards, who participate in massive multi-player online role-playing games (such as Blizzard Entertainment's® *World of Warcraft*, namely:

- Hearts engage in social interaction more so than others;
- Diamonds pursue the objectives of the scenarios within the game, and tend to accumulate more in-game prizes and wealth than the others;
- Spades are explorers (usually "digging around"), and enjoy the act of checking out the world of Azeroth (in *World of Warcraft*'s case), and
- Clubs are fighters, and are most attracted to the drama of individual combat.

Maccoby's players exhibited a preference for certain strategies within the corporate world, just as Bartle's subjects did in the online game world. In the clawing-the-way-to-the-top-of-the-group world, I'm looking at the eight possible combinations from the placement of the three arrows. Let's take them one at a time.

(1) *Low, low, low* (Figure 8.3).

This is the category where we all belong when we enter the world, so I'll refer to them as *Babies*, or *Omegas*. The only structure willing to take them on, typically, is their very own family. Literal babies have little or no concept of their self-worth, meaning that the White Arrow is superfluous for them. For non-infants in organizations other than their families, though, this is the position of the Omega. In wolfpacks, the Omega wolf engaged in strategies that communicated to its superiors that, not only did the Omega represent no threat to the status or well-being of its superiors, it acknowledged and accepted its bottom-rung role.

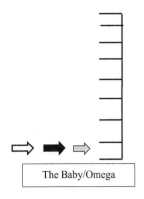

The Baby/Omega

Figure 8.3 Three-Arrow Model Placement of the Omega

Strategies available to the Omega are few. They are basically dependent on the unearned goodwill from the other members of the organization. In actual families, of course, this is the norm; in other organizations, this is an extremely vulnerable position to assume. The Baby (not actual infants, of course) must pour any and all available energies into advancing their Black Arrows, or their demonstrable value to the group they wish to join. Inflating the White Arrow will be perceived as counter-productive, and there is really very little basis for influencing the others, i.e., inflating the Grey Arrow. Advancing genuine personal value is essentially the only strategy remaining.

(2) *Low White, low Grey, high Black* (Figure 8.4).

The Cinderella category is as compelling as it is rare. I say compelling because, as a literary device, it automatically introduces into any narrative – both the group's and the individual's – a dynamic that simply demands to be reconciled. Examples, besides Cinderella herself, include characters like Harry Potter and *Star Wars'* Luke Skywalker. These people are intrinsically valuable, but they don't view themselves that way, nor do those around them recognize their worth. One of the most endur-ing and ubiquitous human characteristics is the holding of the belief that we're really very valuable, but the rest of the universe simply doesn't recognize it, which is why it's easy to associate with these fictional characters. They endure the difficulties nom-inally associated with Omega status, even though, truth be known, they should never have to.

In reality, though, this type is rare. The group, as discussed before, is set up to employ a series of tests to ensure that the best among them are (a) recognized, if not early, then certainly in a timely fashion, and (b) encouraged to develop to their full potential in order to assume a position within the group to help ensure its longevity, if not advancement.

As with all of the other categories, Cinderellas have three general options: (1) advance the Black Arrow (further), (2) try to advance the Grey Arrow, (3) allow an inflation of the sense of self-worth, with its accompanying euphoria (i.e., inflate the White Arrow), or some combination thereof. As in the literary versions, the wisest strat-egy selection is to continue to advance the individual's true value – in other words,

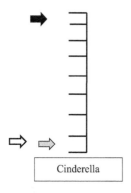

Figure 8.4 Three-Arrow Model Placement of the Cinderella

continue to pursue virtue and expertise. The outside recognition will come later, often unexpectedly.

If this type is unwilling to wait, however, their available strategies will be those designed to reveal their true value to the other members of the organization. Returning to that font of conventional pithy wisdom, the clichés, we retrieve "It isn't bragging if you can actually do it." Put another way, boasting is not a vice if the boaster is actually conveying accurate information about a previously unrecognized talent.

It's still off-putting, though.

(3) *Low White, high Grey, high Black* (Figure 8.5).

Again referring to the social structure of wolves, this is the category of the Beta. The Beta has a sense of its worth to the group, as reinforced by the group itself. However, it lacks the confidence to step up into the true leadership role. The group knows this, however intrinsically, and therefore has a motive to keep this type of individual in the group, even as they share the sentiment that the Alpha is not yet ready to be displaced, or succeeded.

My observation is that it is often the case that, in a time of crisis, the organization will select a Beta to become the new Alpha, and the required transformation entails the infusion of confidence into the Beta to fulfill its new role. In this case, an "infusion of confidence" means, basically, inflating the White Arrow to closer approximate the rankings of the Black and Grey, essentially converting the Beta into the Alpha.

Since the Beta's Black Arrow is already relatively high, its only true vulnerabilities are that (1) its Grey Arrow will be artificially lowered, or (2) its White Arrow will be artificially or prematurely inflated. When I refer to the Beta's White Arrow being artificially inflated, I'm addressing an increase in the Beta's self-perceived ranking that has nothing to do with its actual value. Stephen Colbert may (or may not) have value as a comedian, but his level of expertise in advising the United States Congress on issues surrounding immigration, as he did on September 24, 2010, is next to zero.

The Beta vulnerability of having its Grey Arrow artificially lowered makes this type the most valued target to the Politician archetype, which will be addressed shortly.

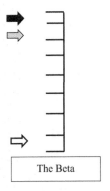

Figure 8.5 Three-Arrow Model Placement of the Beta

(4) *High White, low Grey, low Black* (Figure 8.6).

The polar opposite of the Beta, the Delusional Fool thinks very highly of himself but, in actuality, is neither very valuable to the group nor is well thought of by its members. I actually prevaricated on this name, debating between this title and "Insufferably Arrogant Jerk," but decided on "Delusional Fool" for obvious reasons. Unwilling to acknowledge its true value, the Delusional Fool engages in the previously reviewed ego defense mechanisms so much that it loses touch with reality, as well as the hierarchical ranking in front of its nose.

In antiquity, the official "fool," or court jester, dressed in a markedly silly costume, and fulfilled the role of providing comic relief to the other members of the court. Recall my previous assertion that to engage in humor is an act of submission. In return, the group accords the fool certain prerogatives, namely that he can say things that challenge the existing orthodoxy – even the Alpha – with impunity. He is not propertied, nor a warrior, and not even well esteemed by the other members of the court. And yet, there he is, spouting off his opinions before royalty as if he were of significant value. From the ancient Arabic saying, he is the fool to be avoided.

There is an axiom, that highly successful comedians wish to marry supermodels, but that supermodels do not wish to marry comedians, they want to marry rock stars. The kernel of truth behind this colloquialism is that comedians are today's court jesters. They entertain us, but are really of little objective value outside the world of entertainment. Ah, but isn't the same true of rock stars? Yes, but there is a difference: rock stars do not engage in a form of entertainment that involves a level of self-abasement. Unique among artists are the comedians, since offering humor – even on a large scale, and even when it's well compensated – is a strategy of the Fool. Since Fools are notable for having low Black Arrows, females who are best able to select their spouses from among elite males will almost always eschew low Black Arrows, leaving the Fool on the outside of the mating mansion looking in.

The use of humor in the act of mocking is a slightly different animal. Mocking is an aggressive and belligerent act, designed to present a self-contained case that the one doing the mocking is (or should be considered to be) superior to the target of the

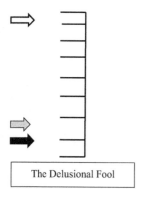
The Delusional Fool

Figure 8.6 Three-Arrow Model Placement of the Fool

mock. That's why Saul Alinsky, in *Rules for Radicals*, so strongly endorsed its usage.[4] In a social construct that's attempting to identify whose Black Arrows are higher than others, the ideal contributors to such an evaluation would be those with (verifiably) high Black Arrows. However, the merit-less, the Omega or the Delusional Fool, can gain access to the ranking process by employing the seemingly innocuous device of humor. The act of submissive entertainment is converted, in an instant, to adversarial confrontation, from those who really do not have any standing whatsoever to even weigh in on the discussion. It's insidious, but that's the kind of nasty tactic that Alinsky correctly identified as effective.

In today's hierarchical structure, of course, the Delusional Fool does not dress in such a way as to make immediate identification of his role intuitively obvious. For that reason, his tactics will include actions that can be undertaken on the sly, such as calumny or gossip. If this archetype does attempt to manipulate his rank within the hierarchy in a manner for all to see, he will usually do so by inflating his Grey Arrow, i.e., attempt to make others think more highly of him than he deserves (or is nominally indicated by his Black Arrow rank).

This category also includes the hopelessly spoiled child. As any experienced parent can tell you, if they were somehow compelled to engage this book's vernacular, the only way to remedy the spoiled child is to deflate his White Arrow, as painful as that is, and then recouple it to the child's Black Arrow. In other words, the misplaced praise and unearned status need to go away, and be replaced by increases in relative rank only when genuinely earned.

There is a variant of the Delusional Fool that I'll name the Victim. The Victim adopts a narrative that, while their Black Arrow may be ranked relatively low, it's only there because of external forces, these external forces being irresistible, powerful, and profoundly unfair. In fact, if not for these unfair external forces, why, the Victim would be readily acknowledged by all (high Grey Arrow) as being virtuous (high Black Arrow) – in essence, a narrative so contrived as to obliterate reality, and allow a continued severely inappropriate inflation of the White Arrow while their actual virtue remains relatively low.

So, when certain seventh-grade American minority students, for example, are taught that, prior to departing their homeland for America, their ancestors could fly (among other, "esteem-boosting" educational tactics, and no, I am not making this up[5]), what is actually happening is an inflation of their White Arrows with no consideration for a concurrent increase of their academic Black Arrows, with the entirely predictable result being that the students so taught will tend to assume one of the high White Arrow/low Black Arrow archetypes.

(5) *High White, low Grey, high Black* (Figure 8.7).

From our previous discussion on wolfpack society, the role of the Lone Wolf was assumed by a member of the pack – usually a male – that was not considered to be of sufficiently high rank for the level of treatment it received. Unable or unwilling to challenge the existing Alpha, the Lone Wolf split off from the pack, often peeling away one or two females while doing so. This little band becomes its own micro pack. As such, it is technically in competition with the pack it just left, and so must find its own territory.

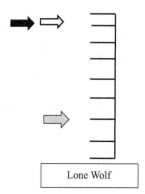

Figure 8.7 Three-Arrow Model Placement of the Lone Wolf

The same sort of scenario repeats itself in the (human) business world all of the time. Key personnel who, for whatever reason, are not recognized for the contribution they bring to the organization, realize that they are in a position to disengage from their current company and provide the products or services that their former bosses did, but better somehow, be it a superior product for the same price, or the same product for a lower price.

Categories 5 through 8 correlate strongly, I believe, with Michael Maccoby's archetypes from *The Gamesman*, in this case the associated archetype being the Craftsman. It's not that the associates of the Craftsman/Lone Wolf think badly of them, as much as it's not in this type to spend the time or energy cultivating relationships on a large scale.

It is to prevent the underappreciated but truly valuable members of the group from readily disengaging that organizations will often embrace and institutionalize strategies that make it more difficult for individuals to leave. Non-disclosure agreements and other intellectual property rules are examples of this strategy's institutionalization.

Returning to the wolfpack, consider a pack that, as a group, has adopted ranking strategies that are not conducive to its long-term viability. For the sake of example, we'll posit that its current Alpha, having been hurt as an adolescent in a pack attack on an elk, now eschews attacks on elk. In this pack's environment, though, elk are a critical source of nutrition for predators – to exclude them entirely from the list of available foodstuffs places the whole pack at a competitive disadvantage. Within the pack, however, this Alpha is unquestionably the most able male, and the other members of the pack are aware of it. As the population of deer, beaver, and smaller mammals is depleted, the pack begins to suffer, especially the non-Alpha or Beta members. The Omega may even starve prior to the Alpha rethinking its no-elk strategy.

In the meantime, an advanced male, not recognized as Alpha or Beta material by the rest of the pack, is seeing 700 lb of fresh elk meat meander by the pack, unmolested, and believes he has an effective tactic for killing and eating it. He may demonstrate his tactic while still part of the pack, or perhaps only do so after having disengaged; in either event, he has adopted a strategy that will serve any pack in which he contributes a leadership role well. Such a pack can be expected to thrive, particularly at the expense of any pack in the same vicinity that cannot (or will not) attack elk.

Indeed, once this male splits off from his former pack, that pack is at a distinct – if not fatal – disadvantage. Its Alpha will never succumb to a former underling in the pack's internal rankings. The Lone Wolf never rejoins its previous pack as its Alpha. The previous pack may, belatedly, begin to attack elk, but the capable but nearly starving members have either joined the new pack, or have become lone wolves themselves – or have stayed, and suffered the effects of a lack of nutrition, which also puts them at a competitive disadvantage. The old pack will go through the death throes of the organization that is nearing the end of its trajectory, and the new social constructs, having adopted the more appropriate strategies for long-term survival within the environment, will begin their lifecycles.

So, going back to the set of strategies a category 5/Lone Wolf character might employ, the set includes, obviously, disengagement. If the pack wishes to head off this selected strategy, it must either convince the Lone Wolf that it couldn't possibly make it outside the confines of the group (lower its White Arrow), or else take positive steps to inflate its Grey Arrow to more closely match its Black Arrow – I don't know, maybe present it with some form of wolf award at a well-attended ceremony. Either option has its problems. Any attempt by the pack or pack leadership to place external downward pressure on the Lone Wolf's White Arrow could very easily precipitate its departure. However, inflating the Grey Arrow without a commensurate lowering of the White Arrow will deliver another Alpha, bringing about a different sort of group hierarchy crisis. From the pack's point of view, the best outcome for the Lone Wolf role player would be to have them convert into a Beta.

From the Lone Wolf's point of view, past actually disengaging from the pack, options are limited. They could spend the energy to change the perception of the Lone Wolf's value to the other members of the society, either by direct solicitation, or by changing the basis of Grey Arrow rank assignment to more closely mirror their true value to the pack (higher level of correlation between the Black and Grey Arrows).

(6) *High White, high Grey, low Black* (Figure 8.8).

In contrast to the Lone Wolf, the Politician must spend significant time and energy convincing the other members of the group that he is extremely valuable, and part

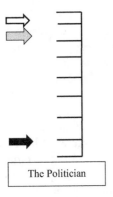

Figure 8.8 Three-Arrow Model Placement of the Politician

and parcel of this core need is to think of himself as extremely valuable. It is reported that Nero's last words were "What an artist dies in me."[6]

The Politician archetype is extremely dangerous, both to the individuals within the group where he resides as well as to the overall group itself. Individuals, because the Politician's true value is relatively low, but that fact must never come to light. The Politician will do virtually anything to prevent an honest assessment of his value, which includes employing deception and calumny to influence others' opinions, both of his artificially inflated perceived value and his unfortunate associates' artificially deflated perceived value.

The Politician represents a threat to the overall group for a variety of reasons, including:

- Should a Politician assume an Alpha role, then the group being so "led" will suffer in relation to competing organizations or groups, perhaps irreversibly.
- As the Politician rises in rank, the members of the pack who are truly deserving of increased rank, but are denied it in favor of the Politician himself or his cohorts, will tend to leave the group, either as Lone Wolves or to join other groups. In economic concerns, this is colloquially known as "brain drain," and is a sure indication of a poorly led organization.
- As any semblance of a meritocracy within the organization fades and disappears from view, an entire series of sociological pathologies will enter in. The ability to make the Politicians within the organization feel safe in their ill-gotten rankings, in the form of displays of twisted loyalty, becomes the determining factor in establishing rank. Sadly, the Politician is never completely comfortable with higher ranks (despite the amount of energy, time, and trouble spent in acquiring them) because they are aware, deep down, that they have not merited their placement – they *know* their Black Arrows are low, and they *know* that if anyone else finds that out, their continued enjoyment of the privileges of rank will be endangered.

The continued practice and enlarging of the capacity for deceiving multiple people on the topic of how the Politician ought to be perceived (higher), and others who are not aligned with the Politician ought to be perceived (lower) eventually lead to a level of self-deception that can easily initiate a downward spiral, first to dangerous levels of delusion, then to out-and-out sociopathology. Groups whose rankings are more subjective (it really does no good to employ deception or manipulations within the chess team in an attempt to raise one's rank) base those rankings on group consensus. Those providing the consensus to the Politician swiftly lose identity as individuals, and become manipulatable nodes in a vast rank-granting network.

While the closest Maccoby archetype is obviously the Jungle Fighter, I believe Shakespeare did a superb job of illustrating this category in the character of Iago from *Othello*. I also believe that this type is far more common than is generally recognized, since, if this type was readily recognizable, their Grey Arrows would (presumably) be quickly lowered in all but those organizations that are, themselves, pathologically backward. Prior to March of 1933, the vast majority of the electorate in Germany probably took a very dim view of the use of murder to advance one's political career, but Hitler's main cronies were probably okay with it.

To those skilled in manipulating or controlling others without the benefit of actual virtue, the path of the Politician can be highly seductive, since

- working hard to attain genuine virtue is, well, hard;
- the inflation of one's White Arrow, through means both valid and invalid, is euphoric;
- the deflation of the White Arrow is excruciating, and
- with a usable portion (if not majority) of the pack believing the Politician to be worthy of a high rank, the available tactics that can be easily invoked to maintain the Politician's erroneously assigned rank are vast.

The strategies the Politician will employ almost always involve deception. Their Grey Arrows did not attain those levels of high rank due to an accurate assessment of the type's true value. In this regard, the Politician will always be opposed to any member of the organization who seeks a higher correlation between the perceived and true values used in assigning rank. In other words, a group where Grey Arrows are consistently placed close to Black Arrows is anathema to the Politician.

To maintain their ill-deserved high Grey Arrow status, the Politician must indulge in one (or both) of two general strategies:

1. They must make themselves appear to be better than others.
2. They must make others appear to be worse in comparison, or at least deserving of a lower rank than the Politician himself.

As for strategy 1, the art of flattering one's self can be very tricky since, if the one doing it is perceived to be engaged in such (literally) self-serving actions, the group will respond in the exact opposite manner from the aimed-for advancement in rank. A relatively safe approach would be to target a few, select and influential team members who can themselves relay a perception of the Politician's "high" value to other members, which is why real-life politicians are so enamored by/terrified of the press. For an outstanding portrayal of this strategy, I would recommend Shakespeare's *Richard III*. For those of you who are not familiar with this play, suffice to say that Richard devotes a great deal of energy promoting those members of the court who indicate high levels of loyalty to him, and an equal amount of energy eliminating (killing off) those who don't.

Strategy 2 is also consistent with the societally destructive Cloward–Piven strategy, particularly the assertion that opposing organizations should be made to exactly meet or surpass all of their stated goals, or else be accused of being either failures or hypocritical. Since no group can possibly meet all of its goals and objectives in the short term, this gives the Politician ample opportunity to look around them, point out the "failures" while attempting some degree of non-involvement (or at least non-culpability), and essentially lower the White and Grey Arrows of all of those around them.

(7) *High White, high Grey, high Black* (Figure 8.9).

Alphas are true leaders: they are (usually) virtuous, in ways that are readily acknowledged or recognized by the other members of the group, and have the confidence needed to fulfill the role. They are analogous to Maccoby's Gamesman, Bartle's Diamonds, and the ancient Arabic story's Wise Man. "Woe to you, O land, when your King is a child" (Ecclesiastes 10: 16) might be expanded to say that any organization is in the lurch if a person who has not established a high-level merit is placed in a position of leadership.

Since acknowledged Alphas are already on top of the group's rankings, their only vulnerability from within is from those who seek to displace them. Unfortunately, this can be (and usually is) just about everybody else in the group, but for different reasons. Leaders who are in place due to their merit must continue to demonstrate that they are making the best decisions for the betterment of the organization they lead; otherwise, the Betas will at least consider whether or not a change in leadership is appropriate.

However, any member of the organization whose White Arrow is significantly above their Black Arrow will resent the true leader, and can be expected to engage in immoral, deceitful, or even illegal tactics to bring the Alpha down. This was the message that Dionysius so successfully imparted to Damocles in the famous legend, about the illusory ease or happiness that is believed to accompany the role of the Alpha.

In those organizations blissfully free of insurrection, overt or otherwise, the main challenges to the Alpha are the same challenges faced by the whole group. For this reason the group will usually fete its Alphas with trappings of ease or comfort, not to encourage idleness, but to dispense with the everyday and mundane difficulties that besot the rank and file in order for the Alpha to address and overcome the larger problems that afflict the entire organization.

(8) *Low White, high Grey, low Black* (Figure 8.10).

The category of the Comedian is an intriguing one. They are well thought of by their packs, even though they are not highly valuable contributors to their packs' success. Since they are outwardly humble, they do not pose an obvious threat to the

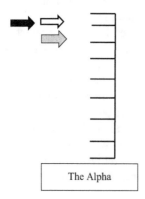

The Alpha

Figure 8.9 Three-Arrow Model Placement of the Alpha

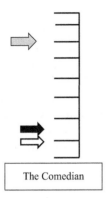

Figure 8.10 Three-Arrow Model Placement of the Comedian

existing hierarchy, and so add to the confidence levels of those who have already attained an acceptable rank. Since I have already invoked the image of the wolfpack, I would like to remind my readers that, within both chimpanzee and wolf societies, the Omegas are noted for being unique in engaging in goofy or entertaining behavior, as if to lighten the spirits of the rest of the group. This is not to say that all who engage in comic relief are Omegas, but all Omegas engage in presenting comic relief to others.

In adding to the previous discussion of the use of humor in group dynamics, I would like to reiterate that, with the exception of mocking, an individual engaging in humor is putting energy and time into an effort to make others feel better. There are several ways of doing this, but the most effective tend to be those uses of humor that reinforce – or actually inflate – what the audience thinks of themselves, either as individuals or as members of a group. It's not for nothing that puns are considered the lowest form of humor – they are amusing at the expense of the nuances of spoken language (though similar gestures in sign language may have their own category of humor, for all I know), as opposed to the foibles of humans or human nature. The act of articulating these foibles, these weaknesses in a non-threatening manner can be of enormous benefit to the overall group. When Osama bin Laden spoke of the need for violent jihad, he was exposing himself as a threat to civilization. When Jeff Dunham voices the ventriloquist doll Achmed the Dead Terrorist to say "Silence! I kill you!" people laugh uproariously.

I do not mean to include the very talented Mr. Dunham in the Comedian archetype. I have no idea what he thinks of himself, nor what his relative value to various organizations or societies would have been had he selected another line of work. That having been admitted, he does do an amazing job of allowing the stated targets of often fatal violence to actually *laugh* at such status, which really could not be accomplished in any way short of total victory over any and all jihadists, except through humor.

The Comedian basically has three paths open to him. Since his White Arrow is (blessedly) low, he may (1) have an epiphany, and decide to put in the time and effort into increasing his Black Arrow. Alternately, he could (2) decide to inflate his White Arrow, based on the input from others (i.e., align his White Arrow more closely to his Grey Arrow than his Black Arrow), and morph into the Politician. Or, he could (3) stay where he is, humbly enjoying the accolades that others place upon him, forever the Comedian.

Part II: the Nature of the Game

The Ranking Game has many versions, and few assertions about how, when, where, and why it's played will have universally valid applications. That's the way reality is, and an automatic application of some sort of strategy relevant in most social interactions among pack animals is going to be illusive, as least as it pertains to humans. And yet, even in Network Theory, with its most dominant feature being Metcalf's Law, as unpredictable and unmanageable as changes in rank and ranking systems can be, certain patterns of individual and group strategy selection emerge, and can be assessed for efficacy. In short, the nature of the ranking game largely depends on the nature and type of organization doing the ranking.

As in individuals' personas, groups can be functional or not, and successful or not. Returning to our friend the payoff grid, see Table 8.1. We would expect organizations pursuing a valid purpose, free of the pathologies of decision making that would either hinder its pursuit or lead to erroneous rank assignments among its individual members to succeed, and do so over a relatively long and stable lifespan (from the Library of Pithy Wisdom, a.k.a. the clichés, "Nothing succeeds like success"). Similarly, organizations pursuing invalid ends, besotted by internal pathologies such as cronyism or tolerance of deceit, will normally end in failure after a shorter lifespan.

Of course, when an individual is in the act of selecting the organization she wishes to join, thereby lending talent to it, and expecting at some point to be rewarded with rank recognition, it's impossible to go by the lone indicator "success." Not only does the meaning of the term change from organization to organization, it also changes within the same organization from time to time. Microsoft Corporation began with its definition of success being to have a significant share of the market of the software that ran on personal computers, for example. Further muddying the waters is something revealed in the payoff grid: not every well-run organization is successful, and not every dysfunctional social construct is a short-lived failure. What other ways do organizations signal their valid functioning (or lack thereof)?

Certainly one of the most elemental organizations in human society is the family unit. Within dysfunctional family units, there are, generally speaking, (wouldn't you just know it?) four main archetypes, or roles played by the individuals so trapped.[7] These roles are:

- The Golden Child/Hero is a family favorite, and is viewed to do no wrong. Often this status is granted without respect to the Golden Child's true potential societal value (high White Arrow, low Black Arrow).

Table 8.1 Functional/Successful Organization Payoff Matrix

	Unsuccessful	Successful
Functional	Victim of unfavorable outside circumstances	Expected (good) outcome
Dysfunctional	Expected (bad) outcome	Beneficiary of favorable outside circumstances

- The Scapegoat (also known as the Rebel) becomes the easily identifiable cause for all that afflicts the family, whether or not he is the proximate – or even material – cause of the difficulties.
- The Mascot/Clown uses humor to dissipate the negative feelings and attitudes within the family unit, delaying a day of reckoning where those negative feelings and attitudes reach a critical point, and initiating a dramatic decline or destruction of the voluntary association of the dysfunctional family's members.
- The Lost Child tends to withdraw from the family in an effort to defend his own sense of self-worth. In non-familial groupings, the existence of a Lost Child type is a clear indication that there are forces in play that are discouraging (or even preventing) voluntary disengagement.

The presence of any individual within a given group exhibiting the behaviors consistent with these roles represents strong evidence that the given group is, in fact, dysfunctional. And yet, it's an unavoidable part of life that we will find ourselves participating in organizations, ones from which we could theoretically walk away, that manifest symptoms of being profoundly dysfunctional. Identifying and decrying them as such, in most cases, is futile. A way must be found to navigate these fevered swamps of dysfunction, at least until a state of affairs can be realized where a suitable exit strategy can be employed.

In forming a strategy on how to advance in a given hierarchy, there are two basic ground rules to be observed.

Basic Ground Rule 1: There's more than One Narrative Going On

I kind of get a kick out of reading various companies' Mission Statements or Corporate Goals documents. They invariably include some reference to providing the best possible service or product to our highly valued customers, blah blah blah, and include references to some combination of the following:

- quality
- value
- worker safety
- diversity
- environment
- efficient use of resources
- contribution to the community (code words for paying taxes).

On occasion, when the firm's accountants are allowed to "contribute," you will see a head fake towards something like "while experiencing advancement of the goals of company's stake/shareholders…" i.e., make a profit.

Look, I don't doubt that the writers of such statements (or those who had them written) genuinely seek those outcomes. What I find striking about them is how similar they all are. But, since the organizations themselves are not really that similar, there's something else going on here.

As a mental exercise, think about how these mission statements would be different should those publishing them be struck with darts containing sodium pentothal. According to MissionStatements.com, this is the mission statement for one R. J. B. Industries, from Clearfield, Utah:[8]

> To exceed our customers' expectations in quality, delivery, and cost through continuous improvement and customer interaction.

Not to nit-pick, but it is rather impossible to do any of these things without "interacting" with one's "customers."

Now, here's me, rewriting this kind of mission statement, as I would imagine it would be if their writers were to be suddenly and completely given over to speaking the truth, the whole truth, and nothing but the truth:

> We intend to have our customers give us a lot of money while fully appreciating the increased value our organization lends to their lives, thereby crushing our competitors and enriching our stockholders.

I don't mean to pick on R. J. B. Industries – for all I know, this is the brutal-truth version of every other company that ever set up shop since the dawning of the free enterprise age. But it does point to a very real and necessary truism for those caught up in a hierarchy: there are multiple narratives being propagated within the organization. One, the main one, is intended for widespread dissemination and recognition; the other is the version that every individual within the organization must recognize as being operable, lest they find themselves ostracized and/or relegated to Omega status.

Basic Ground Rule 2: the Other Narrative Is One that Few Dare Openly Articulate

So far we have the "official" narrative of the organization, and a version that's somewhat sub-rosa, but everyone involved pretty much needs to recognize if they have any chance of advancement. Then, there's the narrative that, in large part, drives much of the interactions that decide rankings within the macro organization, and yet, it's not articulated. This narrative is:

> The organization exists to propagate or maintain the ranks of those who are comfortable with their current or potential status.

If this narrative were to be published or plainly asserted, the owning organization would indicate beyond a shadow of a doubt that it had become unmoored from its original underpinnings. Since hierarchical structures for the sake of hierarchical structures serve no purpose whatsoever, such an organization would, rather dramatically I suppose, precipitate its own demise. Even Stalin, murdering millions of his own countrymen, had to throw out the occasional reference to the "good of the proletariat."

At this point the group member should be aware of at least three narratives:

- The one the organization wants known (usually published or otherwise asserted for external consumption).
- The one that keeps the group going with respect to the facts from its environment. The main analogy here is the wolfpack confronted with a dramatically changing environment, needing to do what it takes to survive as a group.
- The unspoken narrative, that the maintenance of the existing hierarchy is more important than virtually any other organizational goal, even the ones in the Mission Statement.

The maintenance of the third, unspoken narrative has its roots in the previously mentioned reasons motivating the Politician/Jungle Fighter, namely that (a) the inflation of the White Arrow is euphoric, (b) the deflation of the White Arrow is excruciating, and (c) the advancement of the Black Arrow requires a significant investment of time and energy on top of an inherent availability of talent. It follows, then, that anybody serving for a significant period of time in an extant position of high rank in any long-lived organization has little chance of having retained such a position through pure merit. Referring again to the Library of Pithy Wisdom, I'll quote Thomas Jefferson, who said "The tree of liberty must be refreshed from time to time with the blood of patriots and tyrants." I will address the political implications of this model in subsequent chapters; for now it will suffice to paraphrase Jefferson's quote as "by the time the existing power structure has been entrenched for a relatively long period of time, it will be inherently corrupt, and desperately needing of overthrow, even if such an overthrow requires much bloodshed."

Note the similarities of the three organizational narratives to the Berne archetypes.

- The published or disseminated version of the narrative – the Mission Statement – is pretty much what the organization aspires to, and wants each of its members to pursue.
- The narrative that keeps the group operating within the realities of its environment is consistent with the Adult persona, the one that performs the tasks necessary to satisfy the Child persona's emotionally driven needs while showing progress against the Parent persona's goals.
- The unspoken narrative, the one that asserts that the organization exists for the pleasure of its higher-esteemed members, is purely internal, irrational, barely satiable, and is therefore very similar to the Child persona.

Note also that the dysfunctional family roles/archetypes do not come about naturally in a normally functioning familial unit. By definition, the archetypes represent patterns of behavior (or strategy selection) of the members of a dysfunctional organization, one that is difficult or impossible to disengage. In other words, the narrowing of the spectrum of available, acceptable behaviors is being pushed down, from the leaders of the dysfunctional organization to its unfortunate members.

No group of human beings is immune from the social pathologies that work against the achievement of the organization's stated goals, team cohesion, or overall well-being, which is why all man-made organizations have a lifespan. There is no one tipping point when an organization goes from functional and valid to dysfunctional and invalid, any more than there is a tipping point for people to go from healthy to sick, or happy to unhappy. These are all relative terms. That having been admitted, just as we all know when we're relatively healthy or relatively sick, so, too, will organizations present as being based on a largely valid model and adhering to it, or else show themselves to be dysfunctional well before the end of their lifespans. One of the main ways in which a given organization will throw out clues that it is, in fact, dysfunctional is if its higher-ranking members attempt to force its new or lower-ranking members into an equivalent of one of the four dysfunctional family member roles.

I'm not referring here to the act of assigning job duties within a corporation or economic concern, since specialization is a natural aspect of growing a team. I'm talking about a noticeable disconnect in the way ranks are assigned and enforced when the basis is somewhat subjective. Harkening back to the chess team motif, the higher-ranked players have absolutely nothing to gain from attempting to alter the Grey or White Arrows of the other members of the team. Conversely, in a team headed up by the Politician archetype with a subjective basis for ranking, anyone with a Black Arrow rating higher than the leader will be viewed as a threat by the Politician. The Politician can't alter others' Black Arrow placements, but he *can* influence the Grey Arrow and, through different tactics, the target's White Arrow.

Indeed, one way of looking at the dysfunctional family roles is in the context of our triple-arrow graphic. We'll assume that our sample dysfunctional family has at its head a father, who is either a substance abuser, narcissistic, or both, and the four children have each adopted a different role.

- The Golden Child must have at least a middle ranking of her Black Arrow, otherwise it would be difficult to hold them up to the other children as deserving unquestioning respect. However, this role's Black Arrow can't be demonstrably higher than the father's (actually, none of them can) without incurring the put-downs and brow-beatings needed to re-establish the father as absolutely justified in his inflated White Arrow. So, in dysfunctional organizations, it is ironic that the Golden Child, the archetype that can supposedly do no wrong, is likely to have a lower Black Arrow than the other members. The father will seek to artificially inflate the Golden Child's Grey Arrow ranking as long as this Golden Child supports the father's inflated White Arrow, in a sort of twisted quid-pro-quo. The Maccoby archetype that most closely resembles the Golden Child is the Gamesman, who is more apt to take risks than the other archetypes. Since the Golden Child can supposedly do no wrong, they are far less likely to suffer the consequences of pushing the limits of acceptable behaviors, as well.
- The Mascot/Clown, who clearly resembles the Maccoby archetype of the Company Man, takes on those characteristics in order to communicate clearly and constantly that they represent no threat to the existing ranks. Since maintaining the familial ranking system as-is, with the father retaining the euphorically high overinflated White Arrow, is the primary driver behind the enforced ranks, the Mascot/Clown indicates preemptively that such enforcement is unnecessary. The Mascot's Black Arrow placement is mostly irrelevant: as long as he communicates a low White Arrow (remember that the use of humor is a self-deprecating

act), the father need not put energy into forcing this role's White (or Grey) Arrow downward.

- The Scapegoat (again, ironically) is likely to have a high Black Arrow, the recognition of which cannot be tolerated by the father in the dysfunctional family unit. In order to prevent any hint of a revelation about who within the family unit is the most accomplished or valuable, the father will deliberately set out to lower the Scapegoat's White and Grey Arrows, usually via the following tactics:
  - The father will reinterpret historical events and insert causality analysis that points to undesirable outcomes being associated with The Scapegoat.
  - The father will attempt to put the Scapegoat into impossible positions or situations, without actually appearing to be doing so. If the Scapegoat fails, it reinforces the notion that the others in the family ought to view him poorly (lower Grey Arrow). If the Scapegoat somehow succeeds, the achievement is downplayed, and the next set of engineered circumstances becomes all the more difficult.
  - A happy, harmonious, successful familial unit existence will be asserted or articulated – except for how it's just beyond the horizon, and can't be realized because of the actions of the Scapegoat. To the extent that the others in the family buy into this lie, the Scapegoat's Grey Arrow will have severe downward pressure applied to it.
  - Then, of course, there's always the more direct set of strategies of challenging, mocking, and brow-beating the Scapegoat in order to immediately lower his White Arrow, or to ensure its continued low rank.
- The Lost Child will test the limits of the individual members' ability to disengage from the association with the family unit. If the abusive father in this particular scenario is okay with that, her marginalization will be allowed. If not, then not, and the would-be Lost Child will be faced with the decision to either assume one of the two roles of Scapegoat or Mascot/Clown, or else transition from Lost Child to Lone Wolf. To prevent such a transition, dysfunctional family members will often come together to dissuade possible flight risks. The members of the group displaying Lost Child characteristics are also the most likely to have the highest Black Arrows, leading to a further sense of apprehension from the others that group cohesion strategies should be employed, since few organizations can withstand the loss of its most talented members.

"What Are You Doing to Our Children?!"

Academy award-winning actress Meryl Streep asked this question during testimony before the United States Congress (?!) in a silly and hysterical episode from the Alar Scare.[9] I cite it because it does point to a difficult but ubiquitous truth: it isn't just the dysfunctional organizations that attempt to force roles upon its members. *All* organizations will tend to change *every* one of its members in order to meet its overarching ends, even if those ends – trendy as they may be – are profoundly backwards. Sometimes, as in volunteering for the military services of one of the free nations, the change is known prior to signing up and is beneficial to the new members. In other instances, as in joining the ranks of pornographic magazine subscribers, the change is pernicious, but not necessarily known beforehand.

So, the short answer to Streep's question is that we are changing the members of our macro group (or "society") to comport with a series of selected roles that mirror the underlying structure for the group's existence. This is a fairly universal truth; as we covered in Chapter 6, societal constructs take on an existence and persona all of their own. This group persona is obviously influenced by its members, but its members are influenced by the group's persona as well, again, sometimes beneficially, other times not.

This becomes something of a precautionary note, then. From the Vault of Conventional Wisdom I recite the rhetorical question "does a fish know it's wet?" As we continue to discuss the analytic possibilities in reviewing hierarchies and the strategies that influence them, keep in mind that, as we play this game, the game is changing us, possibly in ways subtle and beneficial, but potentially in grotesque and nasty ways, as well. Again, from The Vault: "Power corrupts, and absolute power corrupts absolutely" can be paraphrased as "individuals within a group didn't start out as vile and monstrous when they first joined, but were changed *by the group itself* through a combination of any inherent evil within the group's basis combined with the desire for an advancement in rank."

The subtle but deadly nature of residual evil within the basic framework of the group being evaluated should not be underestimated, and is a key exception to the "power corrupts" cliché. To invoke two extreme examples, the Pope is more powerful within the structure of the Catholic Church than is a local pastor, but that does not translate into higher levels of corruption. Conversely, within the nascent Nazi Party, one gets the impression that had Bormann, Himmler, or Gebhardt supplanted Hitler, the overall outcome would have been pretty much the same.

However, there are limits to the degree to which the organization's persona can influence or change its individual members. This limit was recognized during the Nuremburg trials, where a common defense among the surviving Nazis was that they were simply obeying the orders of their superiors. The court found – correctly – that, (paraphrasing) while an inherently evil organization can exert extraordinary pressure on its individual members to perform acts they would not otherwise do, at some point the individuals are responsible for their own behavior, and are culpable for criminal acts carried out in service to the macro organization.

And the notion that "society" is what enforces male or female gender identity is just plain idiotic.

On occasion a truly insightful individual will recognize the changes within that have been adopted in response to participation in an outside group, realize that these changes do not represent an improvement, and (if possible) disengage from the outside group, regardless of material loss or reduction in perceived rank. Indeed, the stories of the lives of the saints are replete with example after example of men and women born into wealth or nobility, and walking away from such otherwise coveted existences in order to fulfill their superior callings of serving God. This behavior was best captured by Jesus of Nazareth, when He said:

> Again, the kingdom of heaven is like unto a merchant man, seeking goodly pearls: Who, when he had found one pearl of great price, went and sold all that he had, and bought it.
>
> Matthew 13: 45–6 (*The Bible*, King James Version)

The ways in which a given group will change its Alpha can be difficult to undo. When, by whatever means, a member of the group is elevated to Alpha/Leader status, her concerns change dramatically. As noted previously, her worries are no longer centered on improving rank within the group – she's already on top. Her concerns turn to defeating attempts from within aimed at displacing her, and taking on the challenges that pose threats to the entire group. Aaron Nimzovich once wrote that chess is 99% tactics, 1% strategy. However, the group conditions its Alphas to think mostly – if not exclusively – about strategy, rendering them less effective should they ever be returned to sub-Alpha ranking, at least within the same group.

So, before we enter into an extensive analysis of how to advance within a given hierarchy, two additional ground rules should be kept in mind:

1. the hierarchy being joined will change its members, and
2. unless membership is truly compulsory, walking away is always an option, no matter how much the situation appears otherwise.

Now we've set up the pieces on the board, with a rudimentary grasp of how and why they move the way they do. Next up: it's your move.

Notes

1 Simmel, Georg, retrieved from *Thought Catalog*, http://thoughtcatalog.com/madison-moore/2013/05/47-quotes-that-inspire-you-to-be-yourself/, June 26, 2015.
2 Maccoby, Michael, *The Gamesman: The New Corporate Leaders*. New York: Simon and Schuster, 1976.
3 Bartle, Richard, "Hearts, Clubs, Diamonds, Spades: Players who Suit MUDS," retrieved from http://mud.co.uk/richard/hcds.htm, June 26, 2015.
4 Alinsky, Saul, *Rules for Radicals*. New York: Random House, 1971.
5 Hamilton, Virginia, *The People Could Fly*. New York: Knopf, 2001, p. 767.
6 Retrieved from *Roman Empire*, http://www.roman-empire.net/emperors/nero-index.html, May 8, 2015.
7 Retrieved from *PsychCentral*, http://psychcentral.com/blog/archives/2013/08/10/early-wounding-dysfunctional-family-roles/, May 9, 2015.
8 Retrieved from *Mission Statements*, http://www.missionstatements.com/manufacturing_mission_statements.html, December 26, 2014.
9 Streep, Meryl, Alar Congressional Committee, 1988, retrieved from *Speak Up America*, http://www.suanews.com/seldom-heard-quotes/seldom-heard-quotes-population-extremism-ddt-pesticides-part-6-3.html, May 9, 2015.

Chapter 9

Playing the Ranking Game

> That which is not good for the bee-hive cannot be good for the bees.
>
> Marcus Aurelius[1]

First, a word of caution, before any individual seeks to advance their rank within a given organization, the question must be asked:

Why?

And, unlike the college-level philosophy class of urban legend, the answer "Why not?" will not suffice. Motive will be a key determining factor in success rate, the extent that the individual changes the organization, and, perhaps most important of all, the degree to which the organization changes the individual.

The most basic reason anybody voluntarily joins an organization is out of pure selfishness: they seek to advance their station or status in life. From Chapter 1, Crusoe and Friday entered into an alliance because to do otherwise would lessen their chances of long-term survivability. Without passing judgment on the virtue or vice of such motives, selfishness is a perfectly valid reason for attempting to either become a member of an existing group, or else start one anew. However, taken to its extreme, a group made up of members exclusively motivated by self-interest will quickly manifest the organizational pathologies that will spell its doom. The wolfpack that lacks food distribution discipline (every wolf eats as much as it can when presented with the opportunity) will lose its weaker members – generally, females – whenever it encounters lean times, leading to its obvious demise. Manic self-centeredness on behalf of a group's members tends to defeat any advantage that the establishment of the group, with its accompanying distribution of roles and tasks, would otherwise have over unincorporated and non-cooperating individuals.

So, in selecting a social construct to join, sure, it's okay if the primary motive is to improve the individual's standing. However, as discussed in Chapter 5, with the Midtown High School clique that Scott would like to join, the group itself will have assumed a persona, one that selects strategies for its own survival or advancement. Part of these strategies involve attracting members who can help the group achieve *its* goals, while dissuading (or out-and-out preventing) individuals who would represent a drag on achieving those goals from joining. Here is the tacit acknowledgment that (a) the individual's main motive in attempting to join the group is self-enrichment, and (b) the group's main motivation in screening potential members is its own self-interest. To the extent that these two desired outcomes are consistent is the degree to which the potential member and prospective group is a good match. In other words, if the potential inductee can help the group, *and* the group can help the inductee, then just such an association is appropriate. In cases where this overlap of mutual benefit is not as clear-cut, well, things get cloudy.

Shakespeare, again, probably best illustrated this, in *Othello*. If we assume that "Team Othello" was comprised of the following individuals:

- Othello
- Desdemona
- Michael Cassio
- Iago
- Bianca
- Emilia,

whose stated purpose was advancing the interest of Venice in the face of a Turkish attack on Cyprus, then Othello is the Alpha, and the determiner of the others' ranks, either directly or indirectly. Michael Cassio is a virtuous servant of the Moor, and Iago is a treacherous enemy. However, Team Othello believes them to be the exact opposite of their true natures, leading to the tragedy. In our vernacular, Iago was the Politician (low Black Arrow, high White and Grey Arrows), whereas Cassio was the Beta (low White Arrow, high Black and Grey Arrows). By allowing Iago into the Moor's inner circle, Iago, being a Politician archetype, does what politicians do best, and nearly succeeds in destroying all of the legitimate contributors to the team.

In short, Team Othello's inability to exclude members who did not seek to advance the team's goals led to its (in this case, tragic) downfall.

And so, in pivoting back from the group's perspective to the individual seeking to join or advance within a given group, we return to the previous question: why? Why does the individual want to join, or advance within a given organization? And, while there's a common understanding that people voluntarily join groups for their own advancement, there also has to be a demonstrated (or perceived) element of benefit to the target group in order for such acceptance or advancement to take place.

For the purposes of this chapter, we'll assume that the individual seeking to join a given organization or, having already joined, wants to advance in rank, does so for valid reasons, and not entirely selfish motives; that the target organization is worthy of the individual's time and effort in its (at least stated) purpose, or mission statement; and that the group's underlying narratives are not so pervasive as to invite in the plethora of organizational pathologies that will spell its demise in the short term. As we explore how the Ranking Game is played in legitimate organizations, I fully expect to uncover insights that can be of use in even profoundly dysfunctional groups.

Now you are seated before the board and pieces, and the tournament director is about to activate the game clock. What, exactly, should you be doing?

Step 1: Assess Yourself

This self-assessment is a bit more thorough than the review of motives referenced at the beginning of this chapter, but it's not that complex. There are essentially three questions that need to be answered:

1.   Where – truly – are your Black, White, and Grey Arrows?
2.   Where do you want them to be?
3.   Are you willing to do what it takes to attain those levels?

The answer to the first question is important, because it will determine which areas need to be addressed in the act of formulating a strategy to get you where you want to be. You can't truly know where you are going if you don't know your starting point, or where you've been. It's true of travels among locales, and it's true of identifying winning strategies in Game Theory.

So, taking them one at a time, where *are* your Black, White, and Grey Arrows?

The Black Arrow can be the most difficult to recognize its precise rank, even though it's the most objective indicator, and can be the most difficult to move. It's unique in several ways, most notably in that there's only one person in the universe who can change it: the person it belongs to. It's fairly axiomatic that this arrow can be easily moved downward, but requires much time and effort to move upwards. While the implications of rank and archetype changes in literature will be covered in Chapter 13, I would like to take a moment here to point out the allure of a person coming into a sudden and dramatic increase in their Black Arrow placement from superhero lore:

*   Spiderman was weakling outcast Peter Parker until he was bitten by a special spider (either radioactive or genetically altered); afterwards, he possessed super-human strength and speed of reflexes, and is extremely valuable to a society wishing to diminish violent crime.
*   Superman was infant orphan refugee Kal-El until he arrived on Earth and, being exposed to a planet with a yellow sun (rather than the red star at the center of Krypton's system), assumed superhuman strength, the ability to fly, and other powers which made him extremely valuable to a society wishing to diminish violent crime.
*   The Green Lantern was test pilot Hal Jordan who happened across dying alien Abin Sur, a member of an organization devoted to diminishing violent crime across the galaxy. Sur's lantern and ring imparted superhuman powers to its user.
*   Captain America was actually weakling Steve Rogers, who was selected to undergo an experimental process that would suddenly and dramatically increase his strength, speed, and stamina to superhuman levels, significantly changing his value to a society wishing to diminish violent crime and/or tyrannical takeovers.

And so it goes in a genre of fiction mostly associated with very young audiences. Their suspension of belief, after all, is easily achieved. Meanwhile, back in the real world, improving one's value to a given organization can indeed be dramatic, but it is rarely sudden, and it is most often accompanied by significant investments in time, energy, and talent. Obviously, successful chess teams will both attract and be composed of high-performing chess players, competitive track teams attract and develop fast runners, and highly ranked universities wish to demonstrate a superior slate of teachers and researchers. With few exceptions, the higher-performing versions of these organizations have members who have not come by their high-performance abilities due to alien encounters or being munched on by irradiated arachnids. In this regard, most voluntary organizations represent an open invitation to those who are willing to work, and work hard in order to both improve the potential members' standing and help achieve the group's objectives (the openly acknowledged ones, anyway).

The word *dedication* is often used to indicate the level at which the individual is willing to commit time and energy in pursuing an improvement to a particular field of enterprise. When attempting to evaluate how dedicated we are to our pursuits, a monstrous strain of confirmation bias can easily infiltrate such an intensely internal evaluation process, especially if the way that the target group assigns value is somewhat subjective. The member of the chess team whose rank isn't where he wants it to be has only his lack of time studying and practicing, or else his inherent talent level, to blame for it. Professional athletes, on the other hand, who crave advancement within their selected teams, may be lazier or less talented than their team mates; or, perhaps, they are only being perceived that way and, if the truth were known, their coaches would experience some sort of epiphany, and the desired improvement in rank would come about somewhat automatically.

And there's the rub. As I stated earlier, the precise placement of the Black Arrow is difficult to know, being somewhat invisible in organizations with any aspect of subjectivity in rank assignment. The other two arrows are a bit more visible – polls readily (if not entirely reliably) reveal where an individual's Grey Arrow is, and the individual himself will often (inescapably?) provide clues as to where they have elected to place their White Arrow. A natural tendency in the less-than-humble will be to assume a Black Arrow placement somewhere in the vicinity of the other two, while a particularly difficult conceit is to assume that one's Black Arrow is entirely consistent with their White Arrow. Since inflating the White Arrow is euphoric and deflating it – either internally or externally – is excruciating, an honest placement of the Black Arrow is not an easy task.

It is, however, key to formulating a strategy on how to advance within any organization. The proper way of performing this assessment, then, is to assign the Black Arrow the lowest score that does not overturn reliable, objective measures.

The chess team member can reliably place his Black Arrow consistent with his US Chess Federation (or World Chess Federation) score. The athlete has it much tougher – does, say, a certain professional basketball player hit the highest percentages of free throws of any member of his team? Great – but that's an extremely thin basis for assuming the rank of the team's best overall player. The team itself will tend to reveal whom it believes is its most valued member by the amount of money they pay that player. And yet, even here much subjectivity is present, due to the old adage that we don't get, in life, what we deserve – we get what we negotiate.

Okay, but if our player happens to be the best free-throw shooter *and* the highest-paid member, does *that* indicate the highest Black Arrow? Again, not necessarily, and, for the purposes of formulating a strategy for rising within the ranks of this team, our pro player would be best served by collecting all of the data associated with basketball player performance, including:

- speed in the 40-yard dash
- speed running the mile
- weight-lifting capability
- frequency of fouls or other penalties

- percentage of three-point shots made
- percentage of field goals
- percentage of lay-ups
- number of hours spent studying strategy
- amount of time spent weight-lifting, or other training, among others.

Are we then ready for an approximate Black Arrow placement? No, absolutely not. The final, key step is this: to take the least-flattering data as gospel, and reject the most flattering as unreliable, or irrelevant. This is the crucial step in assuming the placement of the Black Arrow, as assuming this arrow is at a low level has few (if any) negative consequences to subsequent strategy formulation, while any artificial or irrelevant inflation simply invites in a plethora of errors. In this regard, assuming the level of the Black Arrow placement is reminiscent of the ground rules from the American game show staple *The Price Is Right*. Aside from the very strange costumes that the studio audience/participant pool wear, the basic component of the show is to estimate the manufacturers' suggested retail price of a variety of consumer goods. However, it's not the closest estimate that's considered the best – it's the closest estimate *that does not go over the true price*. And this is a component of the estimation cycle of the Ranking Game: you need to be able to estimate the placement of the Black Arrow as close as possible, but without *ever* overestimating it.

This is part of what makes the truly humble individual both valuable to the group and formidable in competition. Such people are clear-eyed about their abilities, and can be expected to be entirely free of the behavioral pathologies that so often accompany those whose White Arrows are placed noticeably above their Black Arrows.

The White Arrow's placement, as previously noted, is closely tied with Freud's Id and Berne's Child, meaning that it is irrational, subjective, emotional, inconsistent... and powerful. Extremely powerful.

Yet, in formulating a strategy for advancement within a coveted group or organization, some semblance of a clear-eyed assessment of who we are and what we're worth in comparison to our compadres is essential. As excruciating as the exercise may be, it is essential: before you can assemble a strategy for advancing within your targeted organization, it's simply necessary that you lower your White Arrow.

At this point I'm really not worried about advising an already-feeling-low type that they ought to feel worse, since this type really has no place lower to arrive. No, this is about those who feel pretty good about themselves, but shouldn't. Besides, the internal conflict experienced by those who feel really badly about themselves is the delta between those individuals' current White Arrow placement, and its more appropriate, lower placement, which is, again, an excruciating exercise. Some people would rather kill themselves than experience it, which is the ultimate tragedy all by itself.

I don't pretend to know the motives behind the act of suicide. But I do believe that few who commit that horrendous act think very highly of themselves, nor perceive their value to the groups they adhere to – or humanity at large – is very (or even acceptably) high. I would venture to guess that these had previously experienced the euphoria of the inflated White Arrow, only to have their delusions of being highly valued punctured by "cruel reality," and could not tolerate the externally compelled deflation of their White Arrows. With their sense of perspective and proportion utterly discombobulated, striking against the ultimate gift – that of existence – appears as an alternative.

So, yeah, we're dealing with unfathomably powerful forces here. Still, in order to assemble a workable strategy for advancing within a given organization, the exercise must be undertaken to ensure that the smallest possible gap exists between the individual's Black Arrow and White Arrow. To the truly humble, such an exercise is entirely superfluous. To the rest of us, it's not that far removed from root canal territory in the world of self-selected but painful gotta-dos. It is, however, a safe assumption going forward that the higher an individual's White Arrow is placed, the more vulnerable he is.

The Grey Arrow does not place itself as we would like it, as much as we might want it to. Its placement is based on two things:

- The perceptions of others. Note that this is not necessarily the same thing as the clues the individual exudes – it's how those clues are received by the observing members of the group.
- The narrative, or script, that accompanies the proffered clues. This script provides a framework that observers can use to make sense of those clues, or at least organize them in such a way as to fulfill the previously discussed voyeur instinct.

The individual has some control over the former, but only limited influence with the latter. This often proves to be a key factor, since most organizations depend (at least to some extent) upon the consensus of its members when changes in assigned rank – movements of the Grey Arrow – actually occur.

Grey Arrow movement is somewhat unique among the other arrows in that it usually occurs during times of organizational upheaval. Black and White Arrows can rise or fall without the social construct's visible reaction, or even having taken note; however, when Grey Arrows start moving up or down, somebody's existing Grey Arrow is being displaced. To the extent that those individuals' White Arrows are connected to their Grey Arrows, such shifts can (and often do) introduce significant conflict to the organization.

One sure-fire method of advancing the Grey Arrow in even partially functional organizations is the ability to demonstrably solve a problem that afflicts the entire group. In meritocracies, the ability to solve difficult problems is the essential aspect of rank assignment, with the demonstrated inability to do so a guaranteed path to lower rankings, if not exclusion from the group. Obviously, the ability to solve problems that afflict a large number of a group's members is often predicated on actual capability, which means that this method of advancing a Grey Arrow depends on an at least somewhat advanced Black Arrow.

For the purposes of formulating a strategy for advancing individual rank, though, the accurate placement of the Grey Arrow is not that important (unless the individual in question is pursuing some form of a duplicitous agenda – more on that in Chapter 14). At this point in the game, it is safe to simply assume a relatively low Grey Arrow. Not the lowest possible, mind you – nobody wants to present as ready to accept Omega status – but low enough as to avoid being seen as a threat to the existing hierarchy.

Once some measure of the rankings of the Black, Grey, and White Arrows has been estimated, it raises a couple of questions, to wit: which of the archetypes from

Chapter 9 is most applicable to your score? And, is that a category with which you are comfortable?

Step 2: Formulating the Strategy

We will review several different strategies for advancing the individual through different types of organizations, based on those different types of organizations. Just as individuals can be categorized based on the eight archetypes reviewed in Chapter 8, so, too, can organizations – which take on personas of their own – be assigned categories based on the strategies they select when dealing both with their members (internal) and their customers and/or competitors (external).

While we're evaluating these strategies, however, the highly variable nature of the groups and the groups' members add a level of squishiness that makes universally valid assertions rather rare. In chess, a valuable axiom concerning preferable strategies emphasizes the importance of controlling (or at least contesting) the center of the board (K4, K5, Q4, Q5). However, in the end game pursuing this strategy may not be beneficial, or may actually be detrimental. In a similar vein, I am confident that the results of our analyses and mental exercises will lead to usable, if not valuable conclusions – they just shouldn't be employed blindly. Each group is different, and the same group will be different from year to year, or even week to week. That having been admitted, let's evaluate some strategies in the Ranking Game.

2A: The Nominal Strategy

Restating the assumptions from earlier in this chapter, that:

- the individual seeking to join a given organization, or, having already joined, wants to advance in rank,
- for valid reasons,
- and not entirely selfish motives,
- the target organization is worthy of the individual's time and effort in its (at least stated) purpose, or mission statement,
- the group's underlying narratives are not so pervasive as to invite in the plethora of organizational pathologies that will spell its demise in the short term. In other words, the group is at least partially predicated on a meritocracy,
- add to these two more conditions: (1) that the individual seeks to (eventually) assume the role of Alpha, and (2) the target group's current leader is a legitimate Alpha,

and it's possible to assemble a nominal strategy that should work for individuals in organizations that meet these criteria. This Nominal Strategy has three tactics, to be executed sequentially.

Tactic 1: Raise the Black Arrow

As discussed earlier in this chapter, this tactic typically involves the willingness to spend the time and energy to become a greater asset to the target group as it seeks its own goals. In executing this tactic, care must be taken to keep exercising the dedication necessary to attain the desired expertise, or level of value coveted by the target group. Set the goals based on objective, quantitative standards. Even a ranking system as subjective as the Midtown High School clique that Scott seeks to join has some hard data to go by, ranging from grade point average to status on whatever extracurricular teams Scott might wish to join (including, yes, the chess team).

Of course, the further away the targeted organization is from a true meritocracy, the less relevant this tactic becomes. However, it's never entirely irrelevant, either. When those organizations that depart from their meritocratic underpinnings eventually fail – and fail they will, sooner than their more meritorious competitors – the members of the failed org will either begin anew, or seek to join other groups. And, when they do, they will recall whom they believed to be genuine, and who weren't, and will seek to have their new groups attract the truly meritorious.

Tactic 2: Manage the Grey Arrow

Notice I did not write *raise* the Grey Arrow. The act of attempting to directly raise one's Grey Arrow is almost always highly transparent, except by those adept at deception. That being admitted, as the individual's Black Arrow begins its ascent, those paying attention will notice, and waves of disturbance will be initiated, like waves emanating from a pebble tossed into a pond. The target group's mechanisms for encouraging and promoting the truly valuable and dissuading or demoting the undeserving will begin to kick in, meaning that the energy that goes into shifting internal rankings has been created. This implies two things: (1) that someone (maybe many someones) who is currently enjoying a high rank might be in for a painful deflation, and (2) the upheaval or disruption that the group endures from such rank-adjustment exercises may be about to get underway.

This energy will be initially expressed in newly minted narratives, shared among the group's members like the oral tradition of Greek tragedy. Facts on the ground need to be incorporated into the organization's script that describes itself to itself (Berne's Child narrative), but in such a way that it does not overturn its key provisions, similar to the cycles and epicycles appended onto Ptolemy cosmology to account for the new data being gleaned from telescopic observations (Chapter 7).

When pressures begin to mount on the individual's Grey Arrow as a result of his Black Arrow being demonstrably raised, the execution of the Nominal Strategy enters into a dangerous period. Recall that, even among the group's most dedicated members, the primary reason for their being in a group in the first place is based on self-advancement. Add that to the fact that *any* deflation of the White Arrow is painful in the extreme, and even those with the group's interests representing a significant portion of their motivation will experience some level of rank-lowering angst. Since we're assuming that this target group's leader is a genuine Alpha, the leader will be among the first to recognize the increased value of the aspiring member. Authentic Betas can also be expected to be a natural source of allies. However, every other member of the organization has the potential of spending time and energy trying to tamp down the elevation of the aspiring member's Grey Arrow, for the following reasons.

The Politician is the most dangerous, having both the most to lose and the least care for the group's capacity to achieve its objectives if such achievements do not benefit him. To the degree that the Politician (high White Arrow, high Grey Arrow, low Black Arrow) enjoys his rank within the group, the group has been fooled into not employing its strategies to help prevent the non-meritorious from rising in rank and potentially influence high-level, high-impact decisions. The reassignment of the aspiring member's inter-group rank poses two existential threats to the Politician: (1) the new, higher rank to be assigned the aspiring member may be taken from the Politician, leading to the dreaded deflation of the Politician's White Arrow, and (2) the fact that the group leadership is showing itself capable of recognizing merit, and adjusting rank based on that recognition, bodes ill for the Politician. Even if the Politician keeps his ill-gotten rank throughout the upcoming organizational upheaval, the group is demonstrating that it is, indeed, capable of recognizing merit and, by extension, its lack, meaning that the Politician's eventual day of reckoning may not be as far out into the future as he had hoped.

The next most dangerous archetype at this stage of implementing the Nominal Strategy is the *Comedian*. This is due to the fact that the aspiring member's upward trajectory is based, at this point, upon his Grey Arrow, and his Grey Arrow is susceptible to the narrative currently in vogue within the group. This narrative is primarily influenced – if not out-and-out controlled – by those archetypes who already enjoy high Grey Arrows. The Alpha and the Beta, being concerned for the overall group's well-being, are not the Cinderella's (low White, low Grey, high Black, the point our aspirant would attain if he first set out to raise his Black Arrow, and succeeded) natural enemies. The Politician is, for the reasons set out in the previous paragraph. The Comedian is the last of the archetypes who will have significant influence on the group's narrative. Our aspirant has three basic responses available:

- Gain the Comedian as an ally. Within our little game's structure, this can most readily be accomplished by convincing the Comedian that his Grey Arrow will actually be ranked higher, should he become allies with the aspirant. At the very least, the Comedian should be led to believe that his status will not suffer as a result of the higher ranking of the aspirant.
- If the Comedian cannot be influenced to become an ally, the aspirant has two approaches left open to him, one active, the other passive. The active response is to lower (or threaten to lower) the Comedian's Grey Arrow, rendering him a Delusional Fool, i.e., Omega. This can be accomplished in a variety of ways, including participating in light challenges to the Comedian, or influencing the group's narrative towards one that is more focused on the group's aspirations and goals. This latter will serve to remind the others in the group of the incongruity of having one of its members enjoy a relatively high rank (Grey Arrow) without a solid basis behind having been assigned that rank.
- The passive response is to simply allow the Comedian to influence the group narrative in a way that is at least somewhat harmful to the aspirant. Comedians are in a tentative position within the group's hierarchy, and the smart ones will know it. The amount of time or energy they are willing to put into engaging in calumny against a potentially up-and-coming aspirant is not limitless. In a group displaying healthy strategy selections, there's a chance that the natural upward pull from the aspirant's Black Arrow on his Grey Arrow will overcome the dragging-down impact of a hostile Comedian's influence on the group's narrative.

The aspirant's relationship to the *Lone Wolf* can be highly problematic, as well. Assuming that our aspirant's path proceeds sequentially from Baby to Cinderella to Beta to Alpha and, by the time our aspirant is managing their Grey Arrow they have already seen to the increase in their Black Arrow, this would mean that the only difference at this point between our aspirant and the Lone Wolf is the latter's inflated White Arrow. If this Lone Wolf is disinclined to disengage from the hierarchy, there is a very real possibility that he will perceive our aspirant as a rival, one engaged in the pursuit of higher perceived standing within the group that would more appropriately be simply handed to the Lone Wolf.

Pivoting briefly to the overall group's persona, if its most valuable members – those with high Black Arrows – do not cooperate with each other, then the ability of the group to attain its stated objectives suffers. This being the case, the Lone Wolves our aspirant encounters during this phase of Nominal Strategy implementation should be approached with one (or both, depending on the circumstances) of the following narratives:

- Any upward reranking of the aspirant would benefit the group, leading to an indirect benefit to the Lone Wolf.
- Unlike the bulk of the group, our aspirant recognizes the value of the Lone Wolf, i.e., if the aspirant had his way, the Lone Wolf's Grey Arrow would be higher.

Should either of these assertions get traction with the Lone Wolves, the aspirant would have increased his odds that, not only have the Lone Wolves been eliminated from the potential enemy pool, they may actually be added to the allies.[2]

Even though the organization's *Cinderellas* have low Grey Arrows themselves, and are therefore unlikely to significantly influence your Grey Arrow placement in the short term, they are nevertheless possessors of high Black Arrows, meaning that, at some point, they will become influential in any but the most dysfunctional groups. If seeking them out and cultivating them as allies is not an option, at the very least don't make enemies of them. If your own Black Arrow is, indeed, highly placed, this shouldn't be an issue, since Cinderellas can be counted on to support the pursuit of the group's objectives, and will tend to value those who can (or are) clearly contributing to this shared effort.

This leaves us with just the *Omegas/Babies* and the *Delusional Fools*. Since these two categories share low Black as well as low Grey Arrows, their influence will be minimal. However, harking back to the voyeur instinct, others within the organization can be expected to observe exactly how you treat those to whom you believe you owe nothing. Indeed, it's axiomatic that a person's worth is most clearly displayed by how they treat those to whom they believe they are not beholden.

From the overall group's point of view, a common (if unarticulated) test for prospective leaders (Alphas or Betas) involves how they treat the weakest members of the group. Note, however, that the approach of being automatically kind to such members is not necessarily the winning one, or even the best thing to do for those members. It depends on the group. The wolfpack that assigns an Omega to a key role in, say, an elk hunt is not only lowering the odds they will feast on elk meat anytime soon, they are also endangering the Omega, since bull elk are very dangerous animals. Conversely, in higher primates the act of abandoning the weak, elderly, or very young, even in crisis situations, is considered prima facie evidence of a stunning, even unforgiveable lack of character. Outside of life-or-death situations, however, things become murky. We tend to have fewer qualms releasing from economic concerns (firing from a company) the person who could contribute, but doesn't try (the Delusional Fool) than we would those who try, but are, for the time being, not possessing the level of expertise needed to contribute (Babies). And, when we take into account the potential for the sub-category of Victims to be among this category, then dealing with them can become dangerous due to their tendency to inappropriately invoke the organizations' mechanisms against unnecessarily belligerent behavior against its weakest members.

Again, spend time managing your Grey Arrow, and do not assume that even a truly placed high Black Arrow will automatically pull the Grey Arrow upwards. Images are managed, usually by influencing the scripts or narratives that the target group uses to describe itself to itself. Certainly influences outside of the group can and do influence its narratives, the vulnerability here being that such outside influences can be seen as inauthentic. The ultimate result of this tactic is to deliver the aspirant to the status of low White Arrow, high Grey Arrow, high Black Arrow – the category of Beta.

Tactic 3: Moving into the Alpha Role

For tactics 1 and 2 of the Nominal Strategy, I addressed what the aspirant ought to do with respect to their Grey and Black Arrows. Paradoxically, though, this pattern needs to be broken with respect to the machinations the Beta should engage when seeking to become or displace an Alpha. What's needed at this point is patience, by the boat load, and attempting to manage an inflation of the aspirant's White Arrow is not the way to gain it.

Besides, a highly placed White Arrow is not necessarily analogous to the sort of confidence the Beta needs to assume the ultimate leadership mantle. Douglas MacArthur was profoundly worried that the Inchon Landings would be a debacle, as was Eisenhower about the Normandy Landings. Exhibited confidence in a leadership role is more about convincing the rest of the group that the selected technical approach to accomplishing the group's objectives is the best possible one, and not so much about how well the Alpha sleeps at night after having committed to a certain course of action.

Of course, the main question before Betas everywhere is: does the Alpha need replacing? To attempt to do so prematurely is highly detrimental – even fatal – to the aspiring Beta, but to do so too late often spells disaster for both the Betas involved and the overall group. This is where White Arrow placement comes back into play: an aspirant with a high White Arrow is far more likely to make an attempt to replace the Alpha prematurely than a true Beta. Indeed, part and parcel of exercising the patience needed to remain a Beta-in-waiting is tamping down its own White Arrow.

Treason can be defined as the act of replacing the Alpha by aggressive, or even violent means, and so it is interesting that, when it succeeds, a new Alpha is ensconced; when it fails, rejection on behalf of the remaining members of the group is guaranteed. In Midtown High School's clique environment, Scott, should he prematurely attempt to displace Jeff and fail, can be expected to be shunned by that clique for the rest of his high school experience. At the other extreme, Guy Fawkes and his associates were drawn and quartered.

On the other hand, any group's lifespan can and will be dramatically shortened should the Alpha clearly need replacing, but isn't. Until Ulysses Grant replaced Henry W. Halleck (if you're thinking Grant replaced *who?*, my response is yeah, my point exactly), Confederate General Robert E. Lee was well on his way to demonstrating that the South was more than capable of exacting a prohibitively expensive price from the North in their pursuit of keeping the Union together. After Grant was promoted to Commander-in-Chief of the Union Armies, the Confederacy's trajectory bent downward until their ultimate defeat and surrender at Appomattox. In the time General Halleck was Commander-in-Chief, the Union suffered some of its most dramatic defeats, including Second Manassas, which is, incidentally, only 27 miles from Washington, D.C.

And that's just one example. In politics, war, peace, economies, sports teams... in almost any field of human endeavor, examples of organizations headed by a leader who was either not a true Alpha or had stayed in that role well past their shelf life coming to a dramatically bad – and imminently avoidable – end are legion.

Typically, any successful, functional organization will have mechanisms in place that help ensure a relatively low-conflict way of identifying when an Alpha needs to be replaced, and by whom among the field of available Betas. In those organizations where this is not the case, it is a clear indication that some elements of dysfunction have entered into the structure's underpinnings. As long as no Roman general led their armies close to the city of Rome itself, meaning that the will of the populace would determine their leaders as opposed to whomever controlled the most military resources, the foundation of the Roman Republic was comparatively pathology free. As soon as Julius Gaius Caesar (literally) crossed the Rubicon, that society's basis suddenly changed to something far more barbaric, virtually eliminating the possibility of low-conflict transfers of power. For example, after Julius Gaius Caesar was assassinated on the day the Senate was to vote him Emperor, it is not entirely clear that *any* of his seven (!) successors died of natural causes.

- Augustus may have been poisoned by his wife.
- Tiberius may have been assassinated by Caligula.
- Caligula was assassinated by his Praetorian Guard.
- Claudius may have also been poisoned by his wife.
- Nero committed suicide after having been named an Enemy of the People by the Senate.
- Galba was murdered by his Praetorian Guard.
- Otho committed suicide after losing the Battle of Bedriacum to Vitellius.

And so it went, when the basis for the appropriate time for an Alpha to move along and be replaced by a suitable Beta was destroyed by the entirely predictable machinations of a suddenly and profoundly dysfunctional organization. If Julius Gaius Caesar observed the don't-go-near-Rome-with-your-army rule, we could all be speaking Latin to this day – I mean, nos vires totus exsisto narro Latin hodie.

So there we have the Nominal Strategy. As stated, it assumes a great deal, about the valid functioning of the organization, the legitimate motives of the aspirant, a working mechanism on the part of the group to encourage the meritorious to advance while discouraging the meritless from doing so, and so on. And, just to reiterate, the aspirant would move through a short series of roles, from the Baby (low Black, White, and Grey Arrows) to the Cinderella (high Black, low White and Grey Arrows), to the Beta (high Black, high Grey, low White Arrows), to, finally, the (legitimate) role of Alpha (high, high, high Arrows). Each transition in this cycle has its own challenges to be overcome, both internal to the individual and external to the individual, but internal to the group. Once the role of Alpha has been attained, the challenges come less from internal to the individual, but from the twin threats of internal from the organization itself, and external to both the individual and the group, i.e., the organization's competition.

As we begin to plumb the inky depths of advancing an aspirant's rank within the gradients of the dysfunctional organization, it must be noted going in that these organizations tend to be dysfunctional for a reason. Either their goals and aspirations are not legitimate, or, having legit goals, have nevertheless allowed in such organizational pathologies as to render the chances of their attaining their (stated) goals rather low, if not eliminated altogether.

Recall the discussion on how the organization is not only altered by its members, but its members are also changed by the organization. Groups take on personas of their own, similar to the Berne archetypes, on their paths to self-sustainment. So, as the aspirant considers formulating a strategy to advance within an acknowledged dysfunctional organization, we simply have to return to the overarching question that began the chapter: why?

I'll leave the answer to this rhetorical question to the aspirant. Just know – if you can disengage from the dysfunctional organization, you should. If you can't, then there are some things you need to know about navigating this swamp before you actually enter in.

2B: A Functional Strategy for a Dysfunctional Organization

> To be, or not to be – that be located the query:
> Whether 'tbe located nobler in the mind to hurt
> The hook up and arrows of contemptible fortune
> Or to take arms against a marine of troubles
> And by differing end them. To die, to nap –
> No more – and by a nap to approximately we end
> The heartache, and the many natural tremors
> That covering be heir to. 'Tbe a consummation
> Devoutly to be wanted. To die, to nap –
> To nap – perchance to dream: ay, there be the rub,
> For in that nap of death what dreams may come
> When we have hobbled off this mortal coil,
> Must give we gap.

So, how did I turn among the most noble 13 lines of English literature into rubbish? By taking every non-plural word containing the letter "s," and replacing it with the first Microsoft Word-listed synonym that also did not contain the letter "s" (except for "consummation" – the synonym list, as well as the thesaurus, had a fit with that one).

Dopey? Perhaps. But this is highly analogous to the aspirant seeking a functional strategy in a dysfunctional organization. The natural inclination of those seeking to advance within any organization is to establish an ability to address and overcome the problems and issues that confront the group as a whole. The ability to solve problems, after all, is one of the primary indicators to social constructs that the individual member not only belongs, but ought to be assigned higher and higher ranks. However, in the dysfunctional organization, the overriding concern from those in a position to influence rank is their own White Arrow placement. Any problem "solved" has to respect this aspect in the dysfunctional organization; otherwise, the optimal solution will be dismissed, usually with contempt. This leaves the aspirant in the dysfunctional organization with the burden of not only articulating and selling the optimal solution to any given problem; they must also package it in a way that supports the already overly inflated White Arrows of those in the highest levels of the hierarchy. The results are invariably not only disappointing – they can easily be rendered gibberish.

And the author won't be remembered for greatness.

There are two obvious problems with attempting to advance within a known dysfunctional organization:

- the dysfunctional organization will invariably change the aspirant, and not for the better, and
- the fact that a rational human senses the need to advance within such a group implies that the tactic of disengagement is largely unavailable.

Dysfunctional organizations will tend to force its members to play out the previously reviewed roles, namely the Golden Child, the Mascot, the Scapegoat, and the Lost Child. It should be noted that merit has little to do with the placement within these categories. In other words, the immediate tactic from the Nominal Strategy, that of spending the time and energy to increase the objective worth of the individual within the organization, is, well, almost worthless. The Black Arrow isn't the primary determiner of perceived value here, meaning that, ultimately, such an organization will be overcome by its competitors. That being allowed, I also maintain a contrary axiom: the Second Coming never happens immediately prior to finals week. Yes, the dysfunctional organization will eventually receive its comeuppance, but it probably won't happen in time to relieve the aspirant's immediate need to navigate it, and it most certainly won't occur while the meritorious sufferers look on.

The main thing to know about advancing within flawed organizations is that the coin of this realm is *loyalty*. High levels of technical, moral, economic, or any other type of merit do not come close to the perceived value of loyalty to the existing hierarchy. This is due to the fact that established organizations will tend to drift from their original purposes – whatever they are stated to be – and towards a self-sustaining system of reinforcing the rankings of the organization's upper echelon. For dysfunctional organizations, this effect is less pull than headlong rush.

Before we get into more specific tactics for the flawed organization, another question: why should merit matter not, but loyalty matter above all?

The answer: because those in the higher ranks of the group have very highly placed White Arrows, meaning that they have imbibed of the exhilarating practice of decoupling their view of themselves from the evidence around them that might suggest that they aren't all that. Unless they got there all by their delusional selves, the implication is that they had help, from those around them.

The effect is reciprocal and cumulative. Reciprocal, because the flatterers often receive rewards from the highest-ranked members of the dysfunctional organization. In return for playing the role of drug pusher – in this analogy, the drug being the inflation of the leaders' White Arrows, or providing basis for the prevention of its deflation – these leaders bestow what rewards are available due to their rank. Cumulative, because, as harsh reality begins to impinge on these leaders' White Arrows, the need to avoid the painful deflation becomes all the more acute. The examples are many: from the political arena alone, Hitler, Stalin, Nero – all were convinced of their importance by those around them, well past any semblance of actual insight or leadership ability. Small wonder that Nicolo Machiavelli counseled the elimination of the displaced prince's courtiers – they were all virtually guaranteed to have either obtained or maintained their own lofty positions by perpetrating untruths, lies that invariably weaken any organization that embraced them on the path to selecting its most appropriate leaders.

It should be taken as a given that the leadership of a flawed organization will be comprised of those with high White Arrow rankings. If we eliminate the valid Alpha, this leaves only three archetypes:

- the Lone Wolf
- the Politician
- the Delusional Fool/ Victim.

Lone Wolves won't be plentiful in dysfunctional organizations – they're hard enough to keep within the confines of even valid groups. Similarly, even within flawed organizations there will be mechanisms in place to prevent the least worthy members (potential Omegas, remember) from rising in the rankings. Which leaves us with...

The Politicians.

That's not to say that those in the highest ranks of flawed organizations will always be without merit. But the corrosive effect of being assigned the role of Golden Child (from the roles assumed by members of the dysfunctional family, recall) invariably eats away at the drive providing lift to these people's Black Arrows. As these slowly, almost imperceptibly drop, their White and Grey Arrows stay high. Indeed, organizations that had initially been led by a legitimate Alpha can easily find themselves transformed from valid and robust into weakened and in decline because their leadership allowed themselves to be advised by flatterers. It's one of the reasons why the act of engaging in unctuous or brazen flattery to those above the flatterers in rank is readily perceived as not only being cravenly self-serving, but detrimental to the team that tolerates it. The act is not only damaging to the flatterer's rivals, depriving them of what would otherwise be a fair shot at rank advancement, but is ultimately damaging to the whole group. The advancement of Politicians means that it is they who are put into positions of making decisions that affect the entire organization, displacing those whose merit should have placed them in such positions.

But that's how flawed organizations operate.

If we were to be kind enough, for the sake of setting up a workable strategy for the low-White Arrow set within such an organization, to abandon the dysfunctional role archetypes in favor of the Maccoby archetypes, what one would expect to see in distinctly flawed groups is that they will be headed up by leadership that will tend to repel Gamesmen and Craftsman, and encourage and reward Jungle Fighters and Company Men. As the Gamesmen and Craftsmen become ever shrinking minorities, and the Jungle Fighters increase, the Company Men will begin to undergo a transformation. Recall that these tend to assume the personal of the group around them; in this case, a group that is increasingly taking on the persona of the Jungle Fighter. The narrative that organizational leadership is just swell must be propagated, and any harsh reality that might challenge that kept at bay. In extreme circumstances, you get North Korea, where hundreds of thousands of people are forced into the Mascot/ Company Man role, and any deviation uncovered is brutally suppressed. Admittedly, that's an extreme example, but the trends of organizations that elevate those wretched roles into leadership positions will always be to become vulnerable to just such group pathologies. Just as individuals can be susceptible to psychoses, so, too, can groups, which can (and do) take on their own personalities. A type of tailspin inevitably awaits; but, again, it never seems to happen when it's most needed.

So, for those who do not belong to the categories of the Politician, Delusional Fool/ Victim, or Lone Wolf, and yet need to at least survive in such an organization, the answer lies in selecting a set of canned strategies associated with one of the available roles that people have been using since flawed groups have been in existence. The role of Golden Child is typically unavailable, since it's assigned from above, and only after extreme acts of loyalty. The use of Mascot/Company Man or Jungle Fighter will be covered in the next section, under Dysfunctional Strategies.

That leaves the rational actor caught up in these circumstances with the strategies associated with the Lost Child, Craftsman variety (to mildly mix my archetypes).

The Craftsman places emphasis on the quality of his output, or what would otherwise pass for virtue within valid organizations. In our vernacular, the placement of his Black Arrow is of primary importance. Unfortunately, in the dysfunctional environment, the Black Arrow counts for little; however, it is still important to work at keeping it high, if odds of surviving are to be maximized. All groups – even dysfunctional ones – can be rather harsh on those found to have low Black Arrows. Even if the people assigning the rankings are flawed, any tamping down of a given individual will be rendered more difficult if that individual is, indeed, meritorious.

In the meantime, our aspirant should abandon hope that virtue will be readily recognized, much less appropriately rewarded. With little or no upside to continued participation, the strategies of the Lost Child become more attractive. By disengaging to the extent practicable, the aspirant minimizes the negative effects of associating with a flawed group on the individual. He also avoids being forced into the role of Scapegoat.

The Dance of the Dysfunctionals is quite a thing to behold. The so-called leader can be expected to be bent on maintaining his high White Arrow placement, and to surround himself with those who will help make that happen. The Golden Children will be appointed, usually based on some combination of a significant accomplishment coupled with a signal of extreme loyalty. In fact, if we use our old friend the payoff matrix, we see this in Table 9.1.

Table 9.1 Loyalty/Accomplishment Payoff Matrix

	Low accomplishment	High accomplishment
High loyalty	Mascot/Company Man	Golden Child
Low-to-medium loyalty	Scapegoat	Craftsman/Lost Child

The Scapegoat can't qualify for Golden Child status, at least not right away. Such a one would need to either brazenly establish loyalty to the existing hierarchy (meaning that Nicolo Machiavelli may, himself, come back from the dead and eliminate such a one), or pull off a singular accomplishment. However, within dysfunctional organizations, mechanisms are typically in place to diminish the genuine accomplishments of those out of favor, or, indeed, any data that would help to overturn the narrative that they are correctly placed at the bottom of the hierarchy.

The Company Man/Mascot also needs to pull off an amazing accomplishment in order to even qualify for Golden Child status. However, there are some factors inherently working against such an elevation. For one, attaining a remarkable accomplishment typically involves engaging in high-risk behavior, something the Company Man/Mascot is not known for pursuing. Adding to the difficulties of this move is the fact that there will almost invariably be at least one Golden Child already established, and they, in all probability, will not look favorably on those who seek to displace them. Extant Golden Children will take advantage of their position to spin the narrative adopted by the upper echelon of the hierarchy to minimize the aspirants' accomplishments while exaggerating their faults and errors. In short, the deck is stacked against this exact progression upwards through the ranks.

The Craftsman/Lost Child role, however, is uniquely placed. If this aspirant sought to get ahead, they would only need to make a gesture of loyalty without appearing to be, as we Americans like to put it, boot licking. But this act would signal to the existing Golden Child/Children that the aspirant has become a threat, and the same accomplishment minimizing that the Company Man/Mascot is vulnerable to would become a problem. Rather than risk being forced into the Scapegoat category, the Craftsman/Lost Child may be better off simply surviving as this particular role within the dysfunctional organization. Generally speaking, this is probably best accomplished by maintaining a high Black Arrow, keeping the White Arrow low, and letting the Grey Arrow float where it will. This will increase the chances that the aspirant can stay safely in the Lost Child category, until either disengagement becomes a viable option, or else they lose their sanity, and begin to desire to advance within the flawed organization. For that, we'll need a dysfunctional strategy.

2C: A Dysfunctional Strategy for a Dysfunctional Organization

If the aspirant is willing to throw their ethics (and, in all probability, their remaining peace of mind) to the wind, then there are actually some strategies for becoming the dysfunctional king of the dysfunctional organization, no matter how difficult to understand the motives for doing so.

The primary thing to keep in mind is that this organization's personality is dominated by its Child/Id persona which, again, is highly irrational, emotional, and powerful. At its core is the maintenance of its existing hierarchy, especially among the upper ranks. The Child/Id seeks to satisfy its base needs in both the individual and the group. For the individual, it is speculated that this has to do with sex, food, and other, primal needs. For the purposes of this analysis, we will assume that the primal needs of the dysfunctional organization do not include survival, as counterintuitive as that may sound. However, example after example indicates that leaders of dysfunctional organizations would gladly sacrifice the very existence of the organization if they could possibly maintain their own high White Arrows. Tyrants will allow their nations to be utterly destroyed, CEOs witness their companies slip into bankruptcy, fathers allow the disintegration of their families, sooner than allow their White Arrows be forced downwards into a closer alignment with their Black Arrows.

So, again, the rational strategy here is to disengage. But, since you are still reading, I'll assume that other, non-rational factors are in play, and the aspirant still needs to survive, if not advance in rank. Are there any rational strategies available here?

Yes, but they are rather like the advice to newly condemned prisoners sent to the penitentiary, that they must seek out the baddest-looking dude and, without warning or provocation, smash him in the face. You may get away with these tactics, and they may very well enhance your standing, or odds of long-term survival – but you have to successfully enact them first, and that's the bell-the-cat aspect of these strategies.

The Immature Organization?

In 1989, a process maturity framework was first described in the book *Managing the Software Process* by Watts Humphrey.[3] The Software Engineering Institute from Carnegie Melon University would further develop the Capability Maturity Model® to significant success, which I will address further in Chapter 10. Briefly, the Capability Maturity Model®[4] posits that organizations seeking to advance a given capability will usually go through a series of levels:

- Level 1, Initial, is chaotic. Everyone is doing their own thing, so that, paradoxically, centers of excellence can actually exist in Level 1 organizations, but they would be isolated.
- Level 2, Repeatable, occurs when the processes are common to the organization. They use the same approaches, processes, forms, etc.
- Level 3, Defined, is indicated when, should the "heroes" who delivered this level of capability be hit by the proverbial beer truck, the organization would suffer no loss of capability. The processes are defined, documented in procedures and training programs.
- Level 4, Managed, has been attained when the organization has quantified its performance with respect to the sought-after capability. The organization is now in a position to export the capability to others.
- Level 5, Optimized, is realized when the organization routinely discovers solutions to complex or long-endured problems. Nobody ever really gets to Level 5.

In 1996, U.S. Air Force Captain Tom Schorsch published an article entitled "The Capability Im-Maturity Model" in *Cross Talk* magazine. In it, Schorsch works backwards from the Capability Maturity Model levels, so:

- Level 0, Negligent, is indicated by an organizational assumption that the work will be performed by *someone*, so there's really no impetus to pursue the group's goals.
- Level -1, Obstructive, occurs when specific processes are mandated and pursued, even if they are, in fact, counterproductive, under the assumption that formality of operations directly translates to more effectiveness and, ultimately, a more advanced capability.
- Level -2, Contemptuous, is marked by a tacit acknowledgment that the organization's output is widely viewed as sub-standard, so its individuals seek to obscure this fact, usually by attributing failures to outside factors.
- Level -3, Undermining, occurs when individuals exert time and energy to deliberately sabotage the efforts of competing groups – even those within the same macro organization – in order to mask their dysfunction.

Something that leapt out at me from reading Captain Schorsch's work was that, while the original Capability Maturity Model dealt with the performance of the overall group, the Capability Im-Maturity Model appeared to deal with the behavior of individuals within the group, and how *their* behavior impacted the overall organization. As the unfortunate organizations spiraled down through the negative levels of the Capability Im-Maturity Model, the flawed strategy selections of its members became more and more apparent, until they ultimately reached comical levels (well, to those not directly involved, anyway).

I actually had an opportunity to witness this sort of death spiral first-hand. The United States government has a program stemming from Paragraph 8(a) of the Small Business Act that steers a certain percentage of government spending towards companies that can establish that they are small, minority- or woman-owned businesses. While its original intentions may have been noble, what the Small Business Act actually did was perpetrate an entire group of companies that, by claiming quasi-victim status, enjoyed a nearly competitor-free market in the areas of contracting they pursued. This, essentially, invited the establishment of fundamentally flawed organizations, or, when 8(a) status was assigned to healthy ones, virtually guaranteed a descent into abnormal operation. After some weeks of enduring unemployment, I took a position with an 8(a) firm that performed environmental restoration work. The experience was, to say the least, an eye opener.

I quickly became aware of a vastly more relaxed attitude in this company towards achieving its projects' goals within cost and schedule constraints. Since they had not had to compete with organizations on the basis of superior quality, quicker delivery, nor lower costs, none of these goals were significant factors in the execution of their work duties. However, what energy was absent from rigorous project execution was more than evident in the hierarchical maneuverings of its employees and managers.

When I joined this company, the project and contract backlog was flush with funding, so there was really no need for any Scapegoats. The entire organization was comprised of (few) Golden Children, Mascots (Company Men), and Lost Children (Craftsmen). It became clear early on that advancement was predicated entirely on what those in the highest ranks thought of you, and their perception had virtually nothing to do with the actual job performance.

The thing about the 8(a) program, though, is that a given company can't stay within it forever. The program has a finite cycle, and end date. When the "graduation" date was two years out, the owner began to hire executives who were believed to be able to help the firm survive in the far, far more competitive environs outside this government set-aside program.

Keep in mind that this organization had formed and advanced in a relatively non-competitive environment. It would be analogous to a wolfpack that not only had no other packs of wolves to outperform in order to survive or thrive, but one that was in a target-rich environment with no other apex predators present.

So, these newly hired execs would come in, expecting to take a leading position in a largely workable organization that, in fact, was not. They would all go through a similar cycle: attempt to get a handle on asset and project performance, look over the proposal backlog and targets, and then try to improve each based on the information on hand and on their perceptions of the staff – who was reliable, or talented, and who was not. In a fully functional organization, their efforts may well have been successful; in this one, it was like trying to write at a Shakespearean level without being able to use words with the letter S.

Borrowing from the Maccoby archetypes, the Jungle Fighters – who were invariably highly placed in each department – were in excellent positions to influence the new executive's take on the relative rankings of the staff. And these were fluent in the tactics of calumny and hearsay, the primary variant being the *ex parte* conversation.

There's a reason why *ex parte* conversations are not allowed in legal proceedings. When only one side of an argument is being entertained, it suddenly acquires an appearance of truth, or at least reliable or actionable assertion. Grima Wormtongue had nothing on these people. Translated to our vernacular, their tactics were clever enough to avoid attacking others' Black Arrows, which is quite difficult to do successfully. Instead, when circumstances allowed "advising" the new exec on the characteristics of the staff he inherited, they would simultaneously impugn their targets' Grey Arrows ("such-and-such had this negative experience working with that person, and doesn't think that [target] should be allowed to get involved in [project N]"), while subtly – oh, so subtly – inflating the exec's White Arrow ("Ted [the owner] recognized that trend as a problem, and must have faith in your [the exec's] ability to overcome it").

In this way the sweet, slow-acting poison of neglecting or even abandoning the trappings of a meritocracy and embracing the narcotic of the high White Arrow, even as the overall organization continued its death spiral, was introduced to the new executive. This situation was somewhat unique, though, in that, while companies or other economic concerns can enter into such death spirals, with their ends being somewhat vague, this company knew when its 8(a) status was up: if it wasn't truly competitive with the genuinely functional organizations by a certain date, the whole gig was over.

New executive after another failed to put the company on a truly competitive footing with its anticipated, real competitors as the "graduation" date marched ever nearer. There were simply too many business model pathologies, tightly held, and not to be challenged. The owner's children had high-paying positions, even though none of them (no, really, I do mean none) brought significant value to the organization. The company began to hemorrhage talent, as those who could most easily disengage and seek gainful employment elsewhere did so. Existing contracts were approaching their end dates, and the new ones needed to replace them weren't walking through the door as they had previously. The high-level flailing began to resemble William Butler Yeates' famous "perne in a gyre," as events spiraled further and further from the rational center. The company attempted an Initial Public Offering (IPO), but found out that it was too highly leveraged to do so at a reasonable price. Yet another business pathology, that of declaring an inordinate share of incoming revenues as dividends while neglecting the company's debt, had its inevitable consequence: no investor in their right mind could possibly be attracted to an IPO of a company so mismanaged.

Clearly it would have been detrimental for any of the new executives to go to the owner and say "Look you here, sir. The organization has drifted so far away from a true meritocracy and towards near worthlessness that something has to be done with the way the staff is organized and advanced. Right away I think the better-educated, most capable need to be moved into positions of authority, and the people currently in positions of authority who don't belong there – your kids included – need to be either demoted, or dismissed."

The fact that these execs didn't – or couldn't – say that meant that they were (1) not brave, (2) not competent enough to realize that that was what was going on, or (3) had been seduced by the dark side of the force, i.e., had accepted some aspect of the machinations needed to succeed or survive in the dysfunctional organization, and were okay with it.

I think it was mostly (3). Consistently.

But for those who find themselves, again, in these circumstances, cannot disengage, and are not being brought in as executives, you need to be aware of the strategies being employed by those around you in the failing organization. Not to be macabre, but a most graphic illustration of these tactics involves the scenes from the movie *Titanic*, as the massive ship begins to flounder by the bow. Note the (fictional, but probably actual) behavior of those remaining on board: they headed for the parts of the ship that they perceived would be the last to go down. On a ship sinking by the bow, this is obviously the stern, unless, of course, they were among the happy company of people who were allowed to disengage, i.e., the lifeboat occupants. In a corporation, the last group to be dismissed would be those that the firm needed to exist, e.g., accounting. For other organizations, the last vestiges of the group to be eliminated are those (ironically enough) most closely associated with the reason the group was established in the first place. Why? Because in dysfunctional organizations the people in the leadership roles are not those with highly placed Black Arrows, and those with highly placed Black Arrows are the ones who keep the organization going, even if they are not highly regarded by those around them (low Grey Arrows).

The analogous equivalent of *Titanic* remnants elbowing aside others on their way to the stern would be the Company Men and Jungle Fighters remaining in the doomed organization. Their tactics are entirely predictable: inflate their superiors' White Arrows while exerting downward pressure on their rivals' (read: everyone else's) Grey Arrows. In pursuing the latter, they will engage in *ex parte* conversations with their superiors and, when targets become scarce or unavailable, will become snarky in meetings or other group-level communications. By "snarky," I mean that the manipulators will assert negative comments, shrouded in a kind of pseudo-cleverness, such that, should they be challenged on the content of their words, they can quickly retreat to protestations that they were simply attempting to be funny. Recall that attempts to be funny are the hallmarks of the humble, even the Omega, but mocking is an act of belligerence. Do not be fooled: any who use this tactic are engaged in mocking, which makes them dangerous challengers indeed, no matter their façade.

The dysfunctional organization where the aspirant finds himself may not have the hours-long end date of the post-iceberg-encounter *Titanic*, nor the years known to the example 8(a) company. The downward trajectory can be decades in the offing and, the longer the term period, the greater the chance that the group's errors can be identified, articulated, and reversed or overcome.

Or all the bad guys can just go away, to be replaced with genuine Alphas or Betas.

Often we are not dealing with immature organizations at this point. They can be extremely mature – they simply are progressing towards the ossification of the group-level pathologies that have enabled their highest ranks to keep their White Arrows inflated while maintaining some semblance of loyalty to the reason the organization was founded in the first place. In the United States, labor unions' bosses are typically well paid, even as the membership of their organizations continues downward, for example. Other, political examples abound, and will be further analyzed in Chapter 10.

An important aspect of surviving in the flawed organization is the ability to recognize the roles assumed by those around the aspirant, in order to better understand the sets of canned strategies they are likely to employ. I believe there to be (what else?) four broad categories of strategies that members of a group will employ in their interactions with other members:

- They will present as genuinely cooperative, either in helping the individual to achieve their goals (with some sort of reciprocity assumed), or else in pursuing the group's goals. This is the *Teamwork/Helpful* category.
- Some will act as enablers, seeking to make the act of participating in pursuing the group's goals more enjoyable, or less stressful. These include the roles of Omega and entertainers, and represent the *Humor/Submission* category.
- The opposite of the enablers are those who will engage in various acts of challenging the aspirant, either for the valid reason of testing them to see where they belong in the group's hierarchy, or else in the invalid attempt to drive down members' Grey and White Arrows. These represent the *Testing/Confrontation* sub-group.
- Finally, there will be those who demonstrate a willingness to abandon practices or people they view to be failures, and embrace new ideas in order to incorporate them into usable strategies to pursue the organization's agenda. This set of interactive strategies belongs to the *Initiative Takers*.

For those members of the group who consistently exhibit only one of these types of interactive strategies, classification can be pretty simple. In reality, few people are so staid and consistent – depending on circumstances, almost everyone will exhibit behaviors from each of these four categories, often within a relatively short span of time.

That having been conceded, it's also my observation that people will tend to adopt a certain set of strategies or behaviors based on the relative placement of their Black, Grey, and White Arrows. That being the case, over time the observed preference for a certain type of strategy will provide a fairly reliable indicator of which role the observed members tend towards which, in turn, provides clues on the types of behavior they are likely to manifest in future interactions. Nevertheless, the following are generalizations.

- Both Babies and Cinderellas will avoid testing or confronting others unless they are forced to. Their combinations of low White and Grey Arrows mean that this would be a high-risk strategy for them to employ.
- Alphas and Betas may engage in testing or confrontation, but it's usually not in an attempt to arbitrarily drive down the aspirant's Grey Arrow. These roles would engage in that behavior only for the betterment of the overall group, in an attempt to more clearly define the most appropriate rank for the member being tested.
- Alphas, Betas, and Craftsmen will tend to avoid interactive strategies that have an air of submission attached to them, meaning that they never assume the role of Mascot/Company Man, nor will they use Humor/Submission-type strategies.
- Fools and Politicians will eschew strategies consistent with *Initiative Takers* and *Teamwork/Helpful* categories, though Politicians will often pretend to perform the latter category.
- Both of the low Black and White Arrow archetypes, the Babies and the Comedians, will routinely employ *Humor/Submissive* strategies in order to forge alliances and avoid loss of standing, or exclusion from the group.
- Both of the high Black and low White Arrow roles, Cinderellas and Betas, will select *Teamwork/Helpful* behaviors, and can be expected to disengage from (or even oppose) any member perceived to be failing to work hard enough to attain the group's objectives.
- Craftsmen and Alphas will interact with those around them in ways consistent with *Initiative Takers*.
- Both of the high White and low Black Arrows – the Fools and the Politicians – can be reliably counted on to engage in the strategies consistent with the *Testing/Confrontation* sub-group. Whether or not these have any idea of the delta that exists between their low Black Arrow and high White Arrow, they do have a firm grasp on their need to maintain downward pressure on any perceived rivals' Grey Arrows. These types of tests need not be overtly belligerent – they can even take the appearance of complete innocuousness (see the list of escalating challenges from Chapter 3).
- Lone Wolves, by definition, will be disinclined to act in a way that is supportive of the other members of the pack, so do not look to them for *Teamwork/Helpful* behaviors. However, they will often show their true colors by taking on strategies consistent with *Initiative Takers*.

A summary of the canned strategy categories and preferences of the eight archetypes is in Table 9.2.

Table 9.2 Three-Arrow Model Archetypes and Likely Strategies

Archetype/Strategy	Most likely to use	Least likely to use
Baby/Omega	Humor/submissive	Testing/confrontation
Cinderella	Teamwork/helpful	Testing/confrontation
Beta	Teamwork/helpful	Humor/submissive
Fool	Testing/confrontation	Teamwork/helpful
Lone Wolf	Initiative taker	Teamwork/helpful
Politician	Testing/confrontation	Initiative taker
Alpha	Initiative taker	Humor/submissive
Comedian	Humor/submissive	Initiative taker

I'm afraid I'm rapidly reaching an end point regarding an ability of this analysis to render recommendations for the employment of dysfunctional strategies to advance within dysfunctional organizations. Beyond a description of the flawed groups' members' motives, archetypes, and preferred and avoided tactics, further insights into how the aspirant ought to proceed become difficult. Part of the reason is that a hallmark of dysfunctional organizations is their uneven treatment of their members. A given tactic successfully employed by one member to either get ahead themselves, or push down their rivals' Grey Arrows may easily be absolutely poisonous to the very next member to attempt it.

Which leads me back to the very recommended strategy selection criterion with which this chapter opened. Why? Why are you doing this? Why *this* group? If the reflexive answer is that disengagement is not a reasonable option, you might want to review that conclusion.

Much depends on it, as we shall see more in the following chapters.

A Third Way for the Dysfunctional Orgs

For this discussion, though, there is an option for the member of a dysfunctional organization that entails embracing a set of strategies that are very attractive, but tend to also have a very low percentage of success. That strategy set is this: to put on the superhero costume, and save the failing organization from itself.

Dr. Laura Schlessinger, in her radio program, would refer to this tendency in men to enter into relationships with women who showed signs of being profoundly dysfunctional, with the intent of rehabilitating them, as the "hero syndrome." I suppose there's an intense fascination with the notion that, having saved the dysfunctional organization from its self-imposed pathologies, the "savior" would be instantly recognized for their contributions, and catapulted to the Alpha status. The sad fact is, though, that it virtually never unfolds that way. These organizations have integrated invalid technical approaches for a reason, and that reason is usually to ensure the continued enjoyment of rank of its hierarchy's elite. This effect is probably why Nicolo Machiavelli was so forward in his discussions of eliminating the previous ruler's courtiers in *The Prince*. It's simply easier to find ways of marginalizing or getting rid of the dysfunction-embracing upper ranks than it is to untie the Gordian knot of how they got to the warped structure in the first place, and convince the organization at large that they need to change their ways.

Recall from Chapter 4 the discussion of the Nash Equilibrium. Briefly, it's

> A concept of game theory where the optimal outcome of a game is one where no player has an incentive to deviate from his or her chosen strategy after considering an opponent's choice. Overall, an individual can receive no incremental benefit from changing actions, assuming other players remain constant in their strategies. A game may have multiple Nash equilibria or none at all.[5]

In other words, the members of the dysfunctional organization have embraced their sets of mixed strategies in order to survive, get ahead, or avoid dropping in rank within the ranks of the group, even though the embraced strategies are inherently harmful to the organization as a whole. The would-be savior, presumably, has an understanding of the best available strategies that can be embraced if the organization were to maximize its odds of attaining its stated objectives. The difference between the embraced, failed strategies and the known best-available strategies is typically an insurmountable gulf. It's the wolfpack that refuses to hunt elk, even if the hunting of said elk were the only way the pack could survive in its current environment. The Beta that attempts to recruit others to hunt elk should expect to be presently forced into the role of Lone Wolf, ostracized by the pack that has already accepted the no-elk strategy.

But, for the sake of argument, let's say the Beta successfully maneuvers behind the Alpha's back and, with the help of three or four other wolves, brings down an elk and invites the rest of the pack to feast. There's still the problem of the existing Alpha, and any or all of the remaining no-elk Betas. The Alpha, recall, determines which members of the pack eat, and how much. Let's further posit that our intrepid Beta, needing an additional point of attack in order to pull off a big-game victory, has recruited the Omega. Upon bringing down the elk, the intrepid Beta intends for this Omega to eat his fill. The Alpha, well, doesn't. At the risk of somewhat personifying the ensuing impasse, the dilemma being brought forcefully front and center is this: the Beta could not have executed his successful alternate strategy without the help of the Omega. If he expects future success, the ones who helped implement the non-flawed strategy must be rewarded; otherwise, the strategy will no longer be successful because of the lack of resources in pursuing it. On the other hand (paw), if the intrepid Beta is deciding which pack members are eating now, that is a primary function of the Alpha – yet an Alpha is still heading the pack. If the Alpha relents... well, he can't, and still remain the Alpha, with his high White Arrow and all. The shown-up Alpha really only has two alternatives if he wants to stay in power:

- manipulate the narrative to make it appear to the other members of the pack that the hunt-elk strategy was actually consistent with the Alpha's intentions all along (including taking credit for the actual kill, if possible), or
- defeat or drive off the intrepid Beta.

Any other choice virtually invites the Alpha's overthrow, particularly at the hands (paws) of those members of the pack who suffered the most under the flawed strategy, handed down by the at-risk Alpha.

While the hierarchical construction of shared narratives is the subject of a subsequent chapter, I would like to point out that this scenario is essentially the one presented in the first half of the novelette *Jonathan Livingston Seagull* by Richard Bach. Jonathan has demonstrated an ability to fly much, much faster than the other seagulls in the seagull society can, or will. For this demonstration, Jonathan anticipates being rewarded; instead, he is cast out of the seagull society. And yet, Jonathan Livingston Seagull provides the perfect example of the erstwhile hero that seeks the redemption of the profoundly dysfunctional organization.

What's happening, of course, is that the dysfunctional organization can be counted on to never have at its helm a leader with a high Black Arrow. High White Arrow – absolutely. High Grey Arrow – perhaps, but it's not necessary, past an inner circle of sycophants. Recall the discussion from Chapter 9, of the tactics that high White Arrow/low Black Arrow (Politicians and Fools) leaders have at their disposal to maintain their high White Arrows in the face of possible challenges from high Black Arrow members – none of them are pretty. And yet, again, that's how dysfunctional organizations operate.

Still, a Hero's Got to Be A-Heroing

If, despite having read all of the previous paragraphs, the aspirant is *still* intent on saving the dysfunctional organization from itself, there are a few tactics that may come in handy. In ordering these tactics into a collective strategy, a bit of groundwork is needed.

First off, what is the precise nature of the group's objectives? The answer, in many cases, isn't quite as obvious as it may seem. For example, in an article written by Theodore Dawes in *American Thinker*, he discusses an interaction with a college-level journalism class where he poses the question, "Why are newspapers published?" The answers he received ranged from providing an information-delivery service to their subscribers to giving a voice to their communities. But, when Dawes pointed out the undeniably true purpose of publishing a newspaper – to make money for the publisher – he was met with strong criticism, even from the hosting professor. A friend of Dawes pointed out "If you want to see heads explode, try explaining to people that they are not the customer and the newspaper is not the product... advertisers are the customer and reader attention is the product."[6]

That newspapers exist to deliver reader attention to potential advertisers, while undeniably true, is probably rarely (if ever) taught in college-level schools of journalism. And yet, even a cursory comparison of a typical big-city newspaper from 30 years ago and one from today will provide a strong clue that this realization has sunk in, at least among management. Thirty years ago, the standard style for writing a newspaper article was "inverted pyramid," so named because the writer sought to assert the highest number of the most relevant facts in the opening sentences as possible, since the writer couldn't know at what point the paper's editor(s) would have to truncate the piece based on space considerations. The alternative approach, known as "tabloid style," involves writing the first sentence (irksomely entitled the "lede," a stylistic misspelling of "lead") in such a way as to not convey information, but to pique reader interest. In advertising parlance, this is known as the "teaser," and it is used to induce potential readers to spend more attention on the rest of the advertisement. Thirty years ago, when the word "tabloid" was a pejorative among newspaper editors and writers, the use of this style was considered base and unprofessional. Thirty years later, it's so common as to be ubiquitous, even in the so-called broadcast journalism sphere. Why the change? Well, if it was to advance the level of writing sophistication among the papers that made the switch, it has most certainly failed.

So, when attempting to penetrate the shield of lies that surrounds the flawed organization's true purpose, it behooves the aspirant to recognize that even those in the higher echelons of the hierarchy – one might even say *especially* those in the upper echelons – are vulnerable to misidentifying why they belong to the organization in the first place. Note that this drift from the original, stated purpose to a more poorly understood, but undeniably more powerful driver of group behavior is over and above the previously discussed effect of the group existing only for (a) its own survival, and (b) the benefit of maintaining the ranks of those in the upper levels of its hierarchy. Taken together, these three effects can create cracks in the connections between the practical goals being pursued and the original group's purposes in even the most valid, purpose-aware groups. In flawed organizations, they can cause chasms. Just ask the factory floor worker who joined the United Auto Workers union and bought a house in suburban Detroit in 1968, and is still living there 40 years later.

In returning to the starting point of this discussion, on assembling and executing a strategy for our aspirant to assume the role of hero and save the dysfunctional organization from itself, we have the starting point – virtuous (if insane) aspirant, not currently in a position of influence – and the end point – to rid a dysfunctional organization of its ingrained pathologies and return it to valid (and successful) operations. We're also assuming that simply getting rid of the upper levels of the organization's hierarchy, the presumed keepers of the group's pathologies, is not an option, and that the aspirant is aware that any motivation that entails having attained this objective, automatically receiving accolades, recognition, and an appropriate jump in rank, is, in all probability, destined for profound frustration. With these assumptions lining up like dead ravens falling at the feet of Alexander the Great prior to his entering Babylon, we'll proceed to analyze the strategies most likely to work.

The flawed organization will tend to be composed of people playing the roles consistent with those in the dysfunctional family, with a nod towards the Maccoby archetypes. Among the dysfunctional roles, only the Golden Child/Hero is truly in a position of influence (and no, I did not shoe-horn in the word "hero." That's actually a usage among family therapists). It follows, then, that our aspirant must attain that role, or at least be perceived as having attained it. Recall the payoff grid from the previous section of this chapter, on developing strategies for the functional operator to merely survive the dysfunctional organization (Table 9.3).

The transition to Golden Child from Scapegoat is virtually impossible. It can only come about from one of Nassim Taleb's "Black Swan events," (from the book *The Black Swan*) defined as being (1) completely unexpected, (2) having a high degree of impact, and (3) after the fact those impacted by it are inclined to rationalize the level of its unpredictability. While hoping for an external event that encompasses all of these attributes that would lead to the transformation of the Scapegoat to a Golden

Table 9.3 Loyalty/Accomplishment Payoff Matrix for Three-Arrow Model Archetypes

	Low accomplishment	High accomplishment
High loyalty	Mascot/Company Man	Golden Child
Low-to-medium loyalty	Scapegoat	Craftsman/Lost Child

Child/Hero is futile, some of the characteristics of a Black Swan event can be initiated and managed, and it is those characteristics the aspirant will need if he is to succeed.

There are, then, two paths for our hero aspirant. He can either overtly establish loyalty to the existing hierarchy on a consistent basis, and move into the Mascot/Company Man role, and then perform (again, on a consistent basis) some act of advanced competency that leads directly to the enrichment of the upper ranks of the hierarchy; or, he can perform some act of advanced competency that enriches the upper ranks, moving into the Craftsman/Lost Child role, and then display intense loyalty to the upper ranks until Golden Child/Hero status is attained.

The preferred path will be indicated by the degree of dysfunction displayed by the organization. The team that is somewhat functional, and only mildly to moderately besotted by organizational pathologies will recognize true merit faster than the profoundly flawed ones. In these groups, demonstrating an advanced capability first, and sycophantic loyalty later, is probably the best course. However, in showing advanced capability, remember that it's an advanced capability in the *real* purpose of the organization, which is often something quite different from the stated goals, and can even be somewhat opposed to the published group's objectives.

For example, let's return to the case of a newspaper whose reporters may or may not have a clear idea of its true purpose. This particular newspaper, like so many others, is experiencing a significant reduction in readership, and local advertising agencies are aware of it. The owners and hand-picked executives are not true leaders: their abilities in both business management and journalism are sub-standard. To the extent that the paper is a success has more to do with (a) the start-up costs of beginning a rival newspaper, and (b) the fact that this particular newspaper has been published in this particular city for so long, it has become the regular, familiar source of sports box scores, weather, movie times, and horoscopes.

With no true competition to keep them sharp, and their editorial pages believed to be able to sway state-wide elections, the people in the higher ranks at this newspaper soon had their White Arrows inflated a fair degree above their Black Arrows. Letters to the editor that dared to criticize the paper's baseless support of popular cultural trends without regard to logical public policy were dismissed as being written from the uneducated or partisan. Thus insulated, several pathologies invaded the decision-makers' business model, the first being cronyism.

Offspring of the owners enjoyed high-paying, low-responsibility jobs, with friends and acquaintances of the senior editors and managers following soon after. These people, too, suffered from high White Arrows and low Black Arrows, since they did not attain their positions through merit. Indeed, their placement within the upper ranks of the paper's hierarchy displaced those who would have attained those positions through actual accomplishment, dramatically reducing the odds that the primary decision makers would select strategies on behalf of the entire newspaper that would prevent them from suffering the downward cycle they are currently experiencing.

As nepotism and cronyism displaced the meritocracy, other pathologies came into play. The paper's upper ranks, knowing that they could not expect to duplicate their benefits elsewhere either within or outside the newspaper industry, come to a grudging acknowledgment that the positions they enjoy are predicated on maintaining good will from those above them, as well as preventing those currently beneath them from rising in esteem, and potentially displacing them from their high ranks. These elite members begin to select strategy sets far more consistent with the Maccoby archetypes of Jungle Fighters, and less aligned with Craftsmen or Gamesmen. As merit recedes as a basis for advancement, working to place upward pressure on their own Black Arrows becomes a waste of time, while putting effort into inflating or maintaining the high White Arrows of those above them becomes virtually mandatory. Returning to the vault of commonly held wisdom, a.k.a. the clichés, this tactic is known as "kissing up and kicking down." At the same time, in dealing with those beneath them in rank, the elite must evaluate them in terms of their potential threat level. In almost any hierarchy, a member of lower rank is a threat to the member with higher rank when:

- they are more valuable than the higher-ranking member (the lower-ranked individual has a higher Black Arrow than the elite member), and
- the lower-level worker is not aligned with or loyal to the threatened elite member.

As those seeking to maintain their higher ranks (attained, remember, through means other than merit) become aware of those beneath them who display the characteristics of a potential threat, they generally have two alternatives for interacting with them:

- they can cultivate the potential threat as an ally, or
- they can work to prevent those above them from realizing that the potential threat actually has a higher Black Arrow than is currently recognized.

Note that neither tactic actually improves the ability of the newspaper to realize its goals. In fact, in spending time and effort to tamp down the proper recognition of merit within the ranks, these high-ranking members are actually pushing *against* the collective goals of the organization. As this cycle continues, the Craftsmen and Gamesmen become more and more frustrated, and tend to leave for better circumstances. This leaves the Company Man/Mascot and Jungle Fighter types, who just as quickly discover which strategies lead to rank escalation, and that those strategies tend to have little or nothing to do with actual accomplishments or advancing a capability. The organization filled with Company Man/Mascot and Jungle Fighter types cannot compete against the groups that have a better mix, and is utterly hopeless against competitors that are largely free of these types. The more the newspaper indulges its pathologies, the sooner it precipitates its own downfall.

The solution, then, for our aspirant/hero is to find a way to become responsible for a team or sub-organizational unit over which they have control of personnel. At the newspaper, our aspirant/hero – we'll call him "Mitch" – has arranged to be responsible for the real estate section, which comes out once per week. Mitch immediately reviews the current roster of staff reporters who contribute to this topic, and attempts to ascertain which Maccoby archetype they largely fit. Current standing within the newspaper's hierarchy is largely irrelevant – Mitch needs two things: writing talent, and a behavior/strategy-selection pattern that indicates that his small team might be rid of Jungle Fighters (primarily), or Company Men/Mascots. If Mitch has arranged to read this book, he would also be well advised to eliminate either of the two types with significantly higher White Arrows than Black Arrows, the Politician and the Fool.

Since merit is not typically valued highly within a flawed organization, this step might not be as difficult as it appears. The hidden pools of talent will be those in the Lost Child category, who, as we have seen, are notably lower on the loyalty scale than their Company Man/Mascot counterparts. The precise tactics will, of course, depend on the particular circumstances. Traditionally, the way to rid an organization of a treacherous or underperforming individual is to give them the worst assignments, least attractive offices, lowest raises, etc. I believe that it's somewhat rare for an employee to base their decisions on whether or not to stay with a given organization on an entirely Boolean basis – either 100% in, or completely out. Rather, I think that most members of an organization base their decisions to stay involved or to disengage on a swing in perception of no more than 10–15%. If their circumstances improve a little, the one thinking about leaving will reconsider, as will the one intent on remaining, should reality unfold with a bit more difficulty than they had anticipated.

Next, Mitch must find a way to communicate to his team that his Black Arrow is high, his White Arrow low. This is consistent with my Three Indispensable Attributes of Management Leadership:

- The Leader must have the optimal technical agenda in mind.
- The Leader must genuinely care for his team.
- The Leader must be willing to pursue his selected agenda in the face of opposition, alone if need be.

If Mitch has no idea how to write an article on real estate in such a way as to attract reader attention, he had better learn fast, or else despair of getting ahead in this hierarchy. In other words, his Black Arrow needs to be high, or else there's really no point.

People who think an awful lot of themselves – high White Arrows – often encounter difficulty in experiencing empathy for those they perceive as their inferiors. Such an attitude is not easy to hide, and those who encounter high White Arrows in others soon catch onto the fact. If the team should learn that its leader does not care for them as individuals, it naturally follows that the assigned leader does not have the best interest of their group in mind. Coming to this realization, consciously or not, will lead to the assigned leader having no true followers. In this instance, even with the best possible technical agenda in front of them, the leader's objectives will not be realized.

The third Indispensable Attribute of Management Leadership does have to do with White Arrow placement. Too high, and the difficulties from the previous paragraph are virtually guaranteed. But too low, and the leader will lack the confidence to pursue the identified best technical approach to resolving the problem(s) before the team. Mitch must present as an Alpha to his team, but no more than a Beta to the macro organization at the newspaper at large.

The next step is for Mitch to clearly communicate his intended technical approach to his team, and in such a way as to convey that their mutual interests are best attained through cooperation, not competition. Part and parcel of this approach is to establish that he will not allow any *ex parte* discussions involving other team members. Mitch must establish early on that, should any member of the real estate section team come to him with "concerns" about another member of the team, he will stop the conversation at that point, and invite the person about whom these "concerns" swirl to engage in any accusations or innuendos against them. Only in this way can a foundation of trust among the team members be established, and without trust, true cooperation is impossible.

(As an aside, note that Mitch's path to save the organization from itself is identical to the path through the three arrow placements, from Chapter 9. He must seek first to upgrade his Black Arrow (optimal technical solution), followed by managing his Grey Arrow (demonstrates his concern for the others in the group). Finally, Mitch must discover the confidence to go it alone, and pursue his technical approach unaided, if necessary (White Arrow placement).)

Although it is somewhat clichéd, the pattern of new organizations or groups to go through the phases of Forming–Storming–Norming–Performing is somewhat universal. It's up to Mitch to lay the inter-group communications as openly as possible to minimize the duration of the first two stages. This involves tying his team members' White Arrows to *group* accomplishments, and not to anything they perform as individuals. As counterintuitive as it may sound, it's of less value to Mitch if one of his team receives a Pulitzer Prize than it is if, as a group, they arrange to increase the number of advertisers who want to appear in the real estate section of the newspaper.

As his group moves closer to and into the performing stage, he must be aware of the pitfalls that await him in the dysfunctional group. Other section heads, being either Jungle Fighters or Company Men from the Maccoby archetypes, Politicians, Fools, or Comedians from mine, or improperly ensconced Golden Children from the dysfunctional roles, will attempt to undermine Mitch's accomplishments while highlighting and exaggerating any failures or setbacks. This is where the narrative and those who most effectively influence it comes into play. Former U.S. President George W. Bush was an avid reader, consuming books at a prodigious rate; however, when former Beatle Sir Paul McCartney visited the White House, he made a joke about former President Bush *never* reading books, and those in attendance laughed. The reality in these situations is largely irrelevant – it's how the narrative is created and modified that counts.

If Mitch has selected the optimal technical approach to making the paper's real estate section the best it can be, and advertising revenue is noticeably higher due to his efforts, then Mitch is approaching Golden Child status. If he can keep ahead of those narrative influencers who have a strong motive to keep Mitch from entering into Golden Child rank, then he has a shot at being given greater responsibility. Repeating his previous strategies whenever presented with the opportunity will maximize his chances of repeating his progress and success, enriching the coffers of the paper's upper ranks while helping them maintain their artificially high White Arrows.

In this respect, Mitch will have advanced the capability of his team to deliver reader attention, essentially following the levels proscribed in the original Software Engineering Institute's Capability Maturity Model®. And, as Mitch and his team have advanced this capability to deliver the true objectives of the newspaper, unencumbered by false objectives of the other sections, he and they have attracted a significant amount of attention from some highly placed enemies. Since I'm using the device of fictionalizing my theoretical strategy selections, I'm going to end Mitch's story by having the owner's daughter – placed as a managing editor (of the style section, where she essentially parrots the most recent edition of *Vogue* magazine) and extremely wary of Mitch – realizing she has reached her breaking point. She simply must be rid of Mitch before it becomes painfully obvious to the most casual observer that his approaches are markedly superior to the other section heads, including hers. She takes advantage of the access she has to her father to impugn Mitch's integrity. While she can't really undermine his Black Arrow, she can do serious damage to his Grey Arrow. She does so by initiating conversations with the employees who have a tangential relationship with Mitch, intimating that the highest levels of management have, well, *concerns* about Mitch's writing ability and his personal integrity. These lower-level employees listen eagerly, offering up their own tidbits about how they have observed Mitch failing to keep regular hours, or committing the crime of preferring to avoid tabloid style in his pieces. The daughter, Christina, returns to the row of executive suites, happily conveying these tidbits to all who will listen, and some who don't really want to, but also do not want to be kept out of the loop when section head evaluations are the topic. When Christina's stories appear to have such an accepting audience, she heads back down to the cubicles, where she, again, informs Mitch's rivals of the executive's unease at what appears to be his disappointing contributions. Thus does Christina ping-pong back and forth between the strata, enhancing the Mitch-must-go narrative until it is firmly entrenched.

Since there's no earthly way Mitch can possibly openly oppose someone of Christina's stature, his upward trajectory is doomed. It's only a matter of time.

But that's the way dysfunctional organizations work. And I *did* try to warn him.

Notes

1 Aurelius, Marcus, retrieved from *BrainyQuote*, http://www.brainyquote.com/quotes/authors/m/marcus_aurelius_3.html, July 5, 2015.
2 It should be noted that, if there is a relatively high number of Lone Wolves, then assembling them as allies will likely be interpreted as a prelude to a sudden overthrow of the existing high-ranking members of the hierarchy.
3 "Watts Humphrey," retrieved from *Wikipedia*, http://en.wikipedia.org/w/index.php?title=Watts_Humphrey&oldid=660741835, May 15, 2015.
4 Retrieved from *SearchSoftwareQuality*, http://searchsoftwarequality.techtarget.com/definition/Capability-Maturity-Model, May 15, 2015.
5 Retrieved from *Investopedia*, http://www.investopedia.com/terms/n/nash-equilibrium.asp, January 22, 2015.
6 Dawes, Theodore, "The Fall of Journalism," retrieved from *American Thinker*, http://www.americanthinker.com/articles/2013/01/the_fall_of_journalism.html, January 31, 2013.

Chapter 10

Tearing Down the Organization

The supreme art of war is to subdue the enemy without fighting.

Sun Tzu[1]

As the saying goes, it's far easier to destroy than to create. Since, as we have seen, the creation of some sort of network or group to cooperate in attaining a mutually desired outcome is fairly automatic among humans, it follows that when we're discussing hierarchies, the creation act is also quite simple.

However, once formed, hierarchical groupings of people are extremely susceptible to behavioral and interactive pathologies, pathologies that enter in even in those circumstances where they are not only unwanted, but actively avoided. Think of it as the tendency within human nature of self-preservation trumping any agreed-to understanding that advances the group as a whole. On those occasions where a member executes a duty to the group that supersedes the duty to self, even overriding the survival instinct, such ones are so rare that they receive honor from everyone else in the construct. But, to be clear, such an instinct – or the ability to override the basic self-preservation instinct – is *rare*. In most cases, a member of the organization presented with an opportunity to enrich themselves will avail themselves of it. If such enrichment is entirely consistent with the pursuit of the group as a whole (e.g., members of a small but highly successful company), then everything's okay. If the enrichment is incidental to the pursuit of the goals, then things become problematic – it may be alright, but it might also represent a case of the enriched individual taking advantage of a set of circumstances, circumstances that may or may not have been accessible to others in the organization. Finally, self-enrichment at the expense of the group's ability to attain its stated and agreed-upon objectives represents a real problem. In extreme circumstances, it's treason, punishable by death.

As we examine the ways that a given hierarchy might be torn down, the question of "Why?" must be re-examined, albeit perhaps not as thoroughly as it was in the previous chapter. Why would someone want to destroy the hierarchical underpinnings of a given organization? The most obvious cause would be due to membership in a rival organization, or else opposition to the goals – stated or not – that the target group is pursuing. Tories oppose Labour, Republicans oppose Democrats, civilized sports fans oppose the followers of the Philadelphia Eagles, etc., etc. Indeed, the act of people coming together to more efficiently or effectively attain shared objectives carries with it the implication that others seek the same goals, and a natural opposition is as automatic as the tendency to enter into cooperative hierarchies. The reasons groups are opposed are as many and varied as the reasons groups are assembled.

But, once someone is an accepted member of an organization, why would they want to tear it down? First off, "tear it down" might be a bit strong since, as we have seen, virtually all social constructs have a finite lifespan. The more accurate term might be "accelerate its decline." Second, the implication is that the member wanting to perform this acceleration either does not have the option of disengaging, or else is motivated to act as an agent provocateur, or traitor, in order to be more effective in their intended destruction. Benedict Arnold had shown himself to be a remarkably talented officer, and some historians have suggested that his actions led to the American victory at the Battle of Saratoga. Arnold could have simply switched sides in 1778 (he was said to have been disappointed that Congress refused the Carlisle Peace Negotiations of that year); instead, he obtained command of West Point, and was preparing to surrender it to the British when his treason was uncovered. While acting as a brigadier general for the British after 1780, Arnold did do damage to his former country, but there is no doubt he would have done far more to harm the colonies' cause had he successfully turned West Point over to the Redcoats.

A third circumstance that could lead to an individual member being led to desire the destruction of the hierarchy around them: the perception that the group is not appropriately pursuing its stated objectives, or is doing so in such a manner as to render its original charter invalid. In these cases, the traitor allows himself a level of comfort for these decisions based on the idea that it was the group that really betrayed *him*, and not the other way around.

Again, the reasons why an accepted member of any given organization might want to tear it down (strikethrough) accelerate its demise are varied, and I have no intention of capturing them all here. However, those strategies used *do* tend to fall into patterns, and those patterns can be recognized and evaluated for their efficacy.

To state the obvious, any organization in existence will have access to mechanisms to recognize and eliminate those members who seek its demise. Referencing back to Chapter 1, should Friday have sudden access to the narratives of a grievance industry spokesperson, and come to the idea that *any* interaction with a Caucasian man is automatically exploitive, he might want to either disengage from any cooperative pact currently enjoyed with Crusoe, or, more extremely, seek the ruination of his companion. In such a small group, his options are limited: he could simply leave, and seek his subsistence in a different area of the Island of Despair. He could overtly attack Crusoe at a moment of vulnerability. Or, he could agree to uphold his end of the survival compact, and simply not do so. In any of these selected strategies, it is likely Crusoe would readily perceive the demise of their relationship, and respond accordingly.

In larger groups, of course, such treachery is more easily concealed. Again, I'm conveniently skipping past the morality or virtue of the motives involved, and getting straight to those strategies that are likely to succeed, and in which circumstances.

One of Saul Alinsky's (of whom I have a very low opinion, indeed) published strategies is to "Make the enemy live up to its own book of rules."[2] As discussed earlier, there will always be a delta between what the organization contends is its reason for existence and desired outcomes, and its real-world selection of strategies in order to attain it. Churches may be based on the goal of bringing the maximum number of its adherence into a closer relationship with The Almighty; reality dictates that no societal goal can be achieved without economic help. A readily available barb is there for the taking: by highlighting any and all efforts on the behalf of a spiritual organization to raise funds for its undertakings, the criticism that such a church expends any effort at all along those lines becomes ipso facto evidence that they have cynically abandoned their stated goals and, instead, are only seeking enrichment for those in the upper levels of its ranks. Cheap? Yes. Intellectually vacuous? No question. Effective? Almost always.

So, one of the first acts of analysis for the erstwhile destructor becomes an assessment of the difference between the targeted organization's stated goals and the methods it employs to attain them. Outside agitators may be able to use this delta in published criticism of the organization; but, to truly bring the group down, the destructor must use this insight as a basis for formulating a strategy against it.

The next parameter to come into play has to do with the destructor's place within the hierarchy. A low-ranked member has little opportunity to influence the overall group, much less bring it to an early demise, and Omegas are lucky to simply hang on to membership at all. Conversely, it's fairly easy for the Alpha of the group to bring about its destruction. A well-disguised bad decision here, an unwarranted promotion of the undeserving there, and an accelerated downward trajectory is virtually guaranteed. But for those in the middling middle, there are opportunities as well as threats that need to be addressed and exploited.

It's a mistake to assume that any of the archetypes possessing a high Black Arrow are automatically outside the category of those who would actively seek the sudden demise of the group. The aforementioned Alphas, for example, are perfectly capable of inflicting ruination, which is why those safeguards that the group has in place to guard against treachery are far more attuned to those in the upper ranks, though this does, in itself, present a paradox: yes, there are mechanisms in the group to uncover and eliminate subversion in the upper ranks. There are also mechanisms in place to prevent scurrilous accusations from eliminating a valid Alpha from a leadership role. The successful destructor must be able to (falsely) circumvent the former, while (also falsely) taking advantage of the latter. To construct a set of strategies to accomplish these ends, we must return to the archetypes, and their corresponding arrows.

The Omega is in an inherently poor position to influence the group, one way or the other. An Omega who seeks to do so must find a way out of that role. The Alpha is in a pristine position to wreak havoc on the organization they putatively lead, with many opportunities and strategies from which to select. Everybody else will need a coherent strategy.

Any group headed by a strong leader/Alpha will be more difficult to deconstruct than those that are not, for obvious reasons, including:

- The fact that the group is headed by a valid Alpha indicates that its internal mechanisms for recognizing and acting upon the valid rankings of potential leaders are strong.
- It also implies that its mechanisms for preventing untrue narratives from undermining or eliminating true Alphas in leadership roles are also effective.

- Since valid Alphas have high Black Arrows, the technical direction selected by them for the group is likely to be among the most effective available. In other words, properly led groups will be less vulnerable to the tactics of weakening it in comparison to its more poorly led competitors.

Accelerating the demise of organizations with strong leadership, then, will need to focus on the leaders themselves. This is accomplished by those in a position to do so in one of two ways:

- Work to deflate the leader's Grey Arrow. Indeed, within our framework, almost all of Alinsky's tactics can be reduced to the act of driving down the Grey Arrows of the current leadership, whether they deserve it or not, by any means available. Comedians and Politicians are particularly good at this, since they already have high Grey Arrows themselves (in fact, they are the only non-Alphas or Betas with high Grey Arrows), and can leverage that esteem energy into the creation of narratives that purposes to lower the standing of the Alpha in the group's eyes. Being caught in an act of naked calumny can be very dangerous, meaning that the use of this tactic will require large degrees of patience and discernment on the part of potential narrative influencers.
- The more insidious tactic would be to inflate the Alpha's White Arrow to the point that they become delusional, and detached from the goals and objectives of the organization they purport to lead. The effect being sought here is to convert the Alpha into a Politician – it's far easier for the Betas-in-waiting to displace a Politician than a true Alpha.

What the destructor is looking to do here is to put some space in-between the leader's arrows, either by moving the Grey Arrow a space below the Alpha's Black Arrow, or else inflating the White Arrow some space above the Black Arrow. This space represents the proverbial crack in the door, or camel's nose under the tent flap. Recall also that it's a rare individual who does not experience euphoria at having the White Arrow move upwards, and pain at having it pushed down. We like to feel good about ourselves, regardless of our other circumstances, and will often expend extra-ordinary amounts of energy to get to a place where we can justifiably feel good about our status. Similarly, we will reflexively ignore, or even openly oppose members of the group who seek to diminish us. It follows, then, that others within our selected groups who can make us feel better about ourselves are going to be more attractive to us than those that make us feel like lesser human beings. Of course, it is often in the interest of the group as a whole that its members don't think too highly of themselves, which is why military organizations' basic training almost always includes large doses of humiliating the newest members. More senior members, however, can be expected to be vulnerable to having their White Arrows artificially inflated, which attracts pathologies in decision making.

All the while this gap introduction and widening is occurring, the destructor must be aware of the nominal organizational mechanisms that are in place to prevent the occurrence of the group's destruction. The subverting of the Alpha's Grey Arrow is best (only?) achieved through *ex parte* conversations; however, if such a conversation occurs to an ally of either the Alpha specifically or the group in general, the destructor will be readily uncovered as subversive. If such a revelation takes place, the destructor will need to engage in a further bit of deception: they weren't seeking an illegitimate toppling of the group's leadership, no siree. They were simply attempting to provide an honest critique of the technical direction being taken by group leadership. And, while the destructor may not agree with some of the particulars of that leadership direction, they fully recognize who's in charge, and will expend all appropriate efforts towards pursuing the agenda laid out by the Alphas. Or, at least, that will be the prof-fered narrative that gives the discovered destructor the room needed to back off their efforts – temporarily.

The alternate approach, of inflating the Alpha's White Arrow, also carries with it imbedded hazards. Even if many (most?) people do not recognize it when they are being flattered as part of a strategy on the part of the flatterer to gain an advantage, it's usually readily perceivable by involved third parties. The colloquial expressions for this act have an unfortunate tendency to invoke images of the proximity of the flatterer's face to their target's posterior. Crude, sure, but it does convey the contempt that such third parties feel for those engaging in the practice of offering up unsoli-cited, unctuous flattery.

Another mental exercise: recall a previous time that you were offended that some-one was engaging in what you perceived to be inappropriate flattery, in a situation other than a salesperson attempting to get you to buy something. From my experi-ence, my disgust came from one (or a combination) of three sources:

- I was disappointed in the person pouring out the compliments for engaging in such a practice;
- I was concerned that that person would surge ahead of me in that particular group's rankings, for reasons that had nothing to do with merit; and
- I realized that a group headed by an individual who was susceptible to transpar-ently hollow flattery was not being well led.

Should the destructor succeed in driving down the Alpha's Grey Arrow, the next step would be to take advantage of confirmation bias to create a narrative that keeps downward pressure on that Grey Arrow. Inter-group communications are very com-plex, even between Friday and Crusoe, and many misunderstandings can occur even when all of the parties involved are actively seeking complete understanding. Any member of the group actively seeking to twist such communications or interpret-ation of events away from their intended or true meanings and towards supporting a meme that is damaging to the group's leadership would have little trouble finding opportunities.

In those cases where the destructor succeeds in overly inflating the Alpha's White Arrow, it may very well become the case that replacing the Alpha is no longer neces-sary to accelerate the group's decline. History is replete with examples of truly advanced leaders coming to the conclusion that they were far superior (White Arrow) to their widely recognized (Grey Arrow) actual skills (Black Arrow) and then, as pre-dictable as clockwork, making gobsmackingly foolish decisions that brought them and the hierarchies they led to a sudden downfall, one example being that of U.S. Army General George Custer, whose arrogance led him to the decision to attack up to 2,500 plains Indians with his force of 700 at the Battle of the Little Big Horn, confident of victory. A person within Custer's force, sympathetic to the Indian's plight, rather than seek to remove Custer would have been better off simply letting him execute his flawed strategy.

However, this latter tactic is very difficult to execute should the targeted group have within its ranks valid Betas. Recall from wolfpack society that the Betas, while occupying a lower rank than the Alphas, don't take any nonsense from the Alphas. This form of low-level, background-noise-style threatened rebellion supports the health of the pack by ensuring that the Alpha thinks twice before embarking on any course of action that would not appear to the pack overall as beneficial or necessary for their continued survival or advancement. Canny Betas work not only as brakes against any potential excess that the Alpha may attempt to indulge, but will be able to sniff out (we're still within the wolfpack, right?) underlings who may lead the Alphas into temptation.

One avenue of thwarting this function of the Betas would be to exploit the space between either the Alpha's Grey and Black Arrows, or the space between the Alpha's White and Black Arrows, and to do so before the Betas even realize that these gaps exist (Figure 10.1).

In the case of the delta between the (artificially deflated) Grey Arrow and Black Arrow, the Betas will usually be aware of the narrative that the rest of the group perceives, that pack members are in danger of failing to realize their shared goals, and the proximate cause is the leadership decisions coming from the Alpha. Also known as the Consensus Argument, it can be very powerful, particularly in organizations that are more democratic in nature. Here in the twenty-first century, it's easy to look back upon the foreign and economic policy decisions of Margaret Thatcher and Ronald Reagan as being insightful and courageous. However, at the time, they were extensively ridiculed, from a multitude of angles. Even if the Alpha's selected strategies are sound, the narrative surrounding them can be twisted to make them appear as the height of folly by a sufficiently talented destructor, and the acceptance of such a narrative acts on Betas as an influence towards action, to either challenge or replace the Alpha.

As for exploiting the distance between the Alpha's White Arrow and Black Arrow in an attempt to tamp down the Beta's ability to prevent the destructor from accelerating the group's decline, this must be done in such a way that the Alpha is led to believe that the group's nominal mechanisms for defeating an unwarranted leadership change have been compromised, and that any challenge whatsoever represents an act of treason. This way the Beta's normal, healthy function of keeping the Alpha from straying

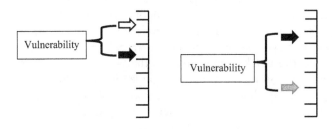

Figure 10.1 Gap Delta-Driven Vulnerabilities

too far into high White Arrow delusion is circumvented, and a group-endangering pathology becomes entrenched.

A near analogy from history involves the Battle of Leyte Gulf, in October of 1944. The overall conflict involved three component battles, one of which involved Admiral William "Bull" Halsey being successfully baited away from his support of troop landings and towards Ozawa's decoy force to the northeast. Once Halsey had steamed away with the body of the Third Fleet, a Japanese force under Admiral Kurita was in a perfect position to utterly destroy the troop transports and most of the forces that had already landed.

As radio traffic reached Admiral Nimitz that Halsey wasn't supporting the landings, he sent an urgent message to Halsey, "Where is the Third Fleet?" However, it was standard practice at the time to put random quotes or non-related words onto either side of a radio transmission, and this was done for Nimitz's message. The radio operator on board Halsey's flag ship happened to include this fluff in the printout given to Halsey, so that what Halsey read was "Where is the Third Fleet stop The World Wonders." Thinking that his leadership decisions were being mocked, Halsey entered into a highly agitated state of mind. Hours passed before he finally elected to turn the Third Fleet around, but by then it was too late to catch the Japanese force that did, indeed, catch the landings extremely lightly defended. Only through an amazing combination of bravery and seamanship did the residual force prevent disaster.

(Just as an aside – the movie *The Hunt for Red October* makes a reference to this incident. During a lull in the torpedo attack against *Red October*, Captain Ramius asks Jack Ryan about what books Ryan had written. Ryan replies that he wrote *The Fighting Sailor*, which he describes as a biography of Halsey. Ramius replies "I know this book! Your conclusions are all wrong, Ryan. Halsey acted stupidly." Since the rest of Halsey's career was somewhat distinguished, I'm assuming that this bit of dialogue could only refer to Halsey's actions at Leyte.)

Now, to engage in the always highly dubious what-if analysis in military history, what would have happened had the filler text not been included in Nimitz's message? The straight question "Where is the Third Fleet?" may have been innocuous enough to tip Halsey off that he was out of position to inflict maximum damage on the enemy, leading to a more spontaneous reversal of course, perhaps in time to catch the fleeing Kurita. But the insinuation that the Third Fleet was being poorly led by its Alpha, and that this was plain to "the world" (Grey Arrow), sent Halsey into a state of highly ineffective leadership. He chose the wrong strategies, to near-catastrophic effect.

Halsey was known as an extremely confident leader. Whether or not this translates to an inappropriately high White Arrow I will leave to historians, both real and fictional. But, at the moment that a significant gap opened between Halsey's White Arrow and Grey Arrow, his ability to select the best available strategy on behalf of the Third Fleet was significantly compromised. I know correlation is not causation, but this series of events does suggest that the ability of a deliberate destructor to exploit a gap between either the White and Black Arrows or even the White and Grey Arrows can lead to a severe compromise on the part of the organization's Alpha to execute the office of leader. Nimitz's message had the unintended effect of placing significant downward pressure on Halsey's White Arrow – another way of putting it was that his confidence was shaken – to the point that some historians suggest that he may have even been on the brink of a mental break.

When Toppling the Leadership Is Not an Option

While toppling the targeted group's leadership is certainly the most dramatic way of accelerating its decline, it is by no means the only way to do so. Referencing back to the analysis of the group's stated purpose and the ways it goes about pursuing that purpose, consider the number of organizational behavior and performance pathologies that can plague any organization so engaged. Many of these are introduced and endured by the organization by accident – an agent provocateur need only accelerate their negative effect on the group's ability to attain its desired goals, and the acceleration of decline can be accomplished.

Take, for example, the nominal resistance of any group to change. In my first book (*Things Your PMO Is Doing Wrong*, PMI Publishing, 2008) I reviewed Carnegie Mellon University's Software Engineering Institute's Capability Maturity Model (CMM®), and noted that the transition between levels often failed due to the difficulty inherent in attaining widespread group assimilation of the desired capability after it had been introduced. I asserted that this was due to the availability of the strategy of the "Silent Veto," which is essentially the act of articulating support for a proffered change in the way the group conducts its affairs, followed by complete inaction on the part of the organization in bringing such change about. My friend and colleague, Dr. Bud Baker from Wright State University's Business School, told me about something similar he had witnessed in military organizations, which he referred to as the "Slow Roll." This was where a new or enhanced capability – a change – to the organization would be announced, and the precise nature of each member of the group spelled out. The members would acquiesce, and actually expend effort in advancing the desired capability – just not quite enough to attain the next capability maturity level. With a finite amount of energy behind the push to get the target group to advance in its ability to attain its articulated objectives, these recalcitrant members knew that failing to expend the necessary effort – even by the smallest of margins – would mean that the desired advancement could be utterly thwarted.

Purely voluntarily joined organizations tend to be immune from this effect. But, in those groups where change is an ever-present factor, and the inability to change to better interact with new environments is key to group success (or even survival), aggravating the Silent Veto or Slow Roll strategies among the rank and file will certainly accelerate the decline of the targeted organization. It could even go so far as to reinvoke the previous phrase, and tear it down.

Another somewhat obvious way of accelerating the demise of the target organization has to do with the previously discussed cliché about the stages of project team formation, of Forming–Storming–Norming–Performing. To elaborate:

- Groups or teams are formed and, in the business world, this is somewhat involuntary. Some management entity has selected a grouping of people, who may or may not be complete strangers to one another, to pursue a certain scope of work.
- Their reflexive response to being put into such a mix is to defend their interests, and to do so as aggressively as they (a) think is appropriate to secure them, and (b) would be allowed under the circumstances. Since each member of the team is inclined to respond in this manner, the "storming" moniker becomes appropriate.

- Once each member of the new organization has a feel for the boundaries of those around them, they become more comfortable in expending effort to pursue the team's articulated objectives. In other words, their selected strategies are normalized as they approach the situational Nash Equilibrium. Conflicts lessen as articulated objectives are approached and attained.
- As each member of the group diverts energy away from defending their individual, personal interests and towards attaining the group's stated objectives, their collective performance leans towards optimization, hence the "performing" reference.

If we view these stages from the leaders' point of view, the first stage – Forming – is both inevitable, and often out of their control. Teams comprised entirely from the preferences of their leaders – like the Manhattan Project (the effort to build an atomic bomb during World War II) – can and do occur, often with amazing results. But usually economic concerns will drive specific teams to include members not selected by the team's leadership, which provides the destructor with no small amount of opportunity.

The span between Storming and Norming can appear as a chasm to the team's leadership. They obviously have a motive to see the group moving from Forming to Performing in the shortest possible time frame, with a minimal amount of hierarchical influence from leadership. The Alpha wolf doesn't want to spend a lot of time teaching new adults how to select, isolate, bring down, and kill an elk. Ideally, the team members would have learned the necessary techniques as older adolescents, allowed to witness how the pack performs in the hunt. But now, with the elk herd stampeded, some of the rookies are running too far ahead, or behind, or misidentifying the best, most vulnerable moving container of food, and the whole herd will suffer for it.

A destructor has an easy opportunity here. Since the group will go through a "storming" cycle anyway, he can take advantage of the fact and elongate this counterproductive cycle. Recall that the inflation of the White Arrow is euphoric, its deflation excruciating. This team that just formed – why were those ranks assigned? Why weren't the higher ranks "given" to those who so unfairly populate the lower levels? Did you see the higher ranks' recent decisions? Aren't they absurd on their face? How can they expect us to pursue such an obviously flawed strategy? Don't they know what the reality of this situation is? In short, any instance of an inflated White Arrow – and they will be all around the group – can be used to delay (or even obliterate) group cohesion, which will elongate the Storming cycle.

And so the destructor adjusts the meme to maximize the length of the Storming cycle.

Sooner or later, though, the transition can be expected to move closer to Norming. Still, Norming is short of Performing, so the more this cycle can be elongated, the higher the odds that the organization will see an acceleration of its decline. The destructor must work against the tendency of the Norming team to become comfortable in the interactions among its members. A useful tactic here would be to introduce a narrative that *any* improved communication among the team members represents some sort of capitulation of one to the other. The concept that, in any interaction, one party represents an oppressor, with the other assumes the role of victim, can be most useful for the purposes of group disruption. Of course, such a narrative is intellectually vacuous, but it does appeal to those whose White Arrows are artificially high. They can't feel good about themselves for reasons completely exterior to their own thought processes, or even control. As a reminder, the set of high White Arrows includes:

- Fools,
- Politicians,
- Lone Wolves, and
- Alphas.

Since we dealt with the undermining of Alphas in the previous section, this leaves the Fools, Politicians, and Lone Wolves. The Lone Wolves are the most valuable target here, since, with their high Black Arrows, they have the most to offer the group once they enter into the Performing cycle. If these can be peeled away, the group suffers far more than from the loss of either the Fools or the Politicians.

Recall from the analysis of the Hawk-Dove Game, that the entire population maximizes its payoff when all of the birds act as doves, collecting their own foodstuffs and either consuming or storing them. And yet, with the introduction of just one Hawk, or a single bird (out of the population of, say, 100) selecting a mixed strategy that includes Hawkish behavior, the Nash Equilibrium for *all* of the birds will quickly assume a 75%–25% mix, with either 75% of the birds assuming Dove strategies all of the time, or the entire population adopting a mixed strategy that maximizes their payoff when they act like Doves in 75% of the iterations. When we overlay the Forming–Storming–Norming–Performing paradigm onto the Hawk-Dove Game, we see:

1. The Forming stage represents the establishment of the population in a set environment.
2. The Storming stage indicates the tendency of the members of the population to act more aggressively as the nominal Nash Equilibrium is being established via trial and error.
3. As false threats are peeled away, the population begins to alter the mix of their selected strategies, away from more aggressive (Hawk) and towards more cooperative (Dove) ones, as examples of working together in pursuit of the team's objectives become clearer and more widely recognized.
4. If the population can be managed via some sort of hierarchy (unlike our model project team, the Hawk-Dove Game assumes no working hierarchy or usable authority), then the remaining instances of competitive strategies can be reduced as the group continues its movement towards strategies that optimize payout.

By pulling into the analysis the Maccoby archetypes, it becomes plain that, while Gamesmen, Company Men, and (especially) Craftsmen can be counted on to eventually come to some sort of cooperative understanding among themselves, the Jungle Fighters, well, won't. Jungle Fighters get ahead, not by actually contributing to the attainment of the group's objectives, but by manipulating the narrative that accompanies the team as the team pursues said goals. The Jungle Fighters do this by diminishing the importance of the contributions of the others, while amplifying their own meager assistances, both acts of aggression. And, to the extent that the Hawk-Dove

Game is analogous to the interactions of newly formed project teams, the introduction of just one Hawk/Jungle Fighter will usually retard, or even reverse, the group's movement towards harmony and, therefore, performance.

The destructor needs to not only be aware of this oft-repeated cycle, but be in a position to take advantage of it. It's like the old joke about the two campers who are awakened by a grizzly bear rummaging through the edge of their camp, and ambling towards the two men. One of them quickly sets to putting on his running shoes.

"You're putting on your shoes? Why? That won't allow you to outrun that bear!"

"I don't have to outrun the bear – I only need to outrun *you*."

Similarly, since most organizations pursue objectives that are shared by other groups, the canny destructor knows that he doesn't have to single-handedly and completely bring down the target organization – he only have to hinder its pursuit of those objectives with respect to its competitors.

The Fools and Politicians in the organization really have little choice when it comes to their selection of strategies to undermine well-led teams. With their low Black Arrows, shifting to a strategy heavy on actual contributions would require extraordinary effort, if it were possible at all. On the other hand, Fools and Politicians have learned that, by employing more deceitful tactics, they can inflate their own Grey Arrows, or at least prevent their low Black Arrows from pulling down those Grey Arrows.

With a Little Help from Friends

In those instances where leadership is weak, the destructor's task is far easier. In Chapter 9 we saw Mitch struggle to advance his team in an organization already steeped in those social pathologies that work so effectively against a return of the group's rankings being returned to a meritocracy. Of course, with "Mitch" and his newspaper being fictitious entities, I had the opportunity to cheat a bit, and write Mitch and his strategies into the failure bin, but that doesn't mean that the pathologies he faced were fantastic. They exist in the real world and, when a destructor perceives them, such pathologies can easily be expanded and grown into team-wrecking inevitabilities.

Take nepotism/cronyism, the act of assigning rank, not according to demonstrated merit, but by preferences that have nothing to do with actual talent or accomplishments. A little bit of unwarranted promotion can go a long way, particularly when it results in Politicians assuming the ranks of Betas. From earlier in this chapter, one of the primary roles of the Beta is to serve as a brake against the potential excesses of the Alpha. When Politicians (or, Heaven help you, Fools) are assigned the rank that would otherwise be occupied by a valid Beta, they will not perform that function – far from it. These will be very much aware that the rank that they enjoy was not attained through talent or hard work, and that they are completely indebted to their sponsor. Challenging the very person you are completely indebted to for your ill-gotten rank over *any* poor decision, even one that clearly endangers the entire group, is not within the set of plausible strategies.

As the various members of the organization become acutely aware of the suspect technical direction being taken by the so-called leaders, the fact that members of the second tier are either unable or unwilling to assume the role of champion for the meritocracy will also become apparent. At this point, how easy will it be for potential destructors to present a narrative that the organization's own leaders no longer have the whole group's best interest in mind, much less the benefit of the rank and file? Such destructors don't even have to dissemble – the truth will be perfectly effective in such instances.

Any deviation the group's hierarchy takes from assigning rank based on merit is damaging, as we analyzed in Chapter 9, and that is unfortunate, as far as it goes. However, such deviations from the meritocracy also allow the introduction of narratives, both accurate and mildly embellished, that can wreck the morale among members. Again, each member of voluntarily joined groups will carry with them the expectation that, in exchange for contributing to the group's stated objectives, they will be able to benefit personally. When it becomes widely known within the ranks that not only have the leaders indulged their own personal preferences at the expense of the overall organization, but that its members now face significantly lower chances of fulfilling their own personal goals, the very fabric that holds the group together is torn to shreds. Project teams in the middle of the Storming cycle are particularly vulnerable – any elongation of this cycle is bound to be detrimental to the organization as a whole.

Meanwhile, Back at Midtown High

Recall the discussion from Chapter 5, and the formation of cliques at Midtown High School. These cliques, or sub-tiered organizations, generally have nothing at all to do with the stated objective of the organization to which they belong, in this case, educating adolescents to prepare them for either gainful employment or further education. They exist solely for the benefit of their members' survival, in some circumstances; in others, social hierarchical advancement. Since members of high schools are at least somewhat compelled to attend, the creation and sustainment of cliques is pretty much unavoidable. In organizations where membership is more voluntary, or even privileged, the power and reach of cliques to influence individuals' behavior may be muted, but it's almost never negated. Inner-city high schools in the United States are often afflicted by gangs, and membership in gangs is often perceived as necessary to simply survive until graduation. Conversely, the bonds of spontaneously formed teams at, say, the United States Naval Academy at Annapolis do not nominally carry with them life-or-death implications, at least not until after graduation.

So, our destructor needs to be able to assess the strength of the bonds of the sub-orgs, or cliques, within the target organization. In corporations, cliques tend to form more often among those with low Black Arrows, to wit:

- Omegas,
- Fools,
- Politicians, and
- Comedians.

Why? Because these are fortunate to belong to the group at all. They can't exhibit their advanced utility to the team, because they don't have any. They *must* form cooperative units within the macro organization to help each other maintain their facades, that (a) they belong, (b) have something to contribute, and (c) deserve whatever rank they currently enjoy.

The remaining archetypes, Alphas, Betas, Lone Wolves, and Cinderellas, may be less inclined to become involved in cliques, but they will not be immune. Indeed, an exhibited inclination to select the disengagement strategy can often serve as a signal to others that the member doing so belongs to the high Black Arrow contingent, at least as far as cliques are involved.

Which brings us back to Scott, at Midtown. After a couple of weeks of regularly interacting with Lori, Phyllis, Tammy, Celeste, Nancy, Audra, Jeff, Mitch, Jim, Chris, Marcus, and Eike, Scott has decided that this clique, as currently constituted, ought to be disintegrated. Not because he dislikes them, far from it. Scott recognizes that these genuinely okay kids have anointed the highly irksome Jeff as their leader, but Jeff is no Alpha. Scott realizes that, if he is ever going to have a chance at developing a relationship with Nancy, he can't risk an overt challenge from Jeff that would demean his budding manhood, personhood, or even qualifications to belong to the clique. Whatever machinations took place previously that led to the clique's current state of affairs, Scott simply must dissolve the bonds that exist that keep Jeff in a high rank.

This clique, as presently constituted, must end, and Scott must do it.

He sets about his task by selecting the following strategies:

- First, he must make more of himself by devoting more energy to his studies (inflating his Black Arrow), and works hard to excel at any extracurricular activities he chooses to engage.
- Next, he must make a conscious effort to keep a reasonable perspective on the challenges before him, and his competition – the other students seeking higher grades. The moment Scott begins to feel comfortable that he doesn't need to expend extra effort to pursue higher placement among his classmates (his White Arrow begins to inflate), he is weakened.
- Finally, Scott needs to undermine the narrative that Jeff rode to the leadership position, since it's obvious that Jeff is no Alpha. Jeff is arrogant and condescending, far more consistent with the Politician archetype than a genuine Alpha.

As Scott pours his energies into his studies, he also develops his relationships with Mitch, Chris, Marcus, and Eike. He communicates that he likes them, and in no way seeks to attain any rank higher than they currently enjoy within the clique. He's happy just to hang out with them, and they know it. Scott does not present as the Omega – he'll immediately challenge any put-down sent his way, but on the same level it was presented. Humor is met with humor, teasing with teasing. Mocks he calls out for what they are, without assuming the role of victim. This happened one lunch hour, with Eike.

"I saw you skate to school this morning," Eike begins. "You don't have better transportation than that?"

"Ja, und auch deine Mutter," Scott responds with the only German phrase he knows. Surprised that Scott knows German at all, Eike is tempted to escalate the challenge. "My mother does not *skate*!"

"Yeah, I remember that. You mentioned previously that she actually drives a BMW, right?"

"Yes, she does," Eike confirms, with some satisfaction.

"Not an Audi?" Scott jibes.

"The 320 series is better than the comparable Audis."

"Even the Quattro?"

At this point Eike realizes that he's unlikely to be able to clearly assert a superior knowledge of cars over Scott; and, in case the reader isn't familiar with the importance of an advanced knowledge of the relative merits of automobiles among pubescent boys, it's, well, important.

"Until I can afford either," Scott continues, "I'm confined to the skateboard. Do tell your Mom to avoid hitting any skateboarders she comes across, would you?"

Scott has signaled a couple of things here, most notably (1) while he's pretty much forced to ride a skateboard for transportation, that's not really a completely acceptable state of affairs for him, and (2) Eike has been granted a way out of presenting like an elitist jerk, should he accept it.

He does.

"I'll pass that along."

As Scott responds to challenges with wit and humor, he simultaneously communicates non-aggression with a refusal to be placed in the Omega category. As he does so, he leaves each encounter with the non-Jeff members of his clique with an overall positive feeling. Conversely, every boy's encounter with Jeff leaves them with a subtle but unmistakable feeling that some amount of downward pressure has been placed on their White Arrows. It's how Jeff, and other non-valid Alpha leaders, reinforce their own feelings of confidence in their ranks. By jabbing the other males in the pack (strikethrough) clique, and seeing that they will not respond in kind, Jeff reinforces his status without having to actually do anything to improve his true value, i.e., inflate his Black Arrow. Jeff is stronger than the other guys in the clique, due to his genes and a willingness to spend time in the gym. However, this being high school, the others will mature into young men at their own pace, even if it's slightly behind Jeff's. As they do so, they will realize that some choices that they had previously rejected out of hand are becoming more available and attractive, namely, either responding more aggressively to Jeff's micro aggressions, or even disengaging from the clique.

This latter option, of disengaging, need not be as dramatic nor final as the Lone Wolf leaving the pack. Other relationships within the clique will not automatically dissolve upon limited disengagement, as would happen in the wolfpack. Also, singular Lone Wolves might be able to peel off some females as they start their own, competitor pack. The choices available to the girls in high school cliques are not nearly so Boolean. Should Mitch, Jim, Chris, Marcus, and Eike join Scott in a widespread act of mild disengagement, Jeff, as well as the girls, will have been forced into a graded choice, with several steps in-between the extremes of enduring an upheaval of the clique's hierarchy, or witnessing its de facto dissolution.

Note that Scott need not embrace any untoward motives – he's just trying to avoid an inappropriately placed low ranking, while influencing circumstances and people to maximize his chances of cultivating a relationship with Nancy. The rankings of the clique as he encountered it were against his achievement of both of these goals, so he set out to change the landscape in front of him to help him realize his objectives.

In this instance, it's really as simple as that, though in other venues some other, more malignant and pungent motives and tactics can readily come into play.

As Scott moves closer to a place where he is better positioned to disengage, he's also signaling that he isn't a Fool, Politician, Omega, or Comedian. While it may remain vague if he's really an Alpha or Beta in hiding, or a Cinderella or potential Lone Wolf, he is producing clues that, at least on some level, Scott is convinced of a higher-than-average placement of his Black Arrow. A belief that one's Black Arrow is higher than average, when coupled with a belief that they're no better than their companions, is properly defined as confidence. Faith that one is superior to their compatriots without a certainty that their Black Arrow is actually higher is arrogance, which is why a critical part of Scott's strategy must be to keep his White Arrow tamped down.

As he pursues these strategies, the others around him begin to get a sense that interactions with Scott leave them feeling a bit better about themselves than similar interactions with Jeff. If Scott can keep this trend going, without some dramatic event by which Jeff performs some act of near heroism that benefits the group as a whole, this particular clique at Midtown High School will experience a hierarchical upheaval, or even cease to function as a closely knit unit at all. Get-togethers, group dates, and parties that would have normally included the entire clique will begin to be held at times when everybody knows Jeff is unavailable, and then at times when he is available, but simply not invited.

As Jeff becomes aware that his rank is endangered, not due to any direct challenge from a specific member, but because the group he supposedly leads is starting to exclude him from some of its functions, his options are few.

- He can react aggressively, but with no target such a strategy would be counterproductive in the extreme. Challenging Mitch (the clique's Beta) to a fight would help exactly nothing, and Jeff has no idea that it's Scott's actions that are undermining the group's willingness to endure his rank-confirming taunts.
- He can attempt to repair the relationships he knows are damaged, such as the one with Tammy, and hope that that quells the overall group's trend away from spending time with him.
- Jeff can perform some act that reaffirms his value to the overall clique (a demonstration of the high position of his Black Arrow), or, as a corollary, can threaten to leave on his own in order to compel the group to consider for themselves what his value to them might mean.
- He can attempt to self-demote, or at least leave off his previous efforts at asserting his Alpha status. This strategy is rather rare, for two reasons: (1) it's painful to have one's White Arrow deflated, and (2) it almost never works. The unasked question will always be, why was Jeff previously highly thought of, but is no longer (i.e., what happened to his Grey Arrow, and why)?
- Finally, he can elect to disengage from the clique himself, and justify it after the fact by any means that prevents a significant deflation of his White Arrow.

Note that most of these strategies play right into Scott's plans. With Jeff seeking to either behave better towards his perceived inferiors, or else disengaging from them altogether, the odds of a dramatic arrow-lowering confrontation with Scott diminish significantly, leaving Scott the latitude to engage in courtship behaviors with Nancy, behaviors that are easily mocked or otherwise abused by rank-coveting competitors.

As fate would have it for our illustrative friends from Midtown, Jeff has decided to spend less time with his previous clique and more time with the members of the school's wrestling team. Mitch's transition to the Alpha role is relatively harmonious, since he never really sought the role, and has little intention of spending energy in reminding the others of his exalted rank. Scott and Nancy do end up dating, and even going steady – briefly. It turns out that Nancy, while pretty, is something of an airhead, and tends to lose interest in most things after a brief period of time, specific boys not excepted.

Years pass, and Scott is the married father of two. He occasionally thinks back to his time at Midtown High, and how most of the kids in his long-standing clique went on to white-collar careers and marriages, while Jeff dropped out of college to become a police officer in a small town. Scott can't help but think – was it the individual pressures involved in staying in the clique that led to his success, or was it something else? Most pointedly, was there something – anything – that Jeff should have done from his early leadership role that would have led to his staying in the clique? How *does* a leader extend the life of his organization, and fend off the pathologies that lead to its early demise, or out-and-out destruction?

Notes

1 Sun Tzu, retrieved from *BrainyQuote*, http://www.brainyquote.com/quotes/authors/s/sun_tzu.html, July 5, 2015.
2 Alinsky, Saul D., *Rules for Radicals: A Pragmatic Primer for Realistic Radicals*. New York: Random House, 1971.

Chapter 11

Preventing the Group's Destruction

> The two most important things to do for self-defense are not to take a martial arts class or get a gun, but to think like the opposition and know where you're most at risk.
>
> Barry Eisler[1]

Actually, this title is also something of a misnomer, since, as we have seen, virtually all organizations have a finite lifespan. A better title may be "Preventing the Group's Destruction in the Near Term," or "Thwarting the Efforts of Those Who Seek to Accelerate the Group's Destruction," but the one I chose is sufficiently pithy for a chapter heading.

So, how *does* one defend the organization against either the deliberate onslaught of its destructors, or the adopting of those organizational pathologies that tend to naturally afflict group constructs, and accelerate their decline?

The first and most important step is to recognize that a problem exists. No matter how harmonious your group, and no matter how swimmingly you are outperforming the competition, there are going to be real forces in play that can and will accelerate the demise of any team. As assessed earlier, The Beatles remain the most successful music group *in history* and, at least throughout the 1960s, its members rather close. According to Jean-Michel Guesdon and Philippe Margotin, by the time *The Beatles* (commonly known as *The White Album*) was released, they could hardly stand to be in the same recording studio with each other.[2]

I co-authored a paper with the incomparable Dave Post on the topic of analyzing the readiness of a given group of people to accept change in the form of an advancement in capability, where Dave made use of a Gaussian Curve to illustrate his take (Figure 11.1).

In this 100-person organization, the As represent those who readily accept change, and were probably those who purchased Beta-Max VCR players (if you don't know what a VCR is, much less a Beta-Max version, ask your parents, since you are way too young). Category B represents those people who are initially opposed to the change, but will come around once they are convinced that it's good for them and/or the organization. The people represented in the C band are those who are actively opposed to change, and will only participate in the enhanced capability being introduced if they are metaphorically dragged into it, kicking and screaming.

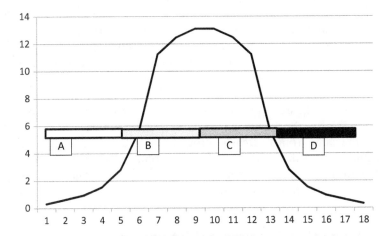

Figure 11.1 Categories of Acceptance/Rejection Model

That leaves the Ds. The people represented in the D band of Figure 11.1 will *never* cooperate with the change being brought into the group. Some of the Ds will disengage, but it's important for the defender of the organization to know that they will never all go away. There will always be at least one member of larger groups who either harbors ill will towards the team as a whole, or else seeks the strategic elimination of a significant part of its leadership for personal reasons.

Possible reasons for a desire to accelerate the decline of the group as a whole were addressed in Chapter 10. Personal reasons for doing so will invariably include issues with the destructor's White Arrow, e.g., the destructor's rank is below where they think they ought to be (gap between White and Grey Arrows), or the leader engages in gratuitous put-downs as a regular part of reminding others of his status (as Jeff did with the Midtown High School clique), which represents a kind of ubiquitous, background radiation pushing downwards on everyone else's White Arrow. There will also be instances where the energy spent in pursuit of a hierarchical upheaval are appropriate, as we saw earlier with the examples of Ulysses Grant during the American Civil War, and Scott versus Jeff in their clique at Midtown High School. As with the possible motives of the destructor, it is rather impossible to catalogue all of the defender's motives, much less pass judgment on their validity. What we can do, though, is to review the likely source of those motives (Chapter 3), common strategies used in the pursuit of the tearing down of the group (previous chapter), and ways of defending against those strategies (this chapter).

Again, a quick assessment for the defender: why should you defend this particular organization, in this particular configuration? Efforts to prop up a failing organization that has swerved into an invalid purpose have the same overall effect of throwing support to an organization that was invalid from its inception, the only difference being the naiveté of the supporter.

As in the case of the destructor, the ranking of the defender will have a significant impact on her ability to defend against the detrimental attitudes, narratives, and behaviors that rend organizations asunder. Omegas are in a very poor position to execute their strategies, one way or the other. Conversely (and also similarly to the destructors), Alphas and Betas are in excellent positions to thwart attempts at organization diminishment – indeed, such thwarting is an inherent aspect of those roles. The remainder of the group – the wolfpack's muddling middle – are far from helpless, even if they do not have access to the same range of strategies enjoyed by group leadership.

Organizing an effective defense requires a structured strategy, and a proactive one at that. Waiting on a potential destructor to move so that a counter-move may be employed is to play the game from a defensive crouch. It also has the added disadvantage of not being able to catch the incidental, almost automatic detrimental influences that afflict groups without being transmitted by a willing destructor. The organization of the defense should take the following steps.

Step 1: Acknowledge that Detrimental Influences Are Present

As stated in the previous paragraphs, the seeds of the group's destruction are already in place, either implicitly or explicitly. I've been studying the martial arts for over 25 years, and have acquired my black belt in Kenpo Karate. I was talking with a colleague when that fact came up, and he was astonished.

"You mean, you could go into any city's downtown, into any bar or lounge, and just order a drink, without being afraid of your surroundings?"

"No, not really. In fact, a key aspect of training to become a black belt involves never putting yourself in that kind of a situation, where you would be in an unfamiliar, potentially hazardous situation. And, if for whatever reason you do find yourself in that kind of a position, you immediately begin searching for avenues of escape, items that can be used as weapons, easily defended positions, and so forth."

There's a well-known study of a number of inmates convicted of violent crimes who were shown videos of cityscapes, of people walking up and down the sidewalks, and were asked, if they were to pick any of those people to attack or mug, whom would they select? The inmates tended to select the same individuals, over and over. When asked why those particular people presented as more tempting targets, the responses were usually along the lines that those people did not appear to be fully aware of their surroundings. In fact, awareness of surroundings (or lack thereof) became more of a determining factor than perceived weakness.

This is why the first step in designing an organization's defense has to be an awareness, or acknowledgment that belligerent forces exist, and, indeed, are already in place. Ignorance of this fact represents one of the biggest, but also one of the most easily corrected, vulnerabilities out there.

Step 2: Identify the Precise Source of the Threat

It's an unfortunate aspect of popular culture to hijack psychological terms to describe everyday attitudes or behaviors, such as an ability to understand or even pursue significantly different ideas or goals simultaneously being misidentified as schizophrenia. However, the perception that an unrecognized yet existential threat may exist is due to a psychosis – paranoia – may be the most debilitating of them all. The threats do exist – the only question is, from exactly where do they emanate, and what is the appropriate response?

Threats to the organization will typically come from three categories of sources, which tend to mirror the Berne archetypes of Child–Adult–Parent aspects of the persona.

- Interior to the organization, i.e., a member of the group will seek to hasten its demise for the reasons addressed above, often centered on advancing or defending their rank, or White Arrow placement.
- Exterior to the organization but interior to its immediate environment, such as the other cliques at Midtown High School, subscribers and advertisers to Mitch's newspaper, or the availability of game animals in the selected hunting ground of the wolfpack.
- Exterior to both the organization and its immediate environment, such as the teams from the other high schools in Midtown's locale, other forms of communication about current events that compete with Mitch's newspaper, or other apex predators which may seek to displace our pet wolfpack, should ours control a more attractive, game-rich environment.

The threats to the organization may come from one or more of these sources and, of course, they may present in such a way as to require simultaneous responses.

Step 3: Reduce or Eliminate the Group's Vulnerabilities

The proactive strategies involve steeling the organization against the nominal threats from each of step 2's potential sources. Each proactive strategy is predicated upon the following essentials:

- The group being defended has a valid reason for existence, and its membership is largely (or even exclusively) voluntary (and yet, even those groups whose membership is mandatory, such as a military organization in time of war, can benefit from many of these strategies).
- The group is well led, or at least has as a fundamental precept of its functioning some form of process that recognizes and elevates genuine merit, while also recognizing members who are not deserving of advanced rank, and also maintaining the machinery that executes rank adjustments in a timely and even-handed manner.
- The group has two key mechanisms in place, in whatever format: (1) a way for leadership to be made aware of facts or occurrences that call into question whether or not they have selected the best technical approach to a given organization-wide problem, and (2) the opposite, or mechanisms that work as a brake on mechanism (1), an accepted process that prevents invalid challenges to the leadership's decisions from leading all the way to an inappropriate hierarchical upheaval.

If these three essentials are accommodated, then a fairly robust defense can be formulated. If not, the target organization's defenses may still be upgraded, though to the point of being effective enough to fend off the inevitable challenges will remain suspect. I refer to the above three bullets as essential because, without these in place, the organization will retain profound systemic vulnerabilities, vulnerabilities which dramatically increase the odds of a successful take-down.

The unavoidable attacks will come from a knowable set of paths. Like the protagonists in the 1986 science fiction thriller *Aliens*, who are forced to retreat to a defensible part of the colony in order to survive the approaching onslaught from the spikey-toothed monsters, each of the possible avenues of attack will need to be recognized and managed, though, one would hope, the failure to do so will not result in being bitten to death.

In preparing for these defenses, the key element has to do with the power of narratives, or memes. While this topic will be addressed in more detail in the following chapter, for now suffice to note that there will be stories or scripts that arise within the target organization that serve as structures to connect occurrences and facts into a consistent story that allows for some level of accurate prediction of how the future of the organization will unfold. Once a widely accepted narrative connects the known facts and interpretations of why the organization's history unfolded the way it did in such a way as to point to its immediate or painful downfall, the target organization is all but lost at that point. In other words, once the *Titanic* began to founder by the bow, nobody wanted to be in the *Titanic* Passengers' Club.

Of course, influencing what people believe about the facts they know and the relationship between the things they encounter is a very tricky undertaking. The avenues that malignant versions of the organization's narrative will take resemble the lines of communication employed by Eric Berne, but with a twist. I would portray the group dynamic as in Figure 11.2. Like the Bernesian model of inter-person communications, the malignant narratives can be mapped as to–from arrows, but, unlike that model, these arrows will automatically represent a type of belligerence.

Attacks against the interior are aimed at sowing discord among the members of the targeted group, and can be initiated from sources both internal and external to the organization (Figure 11.3).

The narratives that undermine the group's shared, interior meme will generally seek to place downward pressure on the members' White Arrows. Examples include:

* Individuals who make up organizations that are voluntarily joined do so for both personal reasons and because they wish to see that organization's stated objectives come to pass. One simple and direct way of undercutting these members'

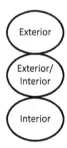

Figure 11.2 Defensive Structure of the Group

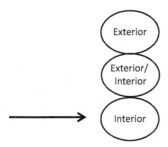

Figure 11.3 Attack Levied against the Group's Interior

initiatives is to propagate the narrative that they will either fail to attain their personal goals through the organization as constituted, the organization will fail to attain its goals without significant internal hierarchical upheaval, or both.

- The ranking system within the group is unfair, or rigged in such a way as to keep the current upper ranks ensconced in their positions, no matter what happens to the organization.
- The target group's leadership does not care about the rank and file.
- The target group's leadership has selected the wrong technical approach to attaining the overall organization's goals, and will lead all involved to ruin.
- At the other end of the spectrum, the group's Omegas are so backward and numerous, and represent such a drag on the group's ability to move forward, that their very presence represents ipso facto evidence that the organization is not truly dedicated to attaining the goals it has set for itself. Shorter version – how do those guys expect to get *anything* done if they have so much dead weight?

The point here is to impress upon the target group's members that the group is already afflicted with one or more fatal pathologies, and the act of continuing to support it is futile.

To defend against this attack variant, insightful leadership ensures that its preferred narrative – hopefully, the more accurate one – displaces the malignant variants. Leadership should engage in a variety of communication venues, aimed at ensuring that the members are confident that (a) the organization is well led, (b) is in place due solely to the workings of a fair and even-handedly enforced meritocracy, and (c) has the interests of each and every *cooperating* member in mind. The malignant narratives can take place within any organization, and there's really no way to completely prevent them from making inroads. However, the odds that these narratives will find traction and become widely accepted can be significantly diminished through employing tactics (a) through (c) above. Reasonable people will tend to accept the explanation that more reasonably fits the facts, which is why the opposite corollary, that unreasonable people will readily accept an unreasonable narrative, and can be led to act on that understanding, helps explain why people acting in mobs can be both extremely dangerous and prone to committing horrific acts.

In this structure, the incitement of large groups of people to commit mob violence represents a cataclysmic failure of a civic organization to communicate its true, valid narrative in such a way as to displace a malignant alternative. And, while police attempting to quell rioters provides a dramatic and unmistakable sign of this type of failure, many organizations have fallen prey to a far more subtle manifestation of this type of breakdown, the failure to prevent an organization's Interior/Child persona from adopting malignant narratives that ultimately undermine the host. And, unlike cases of slander or libel brought before a court of law, truth is not an automatic, unassailable defense. There is no evidence that Marie Antoinette ever said "Let them eat cake." In fact, there is significant scholarship to suggest that, far from insulated and disdainful of the poorer members of French society in the late eighteenth century, she was rather a champion for the downtrodden in King Louis' court. No matter – the Jacobins had a malignant narrative that the majority of the citizens would adopt, and through that adoption would commit horrific acts. In this, and many other cases, the truth had no chance against a readily adopted, malignant narrative.

Could Marie and the rest of Louis XVI's court have been saved if they had taken more aggressive, more effective steps to counter the Jacobins' poisonous memes? Who knows? But the fact that history unfolded the way it did lends itself to such speculation. In any event, I don't believe that there can really be any question that the inability of Louis' court to overturn, or really even effectively challenge, the Jacobin's narrative represented a material cause (if not proximate cause) of his dynasty's downfall. (The power of narratives to influence matters political and, by extension, all of us, will be addressed further in Chapters 12 and 13.)

Attacks against the interior/exterior component of the organization are aimed at interfering with the target group's ability to carry out its function or selected strategies as it pursues its lateral objectives (Figure 11.4). A prime example of this type of attack narrative has to do with those online services that allow customers of corporations to comment on their perceptions of the quality of those company's goods or services. Such services allow for satisfied customers to relay their experiences, as well as dissatisfied ones. It also enables enemies of the company to post malicious comments that interfere with or discourage the company's relationship with potential customers.

Managing the organization's communications is the default defense in these avenues of attack. There are actually companies that will help other companies "manage" their image on the world wide web, in case the target company has been subjected to inordinate, unfair postings. In the project management realm, most successful project teams will have some form of a "zipper plan," which is a structure for how the

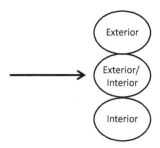

Figure 11.4 Attack Levied against the Group's Interior/Exterior

members of the team interact with their counterparts from the customer's organization. As teeth of a zipper connect with their same counterparts every time something is zipped up, so, too, do the project team's design engineers interact with their appropriate customer counterparts, as do the administrators, foremen, etc. In this way the odds of either a destructor or an inept team member communicating a damaging opinion or incorrect assessment are minimized.

While economic concerns – corporations, or companies – have clearly identifiable customers, other groups whose objectives are not necessarily economic in type will also have those who are neither (a) part of the organization, or (b) a member of a competing organization, who are, nevertheless, important to the group's ongoing concerns. The mid-level avenue of attack that must be recognized and defended, then, has to do with any attempt to interfere with the relationship the target group has with these people.

Attacks against just the exterior component of the organization are aimed at preventing the group from attaining its overarching objectives, and will almost always come from the group's competitors (Figure 11.5). When companies engage in advertising, particularly the so-called vampire ads, or advertisements that specifically name their competitors, they are employing a type of attack against their competitors, with market share being the main gradient. Luring away a competing organization's talent is another form of this kind of attack, as are any tactics that damage or hinder the group with respect to its competition.

Since virtually no organizations (outside of monopolies) have any level of effective control over what their competitors do, no standard set of defenses can be offered up, either. That being said, organizations that rely on any kind of technology to attain their stated objectives are particularly vulnerable to being overcome by competitors who can access and deploy technological breakthroughs in the pursuit of *their* objectives. While this is obviously true in areas like companies involved in consumer electronics or software, it's also (chillingly) true of other, life-altering groups, such as the military, or political parties. The English saw many successes against the French during the Hundred Years' War, even though all of the battles were fought on French soil, and almost always with the French outnumbering the English. Shakespeare would have us believe it was due to the righteousness of the British cause; the truth, however, is more likely to be that the French could not come up with a technological answer to the longbow until muskets became the primary weapon of infantry. When personal

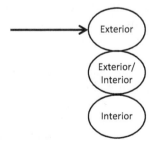

Figure 11.5 Attack Levied against the Group's Exterior

computers first became common, Microsoft® Corporation's Disk Operating System, or DOS, was the only way to invoke the specific software applications you wanted to run. Once Apple® made the point-and-click capabilities of Graphic User Interface (GUI) available, DOS, empire builder that it was, was doomed. Had Microsoft® not followed suit, even though it brought on a lawsuit from Apple®, they would have lost out completely to *any* competition successfully deploying GUI-type systems.

Since technological advances do represent either a profound vulnerability (when a competitor gets it) or an advanced capability (when the target organization gets it first), organizations so situated tend to employ three options:

- invest in obtaining the tech advance yourself (the *Get Smart* strategy),
- invest in the resources necessary to take the advances from your competition (espionage, lawsuits, etc., which I'll name the *Kaos* strategy),
- or a combination of both.

Since advances in capability or technology generally depend on the existence of talent (high Black Arrows) within the organization, and those with high Black Arrows tend to belong to one of the four coveted types (Alpha, Beta, Cinderella, and Lone Wolf), the existence within the group of any of the aforementioned organizational pathologies that take the group away from a pure meritocracy will tend to drive away the very types of members the organization needs to survive in such an environment.

But the tendency of organizations that have veered away from assigning rank based on merit to drive away the very members it needs is only one instance of organizational pathologies leading to a weakening of such organizations. Poor communications, sub-standard recognition devices, the perception that the organization tolerates poor performers within the ranks – these all end up weakening the group, even if the negative results do not come about in a timely manner, or for all to see. Which brings us to step 4.

Step 4: Calibrate the Organization's Internal Defense Systems

I was a columnist for *PMNetwork* magazine for over ten years. In that time the Project Management Institute® editors were really good sports about letting me challenge the conventional wisdom, since those axioms often struck me as little more than eat-your-peas-style hectoring, wrapped in management science terminology. The widely accepted memes weren't wrong, per se, but it was a genuine rarity when a given management-science publication produced a document that resembled a Kuhnsian-style paradigm-shift argument, or theory.

But the things they did say, about the need to improve communications, or to upgrade quality control, all needed to be said, since, when embraced, they would make the embracing organizations stronger and better able to thwart many of the pathologies that tend to afflict project teams. However, I will not simply punt to the idea that *all* of that hectoring should be embraced and attempts should be made at incorporation: a structure needs to be established, that helps add the necessary amount of perspective, or proportion. To help clarify this structure, let's return to our White/Grey/Black Arrow model (Figure 11.6).

From Chapter 8, these are the relative rankings for Scott. Now consider a rank, a level of value to the organization that's considered to be the bare minimum, or floor, beneath which the already admitted member would be recognized as adding no value (Figure 11.7).

In Figure 11.7, I've drawn two thick lines, at the 1.5 and 0.5 marks (on a scale of 1 to 9). The 1.5 line represents that point of actual contribution (technically, Black Arrow, but practically, Grey Arrow) that, should the corresponding arrow drop below that point, the others in the group would recognize that the lower-ranked member is not contributing, and perhaps should not belong to the group at all. The 0.5 floor is the point at which the member's contribution is so low that they represent a drag on everyone else, or else are deliberately engaging in activities to delay, hinder, or even stop the group from achieving its objectives (e.g., treason), and must be actively expunged from the organization.

As stated previously, almost all groups will have some mechanism in place to deal with its low performers, even those teams besot with the pathologies that interfere or undermine a true merit-based structure. The tactics inherent in these mechanisms will kick in when the target member's behavior throws off clues that their Black Arrows

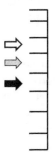

Figure 11.6 Nominal Three-Arrow Model Rank Scale

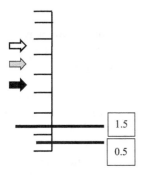

Figure 11.7 Floor Scales

have sunk below these minimum levels. And yet, these mechanisms themselves can readily incorporate the very pathologies they seek to prevent.

The group's auto-immune function, then, will need to be evaluated for its efficacy if the group is to sustain an effective defense. This becomes something of a quality control effort. In quality control circles, two events are sought out:

- The Alpha event (not to be confused with our archetype) occurs when a widget on the production line is identified as faulty when, in fact, it is perfectly within approved product specifications.
- The Beta event (again, not our archetype) occurs when a faulty widget passes all inspections and is made available to the consumer, but is, in fact, faulty.

With respect to building a structured defense against organization-wrecking threats, the mechanisms that the group employs to jettison unbearably poor performers becomes the quality standard, applied, in this case, to the members of the group. Modified, they represent two events:

- Those times when a truly meritorious member is falsely accused of being a poor performer.
- Those occurrences when a poor performer (low Black Arrow) is indulged in their behaviors that are actually detrimental to the organization, but it isn't recognized or, even more insidious, it is recognized, but the response is not appropriate, nor consistent.

Which type of event represents the greater threat will vary greatly based on the organization itself, its environments or markets, the extent it has already adopted non- (or even anti-) meritocracy practices, and hundreds of other parameters. What can be reasonably asserted, though, is that whatever mechanisms are in place to help ensure that organizational threats are recognized and dealt with in a timely manner, they must be both effective and evenly enforced, or else they become an organizational pathology all to themselves.

One of the things I find most interesting about the use of quality control event types in evaluating the way groups assign members' ranks is the nice, neat way that the alpha and beta *events* line up with our archetypes.

- The alpha event – those occurrences where a truly meritorious member is falsely accused of being (or assumed to be) a poor performer can *only* happen to those with high Black Arrows (Cinderellas, Lone Wolves, Betas, Alphas). Assuming a low Black Arrow for one whose Black Arrow is actually low isn't an error.
- Conversely, the beta event – assigning a higher rank to a member who does not deserve it based on merit – can only happen to those with a low Black Arrow (Politicians, Comedians, Omegas, and Fools).

Staying within this structure, then, it becomes apparent that the only way an alpha event can come about is if *somebody* within the organization can successfully bring effective downward pressure on the high performers' Grey Arrows. The overall organization must accept a narrative that the true contribution(s) of the Cinderella, Alpha,

Lone Wolf, or Beta isn't all that. In other words, these archetypes must be made to look like their low Black Arrow counterparts:

- Alphas must be made out to be Politicians,
- Lone Wolves to be Fools,
- Cinderellas to Omegas, and
- Betas to Comedians.

For the beta event, the exact opposite is true: those with low Black Arrows need to present themselves as their high Black Arrow counterparts:

- Omegas need to appear as Cinderellas,
- Comedians pretend to be Betas,
- Fools present as Lone Wolves, and
- Politicians want to be viewed as Alphas.

I'm going to name these two strategies *Rank Impersonating* and *Rank Cutting*. *Rank Impersonating* is the act of articulating or maintaining a narrative that suggests that the impersonator is of more value to the organization than is verifiably so, i.e., their Black Arrow is higher than it is. Since Black Arrow placement has nothing to do with external influences, this works out as an attempt to influence one's Grey Arrow in an upward direction.

Conversely, *Rank Cutting* is the act of introducing or perpetrating the meme that a high-ranking member does not actually possess the ability or willingness to contribute to the group's objectives commensurate with their rank. Since, again, Black Arrows are not subject to narratives, this tactic plays out as an attempt to place downward pressure on the Grey Arrows of the possessors of high Black Arrows, à la Alinsky.

An interesting side note is that, since *Rank Cutting* can only truly manifest as an effort to drive down the Grey Arrows of those with high Black Arrows, the two archetypes with high Black Arrows *but already depressed Grey Arrows* (Cinderellas and Lone Wolves) tend to be resistant to this strategy. Similarly, with respect to the *Rank Impersonating* strategy, since Omegas can't become Cinderellas without attaining some level of true value to the group, their efforts at inflating their Grey Arrows, if successful, will result in their becoming Comedians instead. Fools morph into not Lone Wolves, but Politicians.

For the less ambitious members of the group, a strategy I'll name *Arrow Resting* becomes a tempting selection. *Arrow Resting* involves the afflicted members' ability to recognize and evaluate the mechanism(s) their group employs to reject those whose Black Arrows drop below the minimum level – the floor – and adjust their actual performance to the point just above that one. These members are content to simply remain members of their target group, which is not to say that they are automatically excluded from those who would engage in *Rank Impersonating* or *Rank Cutting*. In times of group-wide duress, the expunging of non- or low performers from its ranks is a common tactic. In our model, it is as if upward pressure is being brought to bear on the floors, with the threat that the floor will be pushed above the arrow resters' exhibited Black Arrow (Figure 11.8).

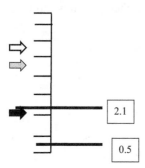

Figure 11.8 Floor Shifting Overtaking an Arrow Rester

When this particular Arrow Rester (who just happened to be a Politician) first analyzed the minimum amount of actual contribution he needed to feel confident the group would not reject him, the floor that the organization was using was set at 1.5 (not that any group would quantify such a subjective parameter, but bear with me). Because the group has encountered difficulties, its reduced benefits distribution has become unacceptably low to its members. The benefits do not appear to be increasing (or increasable) in the near future, so the only answer it sees for itself is to reduce the number of recipients. Naturally, it will seek to keep its better performers, or those with high Black Arrows, which leaves the other four archetypes vulnerable. Within the model, the line representing the floor has been raised, above the point where our Politician's Black Arrow had rested.

Now our Politician has two choices before him. He can (1) quickly put forth the effort to contribute more, but raising one's Black Arrow rarely happens quickly. Or, he can (2) start devoting time and energy into preventing the others in the group from perceiving that his contribution is below the minimum acceptable level. In other words, he must either inflate (or at least maintain) his Grey Arrow, or else prevent the downward pressure on it that comes about as a natural tendency for Grey Arrows to follow Black Arrows. And, in order to do *that*, the two general strategies they must employ if they eschew doing nothing will be either *Rank Impersonating, Rank Cutting,* or some of each.

So, what's the best defense against these strategies? Note that the archetypes whose Grey Arrows are either aligned with their Black Arrows, or with Grey Arrows below their Black Arrows, are naturally resistant to this type of attack. It follows, then, that two natural defensive strategies would be the most effective:

- Remember those mechanisms that the organization employs to prevent the meritorious from being downgraded, and the merit-lacking from being promoted? Work to strengthen the capacity to accurately align the members' perceived value (Grey Arrow) with their true value to the group (Black Arrow).
- Don't allow into the organization poor performers in the first place.

Okay, okay, I know that the second bullet, if doable, would be performed in almost every case, and that it would solve a whole host of issues beyond improving the efficacy of an organization's rank assignment system. But it does point to our last step in constructing a structured group defense.

Step 5: Eliminate the Internal Threats

This is a very tricky step, even if your organization is thoroughly Machiavellian and somewhat cold-hearted when it comes to ridding the group of its poor performers, dead weights, and detractors. The streamlining group runs the risk of committing an act of what I'll call *seagulling*, named after the response from the society of seagulls from *Jonathan Livingston Seagull*. In that novelette, young Jonathan Livingston is a seagull who is enamored with his ability to fly. He works and works at his flying, and experiments with ways of doing it better and faster. Jonathan eventually discovers a way to fly faster than any other known seagull, but, when observed doing so, is banished from seagull society, which perceives his remarkable flying achievement as an aberration. In short, it's important to avoid alpha events. Recall the voyeur effect discussed in Chapter 5 – those with high Black Arrows generally retain the ability to identify others of value, and they are watching the organization's rank-establishing behavior. If they observe that the organization abruptly punishes or even ejects a valid Alpha, Beta, Lone Wolf, or Cinderella, they will draw the easy conclusion, that the so-behaving organization is not currently a meritocracy, if it ever was. Confirmed in their interpretation that, not only is true merit not recognized or rewarded, but that their past contributions have probably gone unrecognized, their confidence in the decision to stay with the group evaporates. The Cinderellas may be used to it – the other three high Black Arrow archetypes will be aggravated, and will probably respond accordingly.

In economic organizations – companies and corporations – most Western nations have laws in place that help protect all employees, contributors and detractors alike, from abrupt or capricious dismissal absent a clear violation of company policy or criminal law. While these laws were created in order to protect employees, they also actually help corporations avoid seagulling its contributing members who have fallen afoul of leadership. On the flip side, though, these laws do make it more difficult for corporations to jettison poor performers, or even active detractors.

In other, non-money making groups, the Alphas or Betas will usually respond to a need to be rid of poor or non-performers by making participation in group activities incrementally less fulfilling for the targeted non-performer. However, since making the experience of participating in (voluntarily joined) group activities less attractive, or even unpleasant, can and will be undertaken by others in the group (as in the *Rank Cutting* strategy), canny Alphas and Betas will be alert to others executing behaviors that are appropriately left to Alphas and Betas. Indeed, the very existence of Cinderellas or Lone Wolves within the organization is evidence that some version of this inappropriate Grey Arrow suppression has already taken place, or is currently operating. And, just for the record, it ought to be noted that the only types likely to engage in Grey Arrow suppression outside of misguided Alphas and Betas are those with low Black Arrows.

So, for the tactics within the Step of Eliminating Internal Threats, they ought to be executed in this order:

1. Make sure you're not seagulling anybody.
2. Go back and redo tactic 1.
3. Get rid of known Omegas. Keeping with tactic 1, make triple-sure they are not Cinderellas in disguise.

4. If there's any mystery about whom remaining has a low Black Arrow, they're the ones actively working to suppress others' image (exerting downward pressure on others' Grey Arrows).
5. If nobody appears to be pursuing the *Rank Cutting* strategy, or if you have eliminated all of those caught using that strategy and there's still some eliminating to do, then the low performers will be those attempting the *Rank Impersonating* strategy. If these are good at it, you will need to go back to tactic 1.
6. If the remaining low Black Arrows are not good at *Rank Impersonating*, then you will know who they are. Steadily increase the pressure on them until they either commit themselves to improving their Black Arrow levels, or leave.

The "pressure" I refer to in tactic 6 can take a wide variety of forms. Within companies or corporations, members generally join in order to earn a paycheck, and the rate of pay is not normally subject to significant variation. However, there are many other variables which go into a person's decision to stay with their jobs. Task assignment, office space arrangements, shift assignments, and dozens of other parameters all the way to parking space assignments can make targeted non-performers more inclined to seek employment elsewhere.

Similarly, for groups that are not in existence to make money, the gradual rejection of undesirable members can take a wide variety of forms. The key, of course, is to discern why the individual is in the group in the first place, and it won't always be for the obvious reasons. On the surface, wolves form packs in order to survive and reproduce, since, as hunters, they are far more effective when conducting coordinated attacks. But Omegas never mate, and are often kept from being allowed to eat with the others by the Alpha if food isn't plentiful, yet they still remain with the pack.

Why did Jeff join that particular clique at Midtown High School? In his case, he wanted to hang out with kids who were smaller or weaker than he, so that he would be perceived as the strongest and, therefore, assume the role of the Alpha. In other words, he started interacting with that particular set of kids because it made him feel better about himself – it inflated his White Arrow. But in the course of his freshman year at Midtown, Jeff's desire to belong to another group – the school's wrestling team – led him away from consistent association with non-wrestling team-associated friends. While Scott didn't perform anything resembling this kind of analysis, he knew that Jeff would be less likely to stick around if the role of Alpha was diminished, or even taken away. Rather than influence Jeff, the easier tactic was to influence the clique to subtly begin to disengage from Jeff as Alpha, making any alternatives Jeff had in waiting appear more attractive.

Takeaways from Chapter 11

We've covered a lot of ground in the discussion on how to defend the organization from an early demise. Here are some of the points I want to re-emphasize going forward:

- The erstwhile defender will have an easier time if he enjoys a relatively higher rank.
- Threats almost certainly exist.
- The precise nature of the threats will need to be identified...
- followed by a structured, concerted effort to minimize the group's vulnerabilities.

- Attacks will come at three levels:
  - against the interior of the organization (targeting its members),
  - against the exterior of the organization, but within its environment (targeting its customers, or peers),
  - against the exterior of the organization, as with competitors.
- The most control is exerted over attacks to the interior; least control is over the organization's competitors.
- The organization's internal defense systems will need to be calibrated, or even upgraded, to recognize and deal with some predictable strategies that may be employed.
- Once the sources of the threats or organizational pathologies are identified, they must be carefully eliminated.

A key component and crucial takeaway from the discussion on organizational defense has to do with the creation, perpetration, and influence of the narratives, or memes that impact how the members of the group see themselves, the group as a whole, and how the group perceives itself and its members. These narratives are identical to the scripts discussed in Chapter 12, and perform several functions, including telling us who we are to ourselves, i.e., the appropriate placement of our White Arrows. Because these narratives have such a powerful influence on White Arrow placement, and White Arrow placement, in turn, has far-reaching implications on group performance and longevity, an analysis of the nature of these memes and their power is unavoidable. So, on to Chapter 12!

Notes

1 Eisler, Barry, retrieved from *BrainyQuote*, http://www.brainyquote.com/quotes/quotes/b/barryeisle621902.html#L3G18pQgFssTe3qg.99, July 2, 2015.
2 Jean-Michel Guesdon and Philippe Margotin, *All the Songs, the Story behind Every Beatles Release*. New York: Black Dog and Leventhal Publishers.

Chapter 12

The Stories of Our Lives

Human behavior flows from three main sources: desire, emotion, and knowledge.

Plato[1]

There has been an unfortunate tendency on college campuses in the United States recently involving something called "micro aggression," which is, as I understand it, a tendency for the intellectually incapable to devolve into near hysterics when exposed to any idea that is not well within the politically correct orthodoxy. The problem with writing on the topic of how and why certain types of scripts tend to be embraced by people, and how that, in turn, influences the strategies they select as they move up and down organization hierarchies is that it simply can't be done without making sweeping generalizations. I am well aware that there's not much in the behavioral or management sciences that can be reliably established predicated on sweeping generalizations; I'm also aware that there are some usable insights that *can* be gleaned from such indulgences. To that end, the reader should be forewarned: this chapter uses broad generalizations as certain concepts are explored and strategies compared and evaluated. If the reader is one who is susceptible to so-called "triggers," potentially leading to near-psychotic breaks when exposed to ideas such as early societies were often based on males having more valuable skills in survival situations, then go ahead and skip to Chapter 13, before I inadvertently melt your face off. If one of my academic colleagues has assigned this part of this book as an assignment, I personally excuse you from this part of it. Just tell your professor that the author himself gave you permission. And now, on to the subject at hand: the way we tell ourselves about ourselves.

The "scripts" that we all run in our heads, that create the stories of our lives, are very real, and very powerful. They may be simple, being little more than the dot-connecting function performed by the hippocampus in order to provide the ability to deal with novel situations by aligning them with analogous situations we have already encountered. Or, they may be highly complex, filled with what-if analyses, speculations, and confirmation biases supporting narratives embracing the entire universe. In Chapter 3, I advanced the idea about the scripts we maintain in our heads with the notion that there are actually three narratives, or the one narrative fulfills three purposes, aligned with the Berne archetypes:

- The Child Narrative tells us who we are to ourselves (White Arrow).
- The Adult Narrative informs our decisions on how we ought to interact with others in our environment (Grey Arrow).

- The Parent Narrative directs us towards who we ought to be (Black Arrow).

While each of these narratives is internally generated, they can be (and are) strongly influenced by exterior factors and people. As our futures unfold before us, our three scripts are either affirmed or challenged, in peculiar ways that depend on how we observe relevant events, attribute their causes, and evaluate their impacts to our lives.

I would imagine that this uniquely human attribute of narrative building was begun concurrently with the ability to speak. Whether it was (depending on your point of view) one of the first family/tribal units in the Middle Paleolithic, or the rapidly expanding first few generations from Adam and Eve, welcoming back a successful hunting party would almost have to involve a transfer of information on how the food was obtained, if for no other reason so that the others could learn which tactics were likely to be successful in future hunts. As with Crusoe and Friday, all the members of the group would enjoy better odds of long-term survival (and, therefore, a higher standard of living) should they enter into cooperative social arrangements, and these cooperative social arrangements naturally lend themselves to a hierarchical structure.

So, before we evaluate the nature and influence of the more sophisticated narratives, let's visit our earliest ancestors as they cook the day's catch and prepare for the night.

"Today's hunt was the most intense one I've been on yet!" begins Eike.

"Why, what happened?" Tammy asks, as she delivers an armful of firewood to the side of the fire.

"That animal you see on the spit there – hey, Scott! What did Grandpa say that animal's name was?"

"A hyena."

"The same, the same. Anyway, Jeff, Scott, Mitch and I were walking a tree line when we saw a group of them, and Mitch identified them as the type of animal that used to attack our camp perimeter at night before we got into the habit of keeping the fire going until morning. We noticed that this one here was lagging behind the others as they were approaching the river, so we followed them to the river bank. As the herd starting moving across, we charged them so as to cut off this laggard. Some of the pack turned to attack us, but couldn't move effectively in the river itself. We stabbed at them with our spears as Jeff killed this one. We drove off the others, and brought this one back, and, *voila*, hyena steaks!"

"So, we have Jeff to thank for feeding us this hyena?" Lori asks.

"Well, like Eike says, I couldn't have killed this one if I had to fend off the others," Jeff begins, "so it really was a group effort."

"I don't particularly care for hyena meat," Phyllis interjects.

"Yeah, I hear you," Scott agrees. "It's only a little better than crocodile."

"True that," Eike replies, "but when we eat them, that means one fewer of them that can eat us. Heck, after they saw what Jeff did, they may even start to avoid us, like the other animals we kill and eat."

"Thanks for the compliment, Eike," Jeff responds, "but I have to admit, this metal thing Scott came up with – what do you call it, a 'knife'? – sure makes our weapons better, and also makes carving up our game animals easier. Whatever possessed you to put that clay mold next to the meteorite the way you did?"

"I was just about to spear an antelope," Scott begins, "when this really loud, fiery object comes crashing down nearby, spooking our dinner for that night. When

I walked up to where it had landed, it had already started a fire in the immediate area, and I noticed that it seemed to be oozing a dark liquid from its red-hot area, and, when that liquid cooled, it assumed the shape of its surroundings as it hardened. I just managed to divert one of those molten streams into a little clay cast of a spear point, and realized right away that I was onto something."

"Really?" Tammy asks incredulously. "Because one of the other groups of people I came across from the other valley said that they became aware of ways to improve their weaponry after one of their hunters came across a large monolith, and went up and touched it."

"And you believed them?" Jeff asks.

"Well, up until now, they *did* have better weapons than we did."

"But you didn't actually see this monolith?"

"No."

"Okay."

"All right."

"Fine."

I've used this little vignette to illustrate some ideas I would like to submit, concerning the nature of hierarchies and relationships, but first I want to draw the readers' attention to some of the things that were communicated around our ancient campfire, to wit:

- If he hasn't already been recognized as the Alpha, Jeff is certainly moving in that direction…
- but it wasn't Jeff who relayed the story that would indicate his appropriate rank. Eike did that.
- While Jeff's hunting strategy and personal courage were the characteristics that enabled the entire group to eat that evening, Jeff readily acknowledged the contribution of the other members of the group, and particularly Scott, thereby signaling a commitment to the group as a whole (just in case his bringing back the hyena for consumption wasn't enough).
- The story of the successful hunt included the contribution of Scott's curiosity and cleverness.
- The girls were interested in the story being told, and not because of the perception that they would, some day, need to know the best strategies for hunting. The voyeurism instinct was in full play, but not for the purpose of evaluating possible future circumstances directly involving the girls. They were trying to figure out who's who in this particular tribe.
- Tammy attempted to introduce a story about how another tribe had also advanced their weapon-making technology, but her story was deemed too fantastic to accept (sorry, Arthur C. Clarke).

These takeaways from the story-telling around the ancient campfire point to two assertions that, I believe, serve as the underpinnings for the best approach to evaluating and comparing strategies for changing ranks within an organization. These two assertions are (1) the narratives (all three of them) determine the nature of our unavoidable organizations and their ranking structures, and (2) the hierarchy and its ranks determine the nature of our relationships with one another. It follows, then, that the narratives determine the nature of our relationships with one another. Graphically,

Personal narratives → rank
Rank → relationships
∴ Personal narratives → relationships

How the Narratives Drive Rank

Before I take that leap, though, let's evaluate the assertions one at a time. In purely voluntarily joined groups, it's rare that a member who thinks highly of themselves (high White Arrow) will remain if everybody else perceives them negatively (low Grey Arrow). In the previous archetype evaluations, these two categories are comprised of the Lone Wolf (who is an inherent flight risk) and the Delusional Fool, the difference between them being their actual contribution to the group (Black Arrow). In groups that are not purely voluntarily joined, e.g., some economic, legal, or survival issue binds its members, these two archetypes are either likely to leave, and peel off some others from the group (Lone Wolf), or fulfill the role of the Omegas.

Conversely, in organizations where a certain member is demonstrably valuable to the group (high Black Arrow), and the stories around their metaphoric campfires point to that fact (high Grey Arrow), that member will invariably rise in esteem, and thereby rank, perhaps even becoming the group's leader, or fulfilling the Alpha role. In-between these two extremes the narratives that the organization embraces will also have a significant impact on its members, the roles they fulfill (or are steered into), and their ensuing ranks. Since a person's rank (depending on the organization) has a direct impact on their realized quality of life, narratives equal quality of life. Put another way,

Personal narratives → rank
Rank → quality of life
∴ Personal narratives → quality of life

So, the narrative that the group embraces is malleable, prone to interpretations of the facts surrounding the events that unfold and verify or refute its particulars. This applies to *all* the group's narratives. It has been speculated that the origins of movies, novels, plays, stories – they *all* came from our ancestors gathering around the cooking fire, and hearing how the day's food was obtained and made available for their consumption. As with our example, these stories fed the overall group's story, of how they survived or even thrived, which strategies were successful, and why, and who originated and/or executed those strategies. What the wolfpack knew instinctively we humans needed to articulate in order to pass from generation to generation, encounters with black, slab-like monoliths notwithstanding.

Speaking of slab-like monoliths, the stories that the group rejects also play a role in its odds of survival. Like the wolfpack in Chapter 4 experienced when they began avoiding elk, human societies that embrace false or suspect narratives lower their chances of surviving or advancing. Much guilty hand wringing has been performed over the treatment of Montezuma and the Aztecs by Hernan Cortes, but the odds of any large-population society that routinely engaged in massive-scale human sacrifice surviving past the sixteenth century were pretty low, Western European-specific intervention notwithstanding. Whatever part of the pre-1519 Aztec shared narrative that asserted that, as a society, it was a good idea to divert significant amounts of time and energy rounding up members of nearby tribes and killing them to appease Quetzalcoatl was clearly not derived from experiences of survival or societal advancement.

Of course, many (if not most) of the stories that come our way have less to do with the evaluation of competing strategies in a survival-critical environment, and more to do with simple entertainment. But, if we don't need to know these stories in order to help ensure survival, why do we watch or listen to them? What's their appeal?

The answer is two-fold: (1) they influence how we think of ourselves (they support or even exert upward pressure on our White Arrows), and (2) they influence or determine our relationships with others.

Now, number 2 above was discussed in an earlier paragraph, evaluating the ways that our internal scripts largely determine the quality of the relationships we have with others. I'm dealing with massive levels of generalizations here, but hear me out. Think back – when was the last time you were privy to the considerations a girl was going through when evaluating a potential spouse, or date? I believe that they go through a step-by-step process, when they are unattached to a man (and sometimes, sadly, when they are), but it begins with seeking out the answer to the question: what is this fellow's rank? (Did that offend you? Go back and reread the first paragraph of this chapter.)

Oh, they may not articulate it exactly that way, but that's what they are trying to figure out. It's all perfectly logical, by the way. In survival-critical environments, like our early tribe members, males are naturally faster, stronger, and far better equipped to attack, kill, and butcher hyenas (and other game, of course, but stay with me). The women know this. They also know that men crave their company, and if one of these men were to fall in love with one of the women, then life becomes better for both involved. However, life is *best* for the woman who attracts the best among the available men, usually the Alpha. At the opposite end of the scale, the woman whose only alternatives are a life alone or as the consort of an Omega will have a more difficult time of it.

So, what's a girl to do? Let me be plain – I have no more idea of how a woman's mind works, or what they want, than any other man (which is to say, next to nothing). Like my previous protestations about my proposed structure explaining *everything* about the selected strategies for getting ahead, in this instance I do not believe that I can explain any such thing. I *can*, however, offer up some insights that appear to be consistent with the structure we've been using in evaluating the behaviors and tactics of people maneuvering for position within a given hierarchy, so here goes.

When women evaluate men as potential spouses, rank is the initial determiner. The most attractive male will be the Alpha, because he has (a) demonstrated his value (he has a high Black Arrow) to the point that (b) others have recognized it (high Grey Arrow), while (c) maintaining the level of confidence to continue performing at a high level (appropriately placed White Arrow). For a woman aware of a life that may or may not swerve into near-crisis environs, her odds of living a good, long life are maximized when she captures the heart of an Alpha.

There are, of course, some additional difficulties here. An Alpha does not perform that role for his entire existence. Nor are either Alphas or Alphas-in-waiting going to clearly communicate their future rank, or potential. In an analytical sense, we're going to have to return to the arrows.

Generally speaking, of course, to a given woman the male with the most attractiveness will tend to be the one with a high Black Arrow. Oh, outward physical attractiveness certainly plays a role, but not as much a one as the subject at hand turns to long-term spousal possibilities (unless our prowling female maintains a pathology that leads her to the conclusion that it's better to have a pretty but ultimately useless mate rather than one who has some actual value to a society or economy). Unfortunately, another's Black Arrow placement is usually highly ambiguous. In order to get a handle on that Black Arrow placement, there are two other indicators, namely the White and Grey Arrows. Grey Arrow placement can be a useful clue of Black Arrow level, since others who interact with the target male will form opinions of him, based on those interactions, and will judge his behavior, leading to the Grey Arrow's placement. Naturally, this placement may be profoundly flawed: criminal organizations, such as street gangs, may think very highly (high Grey Arrow) of a particularly courageous violent enforcer, whose actual Black Arrow is hovering just above the pits of hell. And, as we have seen, the Cinderella archetype maintains a low Grey Arrow, while actually being of very high value, indeed (think Harry Potter, or Luke Skywalker).

Then there's the White Arrow. In most people, the White Arrow is somewhat above the fairly placed Black Arrow, with the difference being the amount or level of delusion with which we indulge ourselves. As discussed in Chapter 3, this is known in psychological circles as the Dunning-Kruger Effect, which tends to lead people into a sense of illusory capability, or even superiority. A person who presents as realistic, clear-eyed, and pragmatic, who nevertheless throws off indications of supreme confidence, makes the inference that this high White Arrow is indicative of a high Black Arrow a fairly easy one to make. Such a one is either an Alpha, or a Politician, with the difference being, in many (if not most) cases, very hard to discern.

Now our theoretical female – let's draft Tammy, shall we? – can pursue this discernment in a structured fashion. She doesn't want any Fools or Omegas as potential spouses, but those are (usually) fairly easy to identify. That being said, there's always the possibility that a given Fool or Omega is actually a misunderstood Cinderella, the type with which they share the low Grey Arrow indicator. The other two low Black Arrow archetypes, Politicians and Comedians, are a bit more difficult to detect, each enjoying high Grey Arrows.

We're essentially proceeding from the premise that everybody, men and women alike, will seek out those who are actually valuable as potential spouses, and eschew those who are not, or at least perceived as not. Of the archetypes, the coveted ones would be:

- Alphas,
- Betas,
- Lone Wolves, and
- Cinderellas,

while the ones to avoid would be

- Comedians,
- Politicians,

- Fools, and
- Omegas.

Knowledge of the true ranking of another's Black Arrow is problematic, at best. If there's a high level of correlation between the White Arrows and Grey Arrows, leaving the valid placement of the Black Arrows to be discerned from only those clues, then the most attractive are Alphas and Politicians, meaning that, even in groups where the prevailing opinion of each member, as well as each member's view of themselves, is accurate, accurately identifying a high Black Arrow is a 50/50 proposition. Obviously, other factors will need to be considered, which brings the middle block of four archetypes back into contention.

From Chapter 10, the Nominal Strategy involves moving ahead by focusing effort at improving one's actual value (inflating the Black Arrow), followed by attempts to cultivate favor with the other members of the organization (inflating the Grey Arrow). On the other hand, attempts to gain rank within the group without having to cultivate any actual virtue is most often accomplished by simply inflating one's Grey Arrow, or deflating others' Grey Arrows in order to appear attractive by comparison. As with the work of assigning valid rankings, those on the prowl for potential spouses might be automatically wary of any who engage in the tactic of disparaging others within the group, except that that tactic also happens to be a legitimate function of both the Alphas and the Betas against those with high White Arrows and low Black ones.

Ultimately, a male's ultimate attractiveness is all about rank, and rank is all about the narratives embraced by the organization to which he belongs. Men are aware of this, and will exert extraordinary effort to attain a higher rank in order to appear more attractive to potential spouses.

Harkening back to Game Theory, an additional game may shed light on this particular set of circumstances. The Pirate Game involves a set of five pirates, all of different ranks, who have acquired a treasure of 100 gold pieces. The gold will be divvied up according to the scheme proposed by the most senior officer. If the proffered plan is rejected by a majority of the pirates, the senior officer is killed, and the next most senior officer makes a proposal for dividing the gold. This continues until a proposal is accepted by at least half of the pirates voting.

Theoretically, in order to maximize his payout, the most senior pirate present ("A," or the captain) would propose the following:

- A would receive 98 gold pieces.
- B would receive none.
- C would receive 1 gold piece.
- D would receive none.
- E would receive 1 gold piece.

This strategy is made plausible because, should the captain ("A") make a proposal that did not meet with the approval of at least half of the other pirates, pirate B would need to make a proposal. Pirate B could conceivably offer pirate D one gold piece, with himself getting all the rest. With the "aye" votes of both B and D, the gold would be so distributed, with C and E getting nothing. Aware that the next alternative for C and E is nothing, pirate A can offer them 1 gold piece each, and expect to carry the vote. As with the Ultimatum Game, I seriously doubt that the calculated "best" strategy would be one that would actually work, but it does point to the gamesmanship occurring in a theoretical game that involves rank.

Back to potential spouse evaluations: recall that virtually all social constructs involve a somewhat automatic rank imposition. The women have a sense of who among them should be considered the most attractive to the available men, or, in this vernacular, where their Grey Arrows ought to be placed. I have found it fascinating to observe how groups of women will enforce their own ranking systems when attractiveness to the opposite sex was a factor. Two insults were prevalent, at least at my high school: (1) that the target girl was "so stuck up" or "conceited," i.e., her White Arrow was placed artificially high, or else (2) that the target girl was a "slut," or one who could not be trusted to be faithful to whomever she would become espoused, i.e., her Black Arrow should be considered quite low, even with no direct evidence to place it so.

These tactics, while being less fatal than the option available in the Pirate Game, serve the same purpose: should a certain female member of the group seek to court a male that the other women believe to be above her rank, they will engage in tactics designed to depress that girl's Grey Arrow, under the assumption that doing so will carry over to the men's perception of her attractiveness, and disengage from her attentions. Also consistent with the Pirate Game would be the expectation that, once "Girl A's" proposition/revealed strategy for capturing the coveted male was ripped to shreds by the others, the next highest-ranked pirate/girl would get her shot. Irrational? No doubt. Does this kind of thinking/script actually happen? You betcha.

All the while this set of strategies plays out on the girls' side of the ledger, the boys have some competing strategies of their own. They also desire the, well, most desirable women as spouses, and the characteristics that define this desirability are as varied as the cultures around the globe. However, even in this near-chaotic environment, certain constants emerge, such as a general awareness that are hard-wired into men: there are two basic attributes that any man who wishes to attract a spouse will eventually have to demonstrate:

1. The ability to provide for her physical security.
2. The ability to provide for her economic security.

There's an old saying, that a woman will never voluntarily marry beneath her status (exceptions covered in the next chapter). Another way of putting it (while translating it into our lexicon) is that any woman who maintains a high White and Grey Arrow rank will not be attracted to a potential spouse with a low Grey and Black Arrow combination. To do so would be a tacit acknowledgment that her high White Arrow placement is inappropriate, and she would have to experience the pain of having it deflated.

Men know this implicitly, which is why their pastimes undertaken during adolescence tend to be highly competitive or even violent in nature. Not only are they engaged in those activities that determine their placement among the other males within their selected social circles, they are also broadcasting their attractiveness to potential spouses. And, when conflict arises as to the more precise nature of those rankings, conflicts which cannot be resolved through ordered, rational means, such conflicts are resolved more brutally and directly, outside the rules and norms of standard conflict resolution.

In other words, they fight.

This being the case, it follows that the efforts to simultaneously push sex education in schools to lower and lower grades (all the way to kindergarten, in the more depraved school systems) is in direct conflict with attempts to tamp down on bullying. The tactics associated with bullying have two possible purposes: assert a higher rank within a group, or drive down another's (or both). Without the need to establish a ranking among the boys for the long-term purposes of being able to demonstrate superior attractiveness to potential spouses, the urge to resort to violence or intimidation in order to assert superiority is, in all likelihood, lessened, or even eliminated, at least for the pre-pubescent years.

How Rank Drives Relationships

While participating in physical competitions or bullying tactics may provide indicators as to a given male's ability to provide for his future spouse's physical security, economic security is a largely different matter. In hunter-gatherer groups they are largely synonymous, but in advanced societies a superior intelligence is a far better predictor of eventual economic success. Recall that even in chimpanzee society a key aspect of rank is the ability to form coalitions. That a demonstrated ability to provide for a potential spouse's physical security tends to be a significantly more attractive trait than observable superior intelligence is fairly intuitive, but, for those who doubt that, consider the following two questions:

1. Remembering back when you were in high school, who do you believe had the easier time securing a date to the prom – the quarterback of the football team, or the captain of the chess team?
2. If you were to conduct a survey of the high schools in your area, 20 years after graduation, who would be more likely to have enjoyed more career success, the quarterback of the football team, or the captain of the chess team?

So we have a somewhat automatically joined situation where the perceived rank of a given male largely determines the pool of potential future spouses. In the United States (and, I would imagine, elsewhere) competitions among chess teams are formally arranged so that the best player of one team ("First Board") plays the best player of the other, the second best ("Second Board") plays the second best of the other, and so forth down to the Seventh Boards. Ironically, something very similar happens in the social interactions of groups of boys and girls, albeit far more informally. I know at least at the high school I attended, the quarterback of the football team dated (and eventually married) one of the prettiest (if not the prettiest) cheerleader.

There is no doubt in my mind that their relative ranks while in high school led directly to the beginnings of their relationship, in that, had either of them *not* occupied their (then) lofty ranks, they probably would have never had a first date. Conversely, I happened to be the First Board and captain of the chess team, and the odds of my receiving an affirmative response to a date request from any of the members of the cheerleaders were remote indeed (at least that was my perception. And, given that none of them rushed up to me at any of my high school's reunions, decrying lost dating opportunities, I'm thinking that perception was fairly accurate).

Rank plays directly into the nature of our relationships because much of our emotional ties to others are based on how those others make us feel about ourselves. Or, put another way, we tend to like those who enable us to provide lift to our White Arrows. Since our White Arrows tend to track slightly above our Black Arrows, the only difference being the self-flattering delusions we indulge, receiving acclaim from those with (perceived) high Black Arrows represents license to feel better about ourselves, i.e., raise the White Arrow, or maintain it if it is already highly placed.

One glaring exception which would tend to overturn the previous assertion on its face would be those many instances where a woman stubbornly stays in a relationship with an abusive husband. However, I would argue that such instances, instead, support my thesis, and here's why.

On the surface, it would appear that any woman who voluntarily stays in an abusive relationship is willing to endure observable and extraordinary downward pressure on her White Arrow. Her husband treats her in such a way as to unmistakably demonstrate that he believes her to be of low value, or rank, and yet she will not disengage from him. I believe that what is occurring (within the confines of our little model) is that our abused wife is somehow convinced of her husband's value, i.e., she thinks his Black Arrow is high. Being the spouse of one with a high Black Arrow generates indirect upward pressure on her White Arrow. Additionally, asserting dominance over others within a social construct is a behavior consistent with Alphas and Betas, both high Black Arrow archetypes, and roles highly coveted as spouses. This effect also lends indirect upward pressure on the abused wife's White Arrow. The direct downward pressures are thus arrayed against indirect upward pressures. As long as the indirect forces counteract the direct ones, the wife will stay. As soon as the downward pressures, or abusive behaviors, overwhelm the upward ones, she will leave. If her White Arrow is already very low, this point of equilibrium shift may never come.

As long as I've come down this road this far, I may as well postulate the obvious, the nominal attraction model implicit in the three-arrow model.

The Nominal Rank-Based Attraction Model

As I stated in the previous section, people are attracted to those who place upward pressure on their White Arrows, i.e., make us feel better about ourselves. For those whose White Arrow is already highly placed, this function is performed by those who help prevent its deflation. In those instances where the White Arrow is placed significantly above the Black Arrow (indicating a high degree of delusion present in the creation of the person's internal narrative), such a one will be naturally attracted to those who can either buttress the White Arrow-inflating delusions, deflect the intrusions of harsh reality that would otherwise deflate it, or do some of each.

This model helps explain a great many things. It adds insight into why breaking up is so excruciating – all of the White Arrow uplift that took place during the courtship phase immediately evaporates, which results in the rather acute pain of having one's White Arrow abruptly pushed downwards. It also sheds light on why men would engage the otherwise insane tactic of striking a beloved woman who is considering leaving him. Driven by pain into a state of rage, with only one arena where he can assert any sort of rank superiority (physical, or violent solutions to potential physical security problems) left to him, he idiotically strikes out, both figuratively and literally.

Indeed, virtually every single traditional tactic involved in attracting a potential mate has to do with inflation of the target's White Arrow. Flowers, notes, coffees, dates, dinners, gifts, humor – it's all directed at conveying a message, directly or indirectly, that the target should feel better about themselves for having interacted with the pursuer. The indirect pressures are invariably directed at conveying the impression of a high Black Arrow on the part of the pursuer, since being the love interest of any of the high Black Arrow archetypes (Alpha, Beta, Lone Wolf, or Cinderella) is a far more attractive prospect than the alternatives. Alternately, demonstrating a high Grey Arrow, i.e., that the pursuer is highly thought of among his or her peers, implies a correlation between the high Grey Arrow and the unseen, but probably highly placed, Black Arrow.

The use of humor deserves its own evaluation. Its overuse can indicate that the pursuer is either a Comedian, or an Omega, since the use of humor is strongly associated with the act of communicating non-belligerence and, therefore, automatic abdication of even appropriate challenges to the existing hierarchy. This would normally be interpreted as the potential spouse with the advanced and oft-used sense of humor as being not a member of the high Black Arrow archetypes. However, the ultimate, core team that any of us participate in is our marriage, and in *that* two-person organization, *someone* has to be the Alpha. A spouse who often engages their sense of humor is transmitting a willingness for their partner to inflate their White Arrow, just as the spouse who abuses their partner is indicating a desire for the deflation of their partner's White Arrow. These are extreme examples, but they do point, I believe, to a truism, that somewhat resembles Eric Berne's notions of what constitutes interpersonal conflict. If you will recall from Chapter 2, Berne's model of the three aspects of the persona, Child, Adult, and Parent, were modeled as three circles, stacked one atop the other. Conflicts arose, he theorized, when the paths of communication between two people crossed over each other, as when Person A's Adult attempted to communicate with Person B's Adult, but Person B's Parent transmitted a communication to Person A's Child.

My advancement on this idea is this: in two-person interactions, if Person A sends off a message, spoken or unspoken, intentionally or not, that they believe (Grey Arrow) Person B's value (Black Arrow) is lower than Person B believes it to be (B's White Arrow), conflict will usually ensue, openly or covertly, immediately or delayed. Graphically, it looks something like Figure 12.1.

In this example, an archetypal Politician (Person A) may be simply conveying a commonly held opinion of the Lone Wolf's (Person B) status within the organization – the Lone Wolf does have a low Grey Arrow, after all. But the implication that this particular Lone Wolf deserves a lower ranking than the Politician is both wrong and insulting. Compounding the level of conflict inherent in any such communication, in this case the Lone Wolf is aware that, despite appearances, the Politician's genuine value (Black Arrow) is significantly below the Lone Wolf's. Even if the Lone Wolf resists the temptation to push back against the Politician, the communication, even if it were as subtle as a glance away, or an avoidance of pleasantries exchanged in passing, will represent an effort at establishing some sort of superiority within a given hierarchy, which translates to conflict.

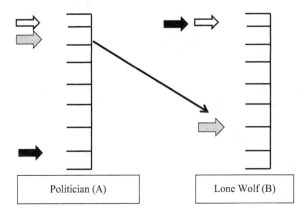

Figure 12.1 A Politician Asserts Superiority over a Lone Wolf

Referring back to Berne's model, the act of Person A's Parent communicating across Person B's Adult to address their Child is not conflict inducing simply because the paths of communication cross. It's conflict inducing because Person A is transmitting that they believe themselves to be superior in rank, and is exerting effort to remind Person B of this perceived reality. To test this hypothesis, I would like to invoke the following mental exercise.

Consider that this Person A – to – Person B interaction happens something like this.

Person B (Scott): "Jeff, I've come across more material like that I used to make the first batch of spear points. For the next bunch, should I try to make them sharper, or larger?"

Just to reiterate, this would represent an example of Scott's Bernesian Adult persona attempting to communicate with Jeff's Adult.

Person A (Jeff): "Why on Earth would you ask me about how you should conduct the particulars of your exploring or tinkering?" Again, this would be Jeff's Bernesian Parent speaking to Scott's Child.

Scott: "Because I'm not the one who will be carrying the spears across the Serengeti and using them for hunting or defense. That's what you do – I'm just trying to equip you better."

Jeff: "Oh, right. Do some of each, and we'll try them out in the next hunt or defense."

Okay, it's fiction (obviously), but not improbable fiction. Both of Scott's communications were Bernesian Adult to Adult, and both of Jeff's were Parent to Child. Yet, no automatic conflict arose. The crossing of the lines of communication does not necessarily lead to reflexive conflict, but the assertion of non-agreed-to rankings within a common hierarchy do. Scott could have just as easily replied along the lines of "Who do you think you are? If not for my 'tinkering,' you would have been eaten alive by that pack of hyenas the rest of us held off from you." Instead, in an acknowledgment of Jeff's physical courage and higher rank, Scott persists in his attempts to gain useful knowledge about the preferred survival strategies going forward.

The primary exception in these types of interactions involves those cases where Person B does not care what Person A thinks, either out of superior, more confident knowledge of their (B's) true value, or out of sheer disdain for Person A's opinion.

However, it's likely that, at the very least, the Lone Wolf from Figure 12.1 will experience some level of resentment towards the maneuvering Politician.

As discussed in Chapter 10, in 1965 Bruce Tuckman published a theory that small groups tend to go through a pattern of stages from the time they are created to the time they attain the purpose for which they were formed in the first place, and called these stages Forming, Storming, Norming, and Performing.[2] The validity of Tuckman's insights are axiomatic in the twenty-first century, but they do raise the question: why should a group of (presumably, voluntarily) enjoined people necessarily go through a time of conflict when the whole point of collecting them together in the first place was to have them cooperate in order to achieve a shared objective? I believe the answer is due to two unavoidable effects in groups:

1.   Some form of a hierarchy will manifest, one way or the other.
2.   Until that hierarchy is created, articulated, and accepted by every member of the group, all sorts of communication will take place that pertain to the way each member of the group sees themselves (White Arrow), and perceives the others (Grey Arrow). These perceptions are susceptible to misunderstandings as well as out-and-out errors when evaluating the true value (Black Arrow) of the other members.

The "Norming" phase occurs as the newly minted hierarchy, with its assigned ranks, is adjusted and manipulated towards an equilibrium of widespread acceptance. Interestingly, the implication here is that the group will not attain the Performing stage unless and until it has gotten past the Storming phase, i.e., reconciled each member's rank within the hierarchy to their satisfaction.

The Abnormal Attraction Model

Now consider an organization comprised exclusively of low Black Arrow holders (Comedians, Omegas, Fools, and Politicians). The temptation to name organizations that I despise as examples is overwhelming, but I'll soldier on. The members of this organization are either okay with having low Black Arrows, or else don't believe that they are of little true value to their respective organizations. What makes these people tick? Or, put another way, how is rank assigned or maintained in such profoundly dysfunctional groups?

Again, it gets back to White Arrow placement. Dysfunctional organizations will find attractive those who either help prevent harsh reality reminding/informing them of their true lack of genuine virtue or, at the very least, allow them to function among organizations without having to face such realities, at least not very often. Of course, this sort of delusion support can't go on forever, for reality, unlike members of a profoundly dysfunctional organization, cannot be fooled.

Back to the Narratives

The story that the group creates about itself and its members is crucial to both the rankings and the nature of the relationships among its members. Recall from Chapter 9 the discussion of how the organization will change its members, by attempting to force them into roles. These roles are not spontaneous. They are the manifestations of the group's narrative, at the three levels of functioning: the script covering who they are to themselves, who they are to the others in their environment, and who they aspire to be. Also keep in mind, from Chapter 8, that among these narratives is the one that cannot be allowed to be articulated: that the organization, to whatever degree, exists not for the reasons stated; rather, it exists to maintain the ranks of those in the upper echelon.

That this is a uniquely human construct is readily revealed by the fact that the wolfpack that exists in order to keep its Alphas and Betas enjoying whatever perks they get from their superior ranking will quickly starve, since the whole concept is, by definition, an abrogation of meritocracy. But the wolves live in a harsh reality, made harsher by the abandonment of even the smallest aspect of a ranking system that swerved away from merit as the sole basis for advancing in rank. Groups of people, on the other hand, can and do create, propagate, and participate in organizations that strongly diverge from a basis in merit, and these groups can and do formulate narratives that justify their existence, chock-full of delusions as they may be. As members of many groupings, most people will experience both joy and pain as their group's rankings change, elevating and deflating Grey and, by extension, White Arrows, reflecting their selected strategies and their outcomes. Such fluctuations take place (1) among members of the group, (2) for the group as a whole as it seeks its own perpetration, and (3) the group as a whole as it competes against other groups seeking the same ends. As circumstances and unfolding events put space in-between the respective White, Grey, and Black Arrows of the individual and group, this inter-rank space creates conflict and energy, conflict and energy that may be reconciled through myriad means, both peaceful and violent, temporary or lasting. Being, as we are, the authors of the narratives we embrace, we can experience the joys and sorrows that naturally stem from the nature of these scripts we write without even realizing that their basis is so powerfully influenced (or even controlled) by the delusions we allow ourselves, and the comparative rankings of our White, Grey, and Black Arrows. The clear proof of this assessment lies in our own observations and experiences. The happiest people I know are those who are truly humble, and yet very capable, or even indispensable within those organizations where they have elected to contribute (low White Arrow, high Black Arrow). Conversely, the meanest, least satisfied people I know think a great deal of themselves, and yet have very little objective evidence to point to that which would indicate their value. These ones will spend an extraordinary amount of time and energy attempting to manipulate others, or engineer circumstances to lead others to believe in their value (high White Arrow, low Black Arrow, leading to energy spent in keeping the Grey Arrow inflated).

This is how the stories of our lives come to us, how we update them and embrace them, and what they mean to our attitudes and states of mind. But, apart from the events unfolding before our very eyes, how are these stories altered?

Notes

1 Plato, retrieved from *BrainyQuote*, http://www.brainyquote.com/quotes/authors/p/plato. html, July 5, 2015.
2 Tuckman, Bruce, 1965, "Developmental Sequence in Small Groups." *Psychological Bulletin* 63 (6): 384–99.

Chapter 13

The Stories of Others' Lives

In this theater of man's life, it is reserved only for God and angels to be lookers-on.

Pythagorus[1]

How the stories we consume for entertainment, either through mass media or via a gossipy associate, affect our lives through our views of ourselves is fascinating to me. In the early days of electronics, some difficulties in circuit design were being experienced due to trace amounts of current occurring on wires or components where they weren't expected. It turned out that, with alternating current circuits especially, wires or components in close proximity were picking up power from energized lines nearby. This phenomenon was named "induction," and accounting for it allowed for significant advances in electrical engineering theory.

Similarly, we may have every reason to believe that our narratives, the ones that we run in our heads every waking hour, are entirely self-generated, created for the purpose of making sense of ourselves and the things that happen to us as our lives unfold. However, much like the A/C energized circuit right next to a supposedly neutral wire, other people's narratives have a significant impact on our internal memes, which go far beyond others' impacts on our Grey Arrows. When we go to see a motion picture, or read a novel, we will usually finish with the entertainment feeling better about ourselves – hence its appeal. But why? Why do we feel better about ourselves? Harkening back to our model, our Black Arrow hasn't budged, nor our Grey Arrow. So, there's upward pressure being brought to bear on our White Arrows. How is this accomplished, exactly?

From the days of Chapter 12 (strikethrough) our ancestors returning from the hunt with something for everyone in the tribe to eat, and informing all about how their dinner came about, all the way to modern times and ranging from classics like *Hamlet* to such idiocies as *The Vagina Monologues*, the stories others tell us entertain us and *change* us, sometimes for the better, often not.

But before we can evaluate how others' narratives affect us for better or worse, we'll have to evaluate how they affect us at all, and that requires returning to the placement of our White Arrows, our affiliations with specific groups, and the voyeur instinct from Chapter 5.

The Use of Plot

In the Anglosphere (among others), children are taught from middle school that good fiction tends to follow a specific formula, known as classic plot structure. Classic plot structure contains the following elements:

- An introduction of the characters, their ranks, and circumstances.
- A problem is introduced that, if left unresolved, can have grave consequences for the protagonists.
- The introduction of the problem usually involves one or more persons who are behind the problem, known as the antagonists.
- As the central problem grows, it begins to have more and more negative consequences for the protagonists, and manifests a trajectory towards the previously alluded to grave consequences. This phase is known as the rising action.
- The protagonist(s) become stronger, either through learning about the limitations of the antagonist(s), or from some other difficulty endured that places them in a better position to overcome the problem and/or the antagonist.
- At a climactic scene, a confrontation occurs, and the protagonist, thanks to the information learned or difficulty endured, overcomes the problem and/or antagonist.
- The so-called falling action phase, also known as the denouement, where the sub-plot conflicts are resolved.
- A conclusion, where we learn the (at least probable, near-term) future of the major characters and their organizations.

Take, as an example, our Chapter 12 hunters, around the campfire as they serve up the barbequed hyena. Eike's story followed this structure, to wit:

- Everybody listening knows the characters, having interacted with them on a daily basis.
- They all need food, which creates the problem they must address.
- The food-finding environs are hostile, and must be overcome.
- As the afternoon progresses, those not involved in the hunt are getting closer to starvation, or at least a situation where they will be going to sleep hungry.
- The targets of the hunt are canny and dangerous, escalating the tensions among the hunters.
- The protagonists (the hunters) become aware of a circumstance where the antagonists (dangerous prey) have exhibited a weakness (one of the pack of hyenas has lagged behind the others, making it more vulnerable).
- The hunters aggressively further isolate their target, and slay it (climax).
- Any tensions among the hunters themselves, about who is most responsible for the kill, are resolved as they bring the food back to camp.
- At the conclusion, the members of the (now) well-fed tribe adjust or reinforce their feelings about the existing ranking system, and now feel better about their chances of a continued, non-starvation future as long as they stay within this grouping, and are reinforced for having been a member of this particular tribe.

Note the last bullet – the listeners to the tale are now happier than they otherwise would be, full stomachs notwithstanding. Also consider the extent to which you, the reader, became involved in the story. It has nothing at all to do with you, since it can be safely assumed that the people who read this are not, nor can be expected to be, in a marginal-survival situation on the Serengeti. Even if you were only marginally involved, enough to take my meaning, the additional point here is that this story was of interest, even though you have probably never even tasted hyena, and may, indeed, be repulsed at the idea. So, in the telling of stories, fictional or otherwise, following the formula of what is known as classic plot structure can be reasonably counted on to produce a happy feeling among its consumers, on a consistent basis.

Now, let's tinker with Eike's story at the Chapter 12 campfire. In order to remove the parameter of whether or not everyone goes to sleep fed or hungry, let's posit that the story comes out much later, after another successful hunting expedition; but, in this instance, the previous hyena kill was not successful and, in this alternate version, *that* tribe did go to bed hungry.

The manner with which Eike connects the dots on what actually happened on the unsuccessful hunt will matter hugely. The group's narrative changes if the cause of the empty barbeque pit is generally accepted as one of Jeff's failing to recognize an opportunity when it presented, or if Scott's experiments with the manipulation of metal ores is related as a waste of time, or if the tribe's failure to encounter and subsequently touch a large, strange black monolith led to their collective inability to thrive (or even survive) in a hostile environment led to their discomfort. If the correct version of the narrative is presented, and the tribe can learn from its mistake(s), then their odds of realizing a future probably free of hunger improve, then they're still hungry on that particular night, but they will all tend to feel less poorly about themselves going forward. In all other cases, everyone's White Arrow is pushed downwards, which, as has been stated previously, is singularly unpleasant. And, when everyone's White Arrow is being pushed downward, hierarchical upheaval is almost guaranteed.

Make no mistake – we are inundated with others' narratives, on a daily basis and, like inductive current's influence on supposedly independent circuits, we are affected by them. Sometimes these narratives are accidental, in that we come across them incidentally. Often, though, we choose the stories we subject ourselves to, and we do so for the exact purpose of making ourselves feel better.

Even non-fiction is vulnerable to this effect – hence, the otherwise self-contradictory expression that "historians disagree." The manner in which verifiable facts are placed into a narrative structure that presents as acceptable to many or most of the members of a group has a profound influence on our personal narratives, the ones that inform us of how we ought to feel about ourselves (the placement of our White Arrows). Examples abound.

- If the ancient Aztecs were peaceful and prosperous, then Cortez's intrusion into Central America was a barbaric act of colonialism. On the other hand, if the Aztecs were bloody savages whose societal practices were virtually guaranteeing its members a horrific fate in the afterlife, then Cortez's actions were positively a godsend.
- If the development and use of the atomic bomb shortened World War II and led to the saving of thousands of lives and the end to the attempts to subjugate millions of others in the Pacific Rim, then the resources so expended were wisely invested. Conversely, if the atomic bomb was so horrific a weapon that its use could never be countenanced by civilized peoples, then those who developed it are unforgivably evil.
- If the romance between Romeo and Juliet would have led to a happy and long-lasting marriage, with the reconciliation of the Montagues and Capulets coming about as a necessary side effect, then their deaths are a tragedy. However, if they

were destined to eventually separate and add to the conflict of their family's feud, then their deaths are automatically reduced to the triviality of the play-within-the-play from *A Midsummer Night's Dream*. (Yeah, I know this last one was from fiction, but I had to include a non-warfare example.)

Since we're on the topic of fictional examples, a review of successful and unsuccessful stories, and why we love, despise, or don't care one way or the other for them can be illuminating in the analysis of how these narratives impact our view of ourselves, others, and entire groups, up to and including nations and global movements. Indeed, a staple of writing for the stage is that there are only three ways of communicating information about a character:

- what they say,
- what they do, and
- what others say about them,

... which are clearly analogous to what we think of ourselves (White Arrow), the actions we perform (Black Arrow), and what others say about us (Grey Arrow).

Theoretically, there are seven basic plots throughout all of literature.[2]

1. Overcoming the Monster, where the protagonist overcomes an existential threat, preventing grave harm to self, loved ones, or homeland.
2. Rags to Riches, where a lowly protagonist advances within a selected hierarchy. Once success is attained, the protagonist will often lose it all before gaining it back, usually by acquiring (or reacquiring) some sort of virtue.
3. The Quest, which involves the protagonist undertaking a mission or project to acquire something of value, and enduring hazards along the way.
4. Voyage and Return, involving the protagonist journeying to an unfamiliar place, enduring trials, and returning as a better person (elevated Black Arrow).
5. Comedy, where non-serious characters overcome adversity in such a way as to leave all or most of the characters in acceptable or happy circumstances.
6. Tragedy, involving a central character who is, usually, the story's antagonist, who, through the trials encountered, eventually gets his comeuppance.
7. Rebirth, in which the central character initially presents as the antagonist but, through trials experienced, morphs into a likeable protagonist.

Here is how each of these standard plots plays out within the model.

Overcoming the Monster

Easily the most compatible with classic plot structure, this story depends on its protagonist having either an already highly placed Black Arrow, or one that can be raised. Installing, say, Richard III as a protagonist in this plot simply would not be effective. Also notable is that, of the seven, this structure is most immune to derivative devices, such as *deus ex machina*. Imagine the groaning and eye rolling that would have accompanied an intervention by a far superior alien race at the climax of the original *Star Wars* film, just as the Death Star was about to blast the forest moon of Endor and, in turn, about to be destroyed by Luke's single proton torpedo, that stopped the whole conflict and set everyone about their affairs, no longer in conflict with each other.

This plot line leaves the consumer feeling better about their analogous relationships with groups that aspire to greater things. To the extent that the fans of *Star Wars* perceive themselves to belong to a society that prizes individual rights and despises tyranny, its denouement has them leaving the theater happier. Fans of evil, planet-destroying emperors were probably less thrilled.

Rags to Riches

Either an Omega or a Cinderella endures difficult conditions until they meet unexpectedly with success, due either to happenstance or a widespread recognition of their inherent value (high Black Arrow, in the case of the Cinderella archetype). Upon losing the success, the Omega will endure further trials in order to attain true merit (work to legitimately elevate their Black Arrow), or else will endure further trials until others recognize (Grey Arrow) their already highly placed value (Black Arrow, as in the Cinderella type).

Consumers of this narrative are made to feel better about themselves based on how readily they associate with the protagonist(s), and get the sense that it's okay for them to place their own White Arrow higher, due to their now-understood own undervalued Black Arrow.

The Quest

This protagonist almost has to have inherent merit, meaning that she will be one of the four high Black Arrow archetypes (Alpha, Beta, Cinderella, or Lone Wolf). The hazards endured while pursuing the object of value only serve to illuminate their value as compared to the other characters in the story.

This story leads its listeners to view themselves better (placing upward pressure on their White Arrows) by leading to the belief that, should the listener be put to the test, their own merit would shine through and be shown to be superior to others'.

Voyage and Return

A protagonist becomes aware that their life experiences are too narrowed or confined due to a lack of exposure to diverse places and cultures – their Black Arrows are uncomfortably low for not having traveled. This implies a low White Arrow in those cases where the voyage is self-initiated, or a low Grey Arrow in those stories where the protagonist is banished, or pressured into leaving. This plot structure is often combined with a rite-of-passage narrative.

The consumers of this story feel better about themselves in empathizing with the protagonist, whose own elevated Black Arrow gives license to enjoy some upward pressure on the White Arrow.

Comedy

Consider an additional tweak to our ancestors' campfire story. Instead of a threat of starvation lingering in the background, the group has more than enough to eat, and can anticipate this situation going forward, because it was actually the hyena herd that came into contact with the large, black monolith, and that has been collecting foodstuffs and delivering them to the humans ever since.

What happened to the narrative? It suddenly shifted away from classic plot structure, in that there's really no issue or central problem threatening the group. Instead, a dose of silliness injected into the narrative points to the idea that much of life is really non-threatening, and that the energy coming from one's low White Arrow driving improvements to their Black Arrow in order to help assure ongoing survival isn't necessary. It's okay to feel better about yourself, because, even if your Black Arrow is lowly placed, it won't necessarily harm you going forward.

Tragedy

An additional tweak to the first ancestors-around-the-campfire story's alternate version, where the hunters came back empty-handed: in that instance, it was, indeed, Jeff's inability to recognize that when one member of the hyena pack became isolated, it was then possible to isolate, kill, barbeque, and eat it. Jeff is lacking a key component – either situational awareness, or straight-up intelligence – that he will need if he is to be a successful leader of a hunting group and, therefore, leader of the overall tribe. Unless and until another member of the tribe challenges him in his position to decide where, when, and how to hunt game, the odds of the whole group suffering the effects of hunger just increased. Depending on the level of the environment's hostility, Jeff's relatively mild deficiency can mean the difference between life and death for the tribe.

This can work out several ways – Jeff can be made to see his deficiency (low Black Arrow), and seek to overcome it; Jeff can maintain his high White Arrow and refuse to accept the idea that someone else fulfilling the leader role would be better for everyone involved, among others – but in all instances Jeff needs to either have his White Arrow lowered, or else he must be eliminated, either through death or banishment. The so-called Tragic Flaw that the central characters in tragedies exhibit can be described as an obstinate refusal to endure the lowering of their White Arrows, which, in turn, precludes an honest assessment of their Black Arrows (or changing circumstances), meaning that even a low-placed Black Arrow will not be addressed and raised. From the original *Star Wars* trilogy, Darth Vader was made to be aware of his evil, and repented. Emperor Palpatine was thrown to his death, convinced of being the rightful ruler of that galaxy far, far away.

Essentially, we feel better about ourselves after having seen a tragedy by reassuring ourselves that *we* would never fail to see the signs that our internal narrative was delusional, and would not, therefore, suffer the unfortunate fate of the tragedy's central character. There's also the feeling of satisfaction from seeing a villain receive their comeuppance.

Rebirth

In what would otherwise be a tragic figure, the realization that their White Arrow is placed well above their Black Arrow occurs early enough in the rising action that they will self-inflict the dreaded White Arrow deflation, leading to the pursuit of Black

Arrow inflation which, in turn, becomes key to overcoming the central conflict. An excellent example of this is the character Severus Snape from the *Harry Potter* series. This story's consumer experiences White Arrow inflation for having empathized with this central character, and convincing themselves that they would have acted similarly.

On Deviating from Classic Structure

The comic poet Antiphanes (408–334 B.C.) was an early critic of the device of *deus ex machina*, literally, "god from a machine." In ancient Greek drama, it was a common plot device that entailed a deviation from classic plot structure. The play so afflicted would proceed along the lines of classic plot structure, but, at the climax of the action, rather than have the protagonists overcome the central problem and/or antagonist(s), a supremely powerful entity would suddenly appear and, with their otherworldly powers, set everything aright. As Antiphanes' criticisms indicate, *deus ex machina* was considered a rather disappointing way of resolving a plot, even in ancient times.

Moving 24 centuries into the future, the 1960s American television series *Star Trek* described the adventures of the crew of the starship *Enterprise*. Producer Gene Roddenberry had marketed his idea to potential network buyers as a "Wagon Train to the stars."[3] I interpret that analogy as asserting that Roddenberry had intended to follow classic plot structure, which was a staple in American Western-genre stories (like "Wagon Train"), with the only significant difference being the futuristic setting. Once American television network NBC bought the idea, Roddenberry was largely true to his word: *Star Trek*'s original series (shorthand: TOS) nominally followed classic plot structure for most of its three seasons.

Star Trek was cancelled in 1969. However, its reruns and intense fan base led to an entire franchise launch, which included four spin-off series and multiple motion pictures. The first television spin-off, *Star Trek: The Next Generation* (shorthand: TNG), began airing in 1987. Besides the changed characters, sets, ships, and quality of special effects – all of which were expected – another change entered in: a consistent deviation away from classic plot structure, most often towards a version of *deus ex machina*. Of the 25 episodes in season 1, I count no fewer than 19 that abandoned classic plot structure in favor of this peculiar version of *deus ex machina*. This particular brand of the plot device substitutes the god "communication" for the Greek Mount Olympus-dwelling variety, being craned onto the stage to fix everything. As the central problem is introduced and the action rises, in most of these TNG episodes it's apparent that, should the central issue's trajectory continue on its expected path, very bad things will happen to our heroes. Then, at the climax, instead of the protagonists overcoming the problem driving the plot, it's revealed that the whole conflict was due to one big misunderstanding. But, since the protagonists aren't bound by traditional methods of overcoming difficulties, don't you know, everything can now be set aright, once everybody understands the true motives and intentions in play. The denouement unfolds apace, as the perceived drivers of the central conflict melt away, and everybody is copacetic with the erstwhile antagonists and each other.

Star Trek: The Next Generation aired until 1994, with this particular plot device invoked often. The frustrations with the storylines led many fans and critics to declare "*Star Trek* is dead!"[4] I must confess that I largely agree with such sentiments. The sub-standard plot lines, combined with odd quotes from Gene Rodenberry himself, along the lines that Starfleet wasn't military,[5] indicated that *Star Trek: The Next Generation*'s producers had abandoned classic plot structure in favor of narratives that pushed a certain point of view, as if entertaining viewers and attracting advertising revenue were to be sacrificed in favor of a more preachy objective. Subsequent quotes from those close to Roddenberry, to the effect that he had come to see himself as something of a visionary, appear to reinforce the notion that the use of classic plot structure had lost its attractiveness to *Star Trek*'s producers.

Another somewhat cheesy plot device is one I've named the psycho-drama. Although instances of it were central to a few movies of the mid-twentieth century, I noticed it to be more prominent following the staging of Peter Shaffer's 1973 play *Equus*. In this play, a psychologist, Martin Dysart, attempts to discover the motives behind Alan Strang, a 17-year-old boy, who has blinded six horses. Many layers of religion, maturation, and sexual realization are piled onto this plot, but the ultimate climax turns on whether or not Dysart can return Strang to a mental state that will allow him to continue with his life on a relatively normative basis.

This variant of *deus ex machina*, where the "god" craned onto the stage is not an Olympus dweller, but a declaration of the overcoming of the central character's neurosis, would be repeated many, many times. The highly successful American television series *M*A*S*H* made extensive use of this device, even using it as the basis for the two-part series finale (aired February 28, 1983, "Goodbye, Farewell, and Amen").

Consider also the classic *Wuthering Heights*. The novel begins with a man named Lockwood arriving to live at Thrushcross Grange, about four miles from Wuthering Heights. His landlord, Heathcliff, strikes him as unusual, so Lockwood has his housekeeper, Nelly Dean, tell him the story behind his landlord and the two manor houses. Her narrative, as remembered in Lockwood's diary, provides much of the plot, and a twisted plot it is. The main driver of the story appears to be who will occupy what rank, and be happy with their lot in life, by the time the novel ends. Along the way, the characters make and break alliances, inherit or make fortunes and lose them, and fall in and out of love. For example,

- Catherine and Hindley Earnshaw dislike Heathcliff when their father initially brings him back from Liverpool. However, Catherine ends up falling in love with Heathcliff.
- … but not enough to marry him. Since Catherine perceives Heathcliff to be base (she thinks his Black Arrow is too low), she marries Edgar Linton.
- Heathcliff leaves Wuthering Heights, and comes back years later a wealthy man (so, in one way, he has proven his Black Arrow was high all along, and others simply did not realize it). However, he sets out to exact revenge against those he perceived had wronged him.
- When Catherine is confronted with evidence that leads her to believe that Heathcliff does not love her, she becomes ill out of spite.

And so it goes throughout the novel. Of the two reasons why people play "games," in order to relive past victories (for obvious reasons), and to relive past defeats, except *this time* the critical error the game player made back then could be corrected, *Wuthering Heights* is completely centered on the latter. The characters are locked into a present where they must experience the consequence of their decisions, with no way of going back and adequately correcting their errors. *Wuthering Heights* is not a "feel-good" novel; rather, it leaves any reader who empathizes with either Catherine or Heathcliff with a sense or feeling along the lines of "if only there were a way to go back and correct situation *n*." To the extent that it is attractive, though, turns on the ability of the reader to come away with the conclusion that *they* would never have made those errors in the first place, therefore *they* will never end up walking the moors on the verge of insanity, pining for lost love.

The ways in which alliances are formed and broken throughout *Wuthering Heights* does serve to illustrate some ways in which the stories that entertain us reflect aspects of the narratives that we run inside our cranium vaults. The characters' ranks change, in dramatic fashion, and their relationships to each other are profoundly affected. Similarly, when our White Arrows undergo a significant change, in either direction, and due to factors delusional or real (the Black Arrow is stuck low, or has been noticeably raised), the impact on ourselves and those around us is almost always profound.

The scripts we run in our heads, the ones that feed the "games" we play, do one of two things:

- They allow us to relive a past success, which reminds us we are "winners," inflating the White Arrow
- They allow us to relive a past failure, except this time we correct the central mistake. This means we are no longer losers, and a successful metaphorical re-enactment removes downward pressure on the game players' White Arrows.

As for the latter – the use of narratives where it's possible to go back and correct a mistake that has led to a present state of suffering – consider this short list of major films that have made use of the implausible technique of time travel:

- *The Time Machine*
- *Back to the Future I, II,* and *III*
- *Star Trek IV: The Voyage Home*
- *Star Trek VII: Generations*
- *Star Trek VIII: First Contact*
- *Star Trek* (2009 film)
- The entire *Terminator* franchise
- *Bill and Ted's Excellent Adventure*
- *Remember Me*
- *Time Bandits*
- *Harry Potter and the Prisoner of Azkaban*

… among literally hundreds of others. Almost without exception they all deal with the notion that past trials can be revisited, only *this* time the critical error corrected, leading to a better present, or future. An example of an instance where a past trauma *cannot* be revisited, and yet continues to generate a powerful influence in the time-now of the story, can be seen in the character of Miss Havisham, from *Great Expectations*, who keeps her uneaten, decaying wedding cake around as a continual reminder of having been stood up at the altar. Her solution to resolving this conflict is to train her beautiful ward, Estella, to be unable to love men, an act of revenge she eventually regrets.

Clearly the narrative of going back and correcting past errors that have led to present difficulties has appeal as entertainment, and I believe the reason is due to two factors:

1. We do run narratives in our minds, which inform our perception of who we are, how we ought to interact with others, what our true worth might be, and, therefore, how we ought to feel about ourselves.
2. Consuming others' narratives, via selected entertainment venues or other sources, can influence our internal narratives in such a way so as to help inflate our self-view, or White Arrow.

Among these influential narratives are the two primary reasons people tend to play "games," i.e., to relive past victories, or eradicate past errors, if only by metaphor.

While these may be the reasons people manipulate others and circumstances in order to collect the memories that keep their White Arrow buoyant, it may also be the reason we seek out certain types of entertainment. For example, pornography, aside from its titillation factor, appeals because the plots – such as they are – are centered around the idea that fornication or adultery are perfectly acceptable behaviors – "cool," even. If that's the case, then any natural feelings of guilt can be relegated to "invalid" status, removing downward pressure on the White Arrow. This removal of downward pressure on the porn consumer's White Arrow may be a factor in the addictive element in the viewing of pornography.

Getting Back to Classic Plot Structure

There are, of course, less extreme examples. Two of the most successful movie franchises ever were *Star Wars* and *Harry Potter*. The central characters of each – Luke Skywalker and Harry Potter – are of the Cinderella archetype, and have a remarkable number of characteristics in common, including:

- Both are orphans, raised by one of their parent's siblings.
- Both are born with inherent superior capabilities (their Black Arrows are already set high).
- But those inherent abilities are not recognized by those with whom they interact, at least not initially.
- They are, however, known to the boys' future mentors, who know of their past, the implications of the circumstances of their birth, and the predictions made of the boys' future.
- Both Luke and Harry are hunted by the ultimate antagonists of their worlds (Emperor Palpatine and Voldemort)
- as well as their main surrogates (Darth Vader and Severus Snape).
- The main surrogates are ambiguously evil,
- and dress in black, head to toe.
- Both Luke and Harry go through an education process to enhance their skills (they must work hard to raise their Black Arrows)
- and are taught by mentors, who are subsequently killed at the hands of the main surrogates (Obi Wan is slain by Vader; Snape kills Dumbledore).

- Both Luke and Harry ultimately confront their ultimate nemesis, and are victorious,
- but not until after the main surrogates have been fatally wounded or killed outright.

So, what made each franchise so amazingly successful? Certainly much of the success had to do with casting, costume design, special effects, setting, direction, production, and hundreds of other parameters.

But I maintain that much of it had to do with the writing, with the observance of classic plot structure, and the ability of these two scripts to reach many people's internal narratives, and influence them in such a way that their White Arrows enjoyed a post-reading/viewing buoyancy. People will pay money for such a buoyancy, and will do so on a consistent basis. Deviating from classic structure is not as successful a literary formula, because it is ultimately unsatisfying, due to the fact that it represents a deviation from the structure of the stories going on inside our heads.

(As an aside, while this book is not intended as a manual for writing fiction, I should point out that the author who creates characters with a clear vision of those characters' White, Grey, and Black Arrow placement, and why those ranks are where they are, will have described deeper, more complex, and more believable characters than the authors that do not do so. Additionally, since the misalignment of the arrows is a natural source of conflict and energy, such an analysis can lead to superior impartation of motive for the various characters' actions and words.)

Contrast these plot lines to the movie *Brazil*. Roger Ebert described the film as "hard to follow," and the box office reflected it. The movie has received much critical acclaim – it's just that people were not willing to pay to see it. Its script did not appeal to, nor mirror, the scripts that most people use to explain to themselves who they are, or how they should expect the future to unfold. In short, it didn't either inflate consumers' White Arrows, nor did it dissipate or relieve downward pressure on them.

That stories that deviate from classic plot structure tend to be less attractive than those that do can be comfortably established through a quick mental exercise. Would the entire *Harry Potter* series have been as successful (spoiler alert!) if, at its climax, Harry had stayed slain by Voldemort, and he and the other death eaters taken sneering, murderous control of the magical realm? Would not such an ending have left its viewers – the consumers of the script – profoundly disappointed?

Similar to the way certain disparate metals, when they come into contact with each other, create an electrical charge (the way in which, incidentally, artificially generated electrical current was rediscovered in the modern age), the gap between the rankings of characters' White, Grey, and Black Arrows creates an energy that drives narratives forward. The resolution of these gaps, i.e., the returning of them to their "proper" place, must reflect what's going on in our own attempts at properly realizing our placement of the arrows, lest they strike us as unattractive or unsatisfying. And, just to reiterate, the "proper" place of our White Arrows is always upwards when it comes to the realm of entertainment.

In short, the role of other people's stories in determining our own hierarchical rank is to create a narrative that is as close as possible a match to the script running inside our own minds, and to then influence it in such a way as to place upward pressure on our White Arrows.

Notes

1 Retrieved from *ThinkExist*, http://thinkexist.com/quotes/with/keyword/theater/3.html, July 10, 2015.
2 "The Seven Basic Plots," retrieved from *Wikipedia*, http://en.wikipedia.org/w/index.php?title=The_Seven_Basic_Plots&oldid=663956116, May 25, 2015.
3 Retrieved from *Roddenberry*, http://www.roddenberry.com/entertainment-star-trek, March 20, 2015.
4 Retrieved from *IGN*, "Review of Star Trek Nemsis," http://www.ign.com/articles/2002/12/12/review-of-star-trek-nemesis, March 20, 2015.
5 Farrand, Phil, *The Nitpicker's Guide for Classic Trekkers*. New York: Dell Publishing, 1994, 121.

Chapter 14

Implications for Management and Leadership

Art is the imposing of a pattern on experience, and our aesthetic enjoyment is recognition of the pattern.

Alfred North Whitehead[1]

Most of management and virtually all of leadership has to do with how we interact with others and, as we have seen, how successfully we interact with others has to do with the nature of the script running in our minds. The script, in turn, is largely based on how we place or perceive our three arrows. In short, the placement of our arrows determines (or at least dramatically influences) how we interpret reality, and convert those elements into a story, or script. The script, then, drives the ways that we approach life and others. So, rank drives script, script drives relationships.

In an article for *American Thinker*, Norman Rogers wrote this about Vilfredo Pareto's book *The Rise and Fall of Elites: An Application of Theoretical Sociology*:

> Pareto believed that men form their beliefs from emotion or sentiment and that rational justifications for beliefs are constructed after the belief has been subscribed to. In other words, the rational justification is window dressing. Pareto also thought that men deceive themselves about the origin of their beliefs, not recognizing that their beliefs are the consequence of sentiment. Men claim, and believe, that their beliefs are the result of rational thought.[2]

To fold the previous paragraph into our model (and, as previously stated), our White Arrows tend to be placed higher than our Black Arrows, the difference being driven by ego defense mechanisms, confirmation bias, the Dunning-Kruger Effect, or a host of other reasons, up to and including out-and-out delusion. From Chapter 3, it's called "harsh reality" for a reason, since the only thing that can be counted on to depress a person's White Arrow to closer proximity with their Black Arrow is an abrupt encounter with the aforementioned reality. Human resources experts whom I've known claim that a person never truly changes unless and until they are confronted with a "life-changing event," similar to George Bailey being visited by his guardian angel, Clarence, on Christmas Eve, and seeing how his home town would have turned out if not for the life he has led in the movie *It's a Wonderful Life*.

Unfortunately, the only way we can raise our Black Arrows is if we first perceive that they are too low – that, in whatever organization in which we find ourselves, we need to make of ourselves a greater value. And *that* perception relies on a low White Arrow since, obviously, if we think we are all that, then there's no reason to devote the time and energy into improving ourselves, i.e., raising the Black Arrow. Why suffer to raise that which is believed to be already high, or at least acceptably ranked?

This dynamic also has an effect on the narrative that the group sets up and maintains. In American football, the Super Bowl champion often encounters a so-called "hangover," where their performance in the following season encounters a notable drop-off. At the same time, it seems that at least one team not expected to perform well at all, or even at a mediocre level, will suddenly find themselves in the playoffs. I believe these are manifestations of the perceived-value/real-value divide, the difference between the White Arrow and Black Arrow at the group level. High-performing organizations are susceptible to their members perceiving themselves as such, and failing (or refusing) to see the need to expend extraordinary effort in order to achieve the organization's stated goals on a continuing basis. Similarly, organizations that are perceived to be poor performers have a better chance of having its members realize that they must work harder to even have a chance at attaining shared goals, assuming that their leadership has any efficacy at all.

This effect represents one of the ironic paradoxes of democratic or republican forms of government, in that those wishing to be elected must find a way of elevating the White Arrows of those who would vote for them, even while the society the politician seeks to lead manifests pathologies that stem from that very artificially elevated group-wide White Arrow. Essentially, the typical person seeking elected office needs to communicate to potential voters that they are great, but he can make them better. An alternative for the cynical would be to communicate that the voters are great, but are made to suffer due to the injustice of "the other," and the office seeker knows how to thwart this "other."

Managers have a similar problem, although they are (usually) saved from the difficulties associated with having to win some sort of popularity contest among those whom they would lead, prior to deflating their White Arrows. Dan Reeves, who played for the Dallas Cowboys prior to becoming a successful NFL coach in his own right, once spoke of the experience of reviewing the film from the previous weekend's game during the time Tom Landry was head coach. "We would have won by 30 points the day before, and we would get out the break and say 'Did we win yesterday? You know, I felt like we got beat!' "[3] I remember reading that one of the Green Bay Packers during their golden era – it may have been Jerry Kramer – once said that legendary coach Vince Lombardi treated him and the other players on those teams "like dogs." And this was during the time that the Packers were winning multiple championships.

And, of course, the first step in preparing men to become warriors and join a group of other warriors is to break them down, to convince them that, individually, they are next to worthless but, as a trained member of the group they are to join, they just might be able to attain some level of value. Translated to our lexicon, the drill sergeants know that their recruits must lower their White Arrows prior to being convinced that their Black Arrows are too low for the tasks ahead of them and their compatriots. Once their Black Arrows have been raised through intensive training, then and only then will they be allowed some bit of White Arrow inflation.

However, both in professional team sports competition and in warfare, what works and is successful, and what doesn't work and results in failure, is unequivocal. At the end of the competition/fight, you and your team either won, or lost. Common elements of the group narrative being propagated appear to be:

- The individuals in the group are sub-standard
- and should consider themselves lucky to be included in the group at all.
- The task before them is next to insurmountable
- and the only chance the organization, as a whole, has to attain that goal is if every single member performs at a higher level than what has been shown, or even fairly expected.
- The competition is very good at what they do
- and, should the competition succeed, very bad things will happen to the group.
- Finally, even in the circumstance of having achieved victory, the winners must not assume that they are superior for any length of time, and that the competition is more likely to win the next time if the group does so.

Compare these to some of the typical elements of the nominal corporate narrative:

- The individuals in the company represent that organization's "greatest assets."
- The company recognized their value, and recruited them for that reason.
- The company is already successful
- and is so not due to any wild stroke of luck, or superhuman sacrifice of its members (though organizations led by the Politician archetype may very well have some element of the amazingly unique qualities of its leaders embedded in the organization's narrative).
- The competition is inferior to the company,
- but, even if they succeed, it's only a temporary state of affairs.
- Should the company achieve its stated goals, it's due entirely to the overall organization's meme, and its members' willingness to embrace it.

With such contrasts, the automatic implication is that there's something else in play here other than the differences in the performing environments.

I think it's arrow placement.

Consider the goal of the leader of the organization that simply must be able to perform at a high level, in the military's case literally being a question of life and death. The organizational pathologies that afflict loser organizations are either introduced or perpetrated by the archetypes with high White Arrows without similarly placed lofty Black Arrows (Fools and Politicians). These pathologies – arrow resting, for one – are beneficial to the other low Black Arrow roles (Comedians and Omegas), who would otherwise be identified and banished if not for those elements of the group's narrative that provide them cover. The pathologies introduced by members maintaining a large delta between their high White Arrows and low Black Arrows must be quickly recognized and rooted out, or else the owning organization will lose in the unforgiving environs where it seeks to survive, if not thrive.

Conversely, organizations engaged in free-market enterprise need only receive more in revenue than they spend in costs to remain viable. Outside of the crucible of allowed-pathologies-equal-death environs, and human nature being what it is, the divide between high White Arrows and low Black ones simply invites the organizational pathologies that, ultimately, weigh down the organization as it pursues its articulated goals, yet fulfills its primary unstated goal, that of maintaining those in the upper ranks in those positions of authority or prestige.

Winning organizations can (and usually will) experience consistent success with the high White Arrow and high Black Arrow archetypes (Lone Wolves and Alphas), but the most successful organizations will be predominantly populated with the low White Arrow and high Black Arrow types (Cinderellas and Betas). This is assuming, of course, that (a) the organization is well led, which in turn implies (b) the primary narrative being perpetrated on (and accepted by) the organization is highly consistent with the best technical approach to attaining the group's objectives. So, to reiterate:

- Narrative = technical approach to resolving the group's problems.
- Technical approach = success or failure.
- Therefore, narrative = success or failure.

The use of the term/symbol "equals" might be a bit strong – I used it for succinctness. A better term for everyday managerial analysis might be "strongly influences," but the logical construct remains largely intact. The chances of managerial success in any of the three types – Asset, Project, or Strategic – is heavily dependent on the scripts that are running in the minds of the group's leader(s), and the narrative that the group as a whole has adopted. When combined with the chain from the chapter's first paragraph, we have:

- Rank drives narrative.
- The narrative determines how the individual or group will perceive and address a given problem, and reflects character.
- The combination of (a) rank within a hierarchy and (b) the narrative embraced by that hierarchy will heavily influence – if not out and out determine – the nature of the relationships among its members.
- As U.S. Senator John McCain wrote, character is destiny.
- Leading to the inescapable conclusion that our rank within a chosen hierarchy, placed accurately or not, attained fairly or not, acceptable or not, and the actions we take to maintain or change it, determines our destiny.

To help illustrate this concept, let's revisit the Hollywood coffee shop from Chapter 1. Should Steve maintain an artificially high White Arrow, he will be far less likely to approach the difficulties associated with running or advancing his business as problems pertaining to providing better service or products to his customers, and instead look to the causal factors of any setback as having something more to do with unfair competitors' actions, unappreciative customers, greedy landlords, unreliable vendors – anything and everything that will help him keep his White Arrow in its lofty place. Conversely, should Steve consistently maintain a low White Arrow, it follows that setbacks will more likely be seen as evidence of his own deficiencies (low Black Arrow), a condition that will require time and effort to remedy. The placement of Steve's White Arrow drives his selection of the strategies he will embrace when faced with setbacks, either to attempt to negotiate better rent rates from his landlord (in the case of a high White Arrow), or encourage his employees to expend extra effort at treating customers with respect and courtesy, should he and they manage to maintain an attitude that their little coffee shop is, indeed, fortunate to have attracted their business in the first place (low White Arrow).

All this is not to say that the truly humble won't attempt to negotiate better rent rates, but it does point to a certain reluctance among the haughty (high White Arrow) set to treat others with genuine consideration or respect, and I think we all can recognize this intuitively when being served in a variety of venues, tiny coffee shops included. Ultimately, the cumulative effect of these decisions will determine the success of the coffee shop, and significantly influence the ability of its owner and employees to realize their own personal objectives.

Indeed, the insight of maintaining an appropriately low White Arrow when interacting with a business's customers, both existing and potential, is arguably more valuable than all of the insights in all of the quantitative analysis in business textbooks ever printed, combined. How do I know? Because, in those instances where comparative raw talent is even close, the business that has embraced a humble narrative with respect to its clients will almost automatically outperform its haughty competitors, and the fluency of their accountants will matter very little. Show me a successful enterprise led by Politicians, or Fools (the high White Arrow, low Black Arrow pair), and I will show you either a company in its decline, or else an enterprise that has zero accountability to its customers, as in a government-enforced monopoly.

The effect of narrative determining the character and likely behavior of the group, and the character of the group in turn determining its success or failure is entirely scalable. It not only occurs in small coffee cafés in California, but in teams, groups, and organizations around the world, and throughout history. Stalin was a criminal in czarist Russia. Unwilling to accept his low rank within that hierarchy, he had a choice: make himself demonstrably more valuable to the existing structure (abandon his criminal ways, and work to inflate his Black Arrow), or topple the existing structure in favor of one that would allow an advancement in rank based on the things he was better at, i.e., treachery and murder. With the economically vacuous ideas of Marx and Engels providing a pseudo-intellectual political hierarchy, Stalin and his cohorts Lenin, Trotsky, Zinoviev, and many others initiated a reign of terror that surpassed the French Revolution by a factor of *1,000* (at least) as they ascended to its upper ranks (estimates of deaths by guillotine during the French Revolution are around 40,000; deaths from the Russian Revolution, including the purges, Gulags, and Holodomor, exceed 40,000,000).

Of course, neither Stalin nor his cohorts simply assumed their ultimate ranks on their own: the others within the macro organization had to either grant them their status, or acquiesce as others did so. One can only assume that the communists' true narrative, of brutal suppression politically and economic quasi-slavery, was successfully cloaked with the proffered narrative of a "workers' paradise," and that the real narrative's horrific nature was completely unknown and unknowable by the majority until it was too late to reverse.

We've Seen These Stories Before

The implications for those who support – let alone embrace – such group narratives can be profound, or even eternal. Grigory Zinoviev was a key member of the

Bolsheviks during the Revolution, and a leader in the Politburo afterwards. He may have had occasion to reconsider the wisdom of embracing the Bolsheviks' narrative when he was arrested and made the key defendant in one of the earliest of the notorious show trials, which ended in his execution. Walter Duranty won the Pulitzer Prize in 1932 for using his position as a reporter to prop up the communists' narrative through communicating their propaganda as factual, while ignoring the Holodomor. While it's impossible to state what would have been the free world's response to the nascent communist government had its horrors been accurately relayed, there can be no evading that Duranty's words supported the narrative that allowed such a widespread monstrosity to continue for decades.

Duranty's Pulitzer has never been suspended.

"Those who do not learn from history are doomed to repeat it." So said Jorge Santayana, meaning we have the same narratives happening over and over. In addition to patterns emerging in the group narratives, consistencies are also apparent in those groups' individual members, or leaders, along the lines of:

- A given organization's leadership is risibly bad, or its inherent structure invalid, or both.
- A challenger (or group of challengers), having endured downward pressure on his White Arrow from the existing leadership/structure, elects to overthrow the same.
- The existing structure employs its self-preservation strategies, typically in increments at first, eventually resorting to any tactic it has at its disposal to repel the incursion.
- A new narrative gains momentum, and is eventually embraced, accepted, or at least tolerated by a majority of the organization.
- The perpetrators or owners of the new narrative solidify the manner in which the narrative's implied hierarchy assigns rank, and (typically) insinuate themselves into the higher ranks based on those rules.
- As with all organizations, the new one has a lifespan. Eventually, its leadership will prove to be risibly bad, or its structure demonstrably inferior to that of other organizations, or both, and the cycle begins again.

Note how closely this pattern resembles that of scientific revolutions, as described by Thomas Kuhn and reviewed in Chapter 7. Note also the central role of the challengers' rank and the organizations' hierarchical system. When the individual's White Arrow is placed above his Black Arrow, the difference between the two creates an energy that must be expended or reconciled. Similarly, when the organization's hierarchical structure or ranking system erodes into an invalid state (e.g., Mitch's newspaper leadership's capacity for rewarding low performers, from Chapter 9), the organization itself generates the delta between its members' White and Black Arrows, also creating an energy of disparity that can only be resolved through conflict, or even upheaval. The feudal system of government probably would not work in most of the world today, but it worked just fine in England for a rather long time. In the early part of the fifteenth century, for example, Henry V was an extremely capable monarch, who just happened to inherit the throne. However, when his infant son was crowned King of England *and* France in 1422, the primary invalidating element of the feudal system was laid bare, not to be reconciled until the War of the Roses had run its course. The possibility that a person might be elevated to a leadership position

Table 14.1 Capability/Narrative Validity Payoff Matrix

Capability/narrative	Low narrative validity	High narrative validity
Highly capable manager	Any success realized is due to the talent of the manager	Organizational/project success
Low capability manager	Failure leading to upheaval	Odds are that the manager/leader will be rejected

of a first-world nation based on birthright, rather than any demonstrated virtue, and would then prove to be unsuitable in that role would be warred over time and again, incidents of wide-scale upheaval pointing to a deficiency in the macro organizations' hierarchical structure.

Reverting back to the game theorists' favorite tool, the payoff grid looks something like Table 14.1.

So, what's the acid test for the validity of the organization's narrative? I believe it has to do with the extent that the target organization embraces its stated objectives vs. the degree with which it has abandoned those goals in favor of maintaining the ranks of its members. On rare occasions, this may be Boolean – Hitler in the bunker had clearly abandoned any pretense to making decisions for the good of Germany. The rest of the instances it will be a slide along a continuum.

What the Continuum Looks Like

In the eighteenth century, Alexander Tytler (probably) noted the following:

> Great nations rise and fall. The people go from bondage to spiritual truth, to great courage, from courage to liberty, from liberty to abundance, from abundance to selfishness, from selfishness to complacency, from complacency to apathy, from apathy to dependence, from dependence back again to bondage.[4]

These steps, then, look like this:

1. From Bondage to Spiritual Truth
2. Spiritual Truth to Great Courage
3. Courage to Liberty
4. Liberty to Abundance
5. Abundance to Selfishness
6. Selfishness to Complacency
7. Complacency to Apathy
8. Apathy to Dependence
9. Dependence back to Bondage

While the degree of separation between some of these stages is somewhat cloudy, the polar opposites, Liberty (3/4) and Bondage (9/1) are clear. Essentially, the organization is on an upward trajectory from Bondage to Liberty but, once Liberty brings with it Abundance, the political entity experiencing this cycle sees its upward trajectory flatten out, if not stall. By the time step 5 manifests, the group has begun its down-ward orientation, which is (theoretically) extremely difficult if not impossible to reverse until step 9, a return to Bondage, has been realized.

This structure is somewhat analogous to our three-arrow model, in that it reflects the changes to the narrative the group has adopted. In the three-arrow model, the polar opposite stages are reflected by a group that (a) has members who have uni-versally embraced a narrative of their shared objectives and devote all of their energy towards realizing them, vs. (b) the organization that exists to maintain the ranks of its (presumably) comfortable members in its current hierarchy, and has allowed sufficient organizational pathologies to crowd out those parts of the shared narrative that serve the original, macro-objective-pursuing variety.

The nature of the group's narrative, specifically which side of the upward/down-ward trajectory line it most closely adheres to, will also determine the types of members it will attract or repel. The organization in its ascendency will attract the archetypes with high Black Arrows (Alphas, Betas, Lone Wolves, and Cinderellas), who are more frequently rewarded for their actual contributions in organizations that are relatively free from common organizational pathologies, such as cronyism. These organizations will also tend to repel those with low Black Arrows (Politicians, Comedians, Fools, and Omegas), since these types must rely on the existence or introduction of narra-tives that are at odds with both the organization's stated goals *and* reality in order to create a hierarchy where they may advance, despite having little to offer in the actual furtherance of the group's goals. Similarly, organizations about to enter onto (or actu-ally experiencing) a downward trajectory will tend to repel high Black Arrows, since any rewards that the group is in a position to bestow are less likely to go to those who actually deserve them, and instead be awarded to their low Black Arrow associates.

Of course, economic entities differ from political ones in that their members are not permanent, and neither is their existence nearly as long term. The truncated ver-sion of Tytler's structure as it applies to corporations will usually see the company come to bankruptcy prior to step 8, since the corporation riddled with apathy and dependence will have almost certainly been displaced by those organizations with an upward trajectory, the exception being government-maintained monopolies. And yet, from the earliest pages of this book we've been working with the assumption that virtually all organizations have a set lifespan. What is the identifiable point in the organization's lifespan that represents its descent into oblivion? That has to do with the narratives it operates under: the first, the organization's stated goals, shared by its members; the second, its unstated goals, that of maintaining its existence apart from legitimate pursuit of those goals, and no longer universally shared among its members. The organization that gradually, by observable degrees, has made the transition from the former to the latter is in its downward trajectory, which is, in all likelihood, irre-versible. Admittedly, the Christian Church teaches that no individual is irredeemable, though that notion was probably a tough sell during the reign of Diocletian or Nero.

If, however, the downward trend for either the organization or the person is *not* irreversible, how can that be determined? There are far too many parameters and data points to evaluate to come up with a single set of triggers that would indicate a person or organization has definitively slipped into irredeemable space. Rome was a republic, clearly in its ascendency when Gaius Julius Caesar illegally crossed the Rubicon with a legion in 49 B.C. By 476, when Odoacer deposed the Emperor Romulus, the Roman

Empire was finished as a power, but the goings-on in the 525 years that separated these two events have led to a great deal of discussion about which trends combined into movements combined into nation-state-toppling cataclysms will be the subject of historical debate for as long as Western civilization lasts. Which is not to say that simpler models of ascendency and decline don't exist – they do. In fact, our little arrow model, reflecting the nature of the scripts that we run in our minds and embrace as part of a group, provides a potentially highly useful one.

For each of Tytler's stages, we assume that the society so placed largely shared a set of values and macro objectives – they had a group narrative. Using the arrow model to lend structure to this narrative, such societies' narratives had three components:

- What they thought of themselves, as individuals within the society.
- What the group as a whole believed about themselves.
- What their actual value to civilization overall was.

At the two extremes, some extreme societal behavior can be expected. If a society or nation-state is filled with individuals who think very highly of themselves, believe that their nation-state is superior to others, and that nation-state *is* actually superior (usually in technology and tech-driven advances in its military), then it will usually engage in marked territorial expansion or imperialism. Conversely, a society filled with those who think themselves weak, believe their countrymen also weak, and have good reason to believe so, will be vulnerable to the expansion of their neighbors. Since the nature of the narrative that the macro organization embraces has a dramatic influence on its future and prospects of success or failure, those individuals with a gift for oratory, who can actually change the group's narrative towards one that favors the orator's (or his political party's) position, have a distinct advantage over those would-be leaders who are not as adept at macro-script changing.

Based on the hypothesis that the arrow model is scalable, its (admittedly rough) alignment with Tytler's progression looks something like Table 14.2.

To the extent that the two models are similar, several implications follow. As with the "Nominal Strategy" from Chapter 10, the progression through the categories is at least partially driven by the energy created by the separation of the arrows. The

Table 14.2 Alignment of the Tytler Progression and Arrow Model

Tytler progression		Arrow model	
From	**To**	**From**	**To**
Bondage	Faith	Omega	Cinderella
Faith	Courage	Cinderella	Beta
Courage	Liberty	Cinderella	Beta
Liberty	Abundance	Beta	Alpha
Abundance	Selfishness	Alpha	Lone Wolf
Selfishness	Complacency	Lone Wolf	Politician
Complacency	Apathy	Politician	Comedian
Apathy	Dependence	Comedian	Fool
Dependence	Bondage	Fool	Omega

Omega society, assuming it's not comfortable with its circumstances, will seek to actually improve its capabilities – it will put collective energy into raising its collective Black Arrow. Once it has attained a measure of objective virtue or capability, the members of the group will recognize it, raising its Grey Arrow, and moving from Cinderella to Beta, Faith/Courage to Liberty. As the society attains its zenith, with all three arrows highly placed, those pathologies associated with the high White Arrow are introduced and take root, leading directly to an eroding of the Black Arrow, and initiating the downward trajectory, if not spiral.

On the Symptoms of a Downward Trajectory

Typically, the macro organization will tend to show signs or throw out indicators of which side of the upward/downward trajectory divide it inhabits. One of my favorite examples has to do with a high-tech company that had invited me in for an interview for a senior position. I was already working in a senior position with an organization that I liked very much, but went for the interview anyway, more out of curiosity than anything else, since this company had been started by an associate I had known previously.

I was interviewed by an eight-member senior management team, including their human resources director, a relatively young woman who was dressed somewhat more revealingly than I would have expected (a hint in and of itself). The other members of the team were interested in my education, experience, background, publications. Not the HR director. When it came time for her to pose her questions, it was clear to me that she was used to applicants who not only wanted to have an offer made, they must have been absolutely desperate for one. Her attitude exuded a sense that she believed that *anyone* who worked for this company was very lucky to do so.

"Why do you want to work here?" she asked, imperiously.

"I'm not sure that I do," I replied flatly. "What can you do to make it attractive for me?"

She was flabbergasted, almost speechless, which told me all I needed to know: this organization wasn't interested in attracting talent – it was already at a stage where it was telling itself how wonderful it was. Its narrative had drifted to a point where sheer rankism would be in play in most (if not all) of its business model components.

Other signs of a commercial organization in decline include:

- Leaders are not Alphas or Betas (or even Cinderellas or Lone Wolves).
- Politicians or Comedians are in highly ranked positions.
- A marked difference between its stated agenda and how it treats employees, customers, or competitors.
- Cinderellas, Lone Wolves, or Betas are occupying lower ranks.
- Any other signs of an abandonment of a meritocracy, most notably nepotism or cronyism.
- Actions from leadership that appear to enrich them personally, at the expense of the rank and file.
- The acceptance of Omegas (or other demonstrably low performers (low Black Arrows)) in the group.
- An absence of lines of communication that would alert the upper ranks that their chosen technical direction is in need of adjusting, or even abandonment.

- A marked inconsistency in the manner in which those who attain the organization's stated goals are rewarded.
- The assignment of awards to those who do not demonstrably or directly help attain the organization's stated goals.
- Obvious instances of the organization behaving contrary to its stated mission or goals.

Many of these pathologies occur simultaneously, or in harmony, for a reason. For example, blatant nepotism or cronyism would damage group morale if it were to be honestly evaluated for its impact on organizational efficiency or effectiveness. Therefore, any lines of communication that would highlight the damage of this particular pathology – up to and including cost or schedule performance information systems – must be downplayed, if not eliminated altogether, leading to yet another business model flaw being introduced.

Additionally, the various archetypes will tend to interact differently, based on the validity of the overall narrative. A strong, valid narrative, relatively business-model pathology free, will see the Alphas and Betas making strides towards the realization of the organization's goals, working to attract Lone Wolves and encourage Cinderellas, while setting up or maintaining the devices that either correct or eliminate poor performers from joining or advancing within the organization. Conversely, in organizations headed on a downward trajectory, at least some of the upper ranks are occupied by Politicians, or Comedians. How did they get there, being low on merit (low Black Arrow)? By the contributions of others, misattributed to themselves. Since Alphas and Betas are not likely to leave their contributions unrecognized, the natural prey for these invalid leaders would be the Lone Wolves and (especially) the Cinderellas. However, the Politician/Comedian must take steps to ensure that the Lone Wolf/Cinderella will not be recognized for their contributions in their own right, and potentially be promoted to a higher rank than the Politician/Comedian. This will often take the form of insisting on some sort of mentor/trainee relationship, or some way that the Politician/Comedian can control the narrative so that the Lone Wolf/Cinderella does not receive the recognition deserved, which, instead, goes to them.

A Quick Return to Game Theory

Recall the Hawk/Dove Game from Chapter 4. A quick recap: we have two birds who can select a passive strategy of foraging for food and keeping or eating all they accumulate (dove), or else engage in aggressive behavior, either taking the other bird's food away or preventing it from foraging in the first place (hawk). Alternately, the birds can engage a mixed strategy, where they behave as dove for some of the iterations, and hawk in others. In a 100-bird population, the Nash Equilibrium ends up being around 75% dove and 25% hawk, meaning that the birds will tend to divide 75–25 into dove-hawks, or else will engage in mixed strategies where they behave as dove 75% of the time. Notable is the fact that the overall population's payoff is maximized when they all behave as dove all of the time; however, with the introduction of just one hawk, the Nash Equilibrium will quickly assume its 75–25 profile.

Granted, the Hawk-Dove Game operates under a severely limited set of parameters, narrowing its analogy utility significantly. However, if a lesson from the analysis of this game is to be gleaned in assessing the dividing line between organizations in their ascendency and those in decline, it would have to be that point in which the organization's narrative changes from the legitimately pursuing its stated objectives, and over to cynically pursuing those objectives while in reality the hidden agenda is truly being sought. In other words, the organization has moved away from pursuing its nominal objective and has devolved into merely maintaining its own existence, with its higher-ranking members enjoying their roles in the group's upper echelons.

There are, of course, other indicators that a given group has entered into decline, but the presence of any of these should serve as an indication that the organization has reached or even passed the tipping point, from being all about its stated goals, and towards its unstated goal, usually that of maintaining the existing hierarchy and those who enjoy places in its upper ranks.

The Essential Impact of Project Management

When project management as a distinct discipline began to become commonly recognized, it was largely presented as a novel set of business tactics germane to better execution of projects, as opposed to organizations or functions. It wasn't only that – it was, rather, a Kuhnsian paradigm shift, a radical challenge to the consensus within the management sciences. Looking back, this challenge was primarily against two strongly held narratives, one open, and one covert. These two were (1) that all relevant management information dealing with cost performance should originate with the general ledger, and (2) the point of *all* management is to "maximize shareholder wealth." Even before the widespread introduction of project management as a discipline, it was clear that at least one aspect of management was to execute the documented, agreed-upon project scope, efficiently and effectively, shareholders notwithstanding.

While (2) above was commonly published in business college texts as absolutely true, it was – and remains –false. And yet, at least at the major university level, to assert that represents a significant career-limiting move, since the ongoing consensus within management science circles is so strongly invested in the maximize-shareholder-wealth narrative. Now, consider the earlier discussion, of how an organization's trajectory transitions from upward to downward once the adopted narrative moves from accomplishing goals – scope – to maintaining the ranks of those in the upper levels of the group's hierarchy. Project management, as a distinct discipline, is all about accomplishing scope, first and foremost. Indeed, given the transitory nature of virtually *all* project teams, the attainment of a certain rank within the project team is similarly transitory. Today's senior project engineer was yesterday's junior project engineer, or tomorrow's project manager. Same with the next project. Projects (successful ones, anyway) by their nature *cannot* exist merely for the maintenance of rank, nor for the purpose of their own continued existence.

In 1984, David Cleland published on the topic of Matrix Management,[5] or the organizational structure that enabled an alignment of the corporation's resources to its project needs. A "strong matrix" pertained to those organizations whose structures favored the project teams' requirements as priority, while a "weak matrix" placed a premium on the organization's resources needs.

Its resources needs.

After the material we have covered together, dear reader, I will leave it to you to determine which version of the Matrix Managed organization is more conducive to being on an upward trajectory, and which has reached the tipping point of pursuing the unarticulated agenda.

Another Recognizable Pattern

Having worked for a few large, long-lived organizations, I noticed a pattern when it came to the way they handled certain functions, most notably safety management. This pattern would often manifest via the following steps:

- An accident would occur, leading to serious injury.
- The corporation would react, sometimes dramatically, and notify all of the employees of what had happened.
- Safety experts and consultants would be brought in to evaluate *all* engineering practices and, often, clerical operations as well.
- The experts would return their evaluation, which would include specific actions they wanted management to enact on the rank and file.
- These actions would be introduced through meetings, memos, and other communication venues, culminating in updated corporate procedures.
- The new procedures being in place, some innocuous versions of infractions would be cited, and acted upon.
- Some time would pass, with no serious accidents or on-the-job injuries.
- Members of the organization would become progressively more complacent on matters dealing with safety, until...
- another major accident would occur, reinitiating the cycle.

Interestingly, this cycle has the identical number of steps as Tytler's progression.

I came to realize that something very similar would happen in project management space, in organizations that dealt with a significant amount of project work.

- A project would come in late, or dramatically over budget.
- The corporation would react, though they would rarely communicate the failure to those members not involved.
- Project management experts would conduct an evaluation, returning the opinion that the company had failed to enact even the most basic of project management techniques.
- A new initiative to perform basic project management techniques would be launched for the ongoing projects in the portfolio.
- These actions would be introduced through meetings, memos, and other communication venues, culminating in updated corporate procedures.
- The new procedures being in place, some innocuous versions of infractions would be cited, and acted upon.
- Some time would pass, with no serious overruns or delays incurred.
- Members of the organization would become progressively more lax (or even antagonistic) on matters dealing with project management, until...
- another major overrun or delay would occur, reinitiating the cycle.

From the perspective, though, of the organization approaching and retreating from the tipping point, of embracing the execute-the-scope narrative over to the maintain-the-hierarchy script, this pattern represents the contest between group narratives, with the winner determining the entire group's future. During those times that the project management techniques are coveted, the organization is on an upward trajectory, being vested in pursuing the scope – the *articulated* scope – before it. When project management, as a discipline, is abandoned or neglected, the organization has entered into its downward trajectory, embracing the pseudo-secret narrative towards a maintain-the-hierarchy mode.

So, what's a manager or leader to do with this kind of insight? If involved in an organization on an upward trajectory, and any of these pathologies begin to manifest, the best probable course of action is to identify them early, and address them as expeditiously as possible, as discussed in Chapter 11. Unless, of course, you are of a mind to accelerate the organization's demise, in which case you would either want to introduce or assist the already present pathologies, as discussed in Chapter 10. Conversely, should you find yourself involved with an organization approaching or already set upon its downward trajectory, and wish to reverse it, the best counsel I can provide would be to evaluate whether or not it's too late for the organization, and respond accordingly. If it's not, execute the strategy from earlier in this paragraph. If it is too late, decide if disengagement is an option. If so, so. If not, then find a way to position yourself so that, as the organization endures its death spiral, you are least affected by the inevitable.

Not to sound overly cynical, but that's the way of organizations. They have definitive lifespans, and will behave differently based on whether or not they are in their ascendency, or in decline. The narratives embraced will have a direct impact on the types of managerial decisions that will land the decision maker in the good graces of the surrounding organization, or in its cellar. The organization's script and behavior will produce a bevy of clues as to the most appropriate approach to take – the onus is on you, the manager, to read these clues, and select the most effective strategies for getting to where you want to be, even if that means disengagement.

Notes

1 Whitehead, Alfred North, retrieved from *BrainyQuote*, http://www.brainyquote.com/quotes/keywords/pattern.html, July 10, 2015.
2 Retrieved from *American Thinker*, http://www.americanthinker.com/articles/2015/03/pareto_speaks_to_us_about_ environmentalism.html#ixzz3ViBvWpPd, March 28, 2015.
3 Reeves, Dan, quoted from NFL Films, "A Football Life: Tom Landry," season 1, episode 8.
4 Collins, Loren, *The Truth about Tytler*, retrieved from http://www.lorencollins.net/tytler.html, April 18, 2015.
5 Cleland, David, *Matrix Management Systems Handbook*. New York: Van Nostrand Reinhold, 1984.

Conclusion
What Have We Learned?

> There will be no end to the troubles of states, or of humanity itself, till philosophers become kings in this world, or till those we now call kings and rulers really and truly become philosophers, and political power and philosophy thus come into the same hands.
>
> Plato[1]

The short answer to the question in this chapter's title, essentially, is that most everybody's White Arrow is too high, and that tends to lead to bad things happening on scales both large and small.

How we arrived here involved a bit more of an intellectual journey.

We have seen how virtually all interactions we have with others carry with them a form of hierarchy, and this hierarchy is fairly automatic, unavoidable even. The nature of these hierarchies is sometimes openly articulated, often assumed, and almost always carries an undisclosed element. Based on these hierarchies, a person's rank within them can easily become a source of conflict.

The reasons for this common conflict are rooted in unchanging human nature, inherited through millennia of assimilated pack behaviors which provided the best chance of ongoing survival. Removed from essential survival environs, these reflexive behaviors and strategies continue to hold sway over our everyday lives and relationships with others.

However, independent analysis of those behaviors shows that they fall into patterns, much like the sets of canned strategies that are observed and can be quantified through Game Theory. The patterns of these strategies are rooted in three basic rankings: how we view ourselves, how others perceive us, and our true value to the groups to which we belong. The misalignment of these three ranks, which we've illustrated using the three-arrow model, represents the energy that naturally flows from unresolved conflict. As this energy is dissipated or directed, those behaviors and strategies are modified, pursued, or discarded.

As these choices are made, and strategies executed, their impacts to ourselves and the organizations to which we belong can have positive effects and outcomes, or may devolve into pathologies that harm us and/or the groups in which we participate. The strategies themselves are morally and intellectually neutral – it's the circumstances in which they are selected that make them beneficial or detrimental, right or wrong.

In this regard, voyeurism is also morally and intellectually neutral; indeed, it's hard-wired in us to want to become informed of the strategies that others within our hierarchies are invoking, to inform us of the nature of the organization, to provide clues as to our ranks, and to evaluate their effectiveness, for when we find ourselves in analogous situations.

The three-arrow model is scalable. It can be used to not only structure the analysis of our own placement within these hierarchies, but to evaluate the nature of the group as a whole. Like individuals, whole groups will embrace certain narratives that can be beneficial or detrimental, to itself and its members. Thomas Kuhn wrote of how these group-wide behaviors tend to manifest in observable and repeated ways within the context of the advancement of scientific knowledge, but his noted patterns repeat in most other arenas of groups pursuing an objective, even when that objective is to simply keep the group in existence.

As the group pursues these objectives, its members tend to select strategies consistent with categories that reflect the eight possible combinations of their three rankings within the three-arrow model.

All of these hierarchies have lifespans, and tend to follow a pattern from their beginnings to their ultimate demise. The rate at which these hierarchies move from stage to stage is predictable based on the nature and acceptance of its underlying narrative. This narrative changes, and the point at which it has changed in such a way as to indicate a transformation of a group in its ascendency over to one in decline is knowable from the clues it transmits. These clues come from the group's observed choice of strategies, which reflect the nature of the narrative underpinning its actions. These actions fall into three broad categories: how the organization treats is members, how it interacts with those on whom it depends who are outside of the organization, and how it interacts with competing groups.

Taken together, these clues can then point to the best technical approach for individuals to rise within the hierarchy's ranks, to tear it down, to defend it, or to advance its objectives, stated or not. Even those organizations that show indications of being dysfunctional, i.e., having abandoned any semblance to a meritocracy, can be analyzed using the three-arrow model, and best tactics derived from the results.

However, even organizations with valid underpinnings are susceptible to pathologies generated by its members' attempts to advance in rank through means other than performance or virtue. Like their biological counterparts, these pathologies can be addressed and eradicated in most instances, but must be recognized first. By their nature, though, the tactics used to advance the undeserving within the hierarchy will not be obvious. The clues that such pathologies are present will be observable, however, to those who know where to look, and what to look for.

The narratives, or scripts we run in our minds are very real, and very powerful. They will influence how we view ourselves, our relationships, our goals and objectives, and how we plan to advance them. A plethora of factors erode the accuracy of these narratives, and can easily lead to a state of near or total delusion, both by individuals and entire groups, up to and including nation-states. How these narratives, and their accompanying strategies play out in a near-chaotic world are modeled in entertainment venues, such as novels and movies. Even here, though, patterns arise, reflected in the types of plot structures that serve as the foundation of their stories, or scripts. Their very entertainment value is an indication of how closely these scripts parallel the basic structure underlying the narratives we embrace, both as individuals and as members of our various hierarchical groups.

The implications for management and leadership are profound. A highly simplified summary would be that our ranks determine our narratives, narratives drive our strategy choices, and our strategy choices result in success or failure, so that, essentially, our ranks – both perceived and actual – determine success or failure, both individually and in groups. While we may have a direct impact on our own ranks or narratives, influencing others' is far more complex, and yet is a key component in successfully leading or managing virtually any endeavor.

Much, if not most of modern-day management science scholarship focuses on the quantitative analysis of business transactions, while neglecting or ignoring the central tenet of (1) the validity of the performing organization's narrative, and (2) the degree to which it is observed or embraced by the organization's members. In a rough parallel to Tytler's progression of nation-states, economic hierarchies – corporations – will tend to perform in observable and repeatable patterns, moving in an upward trajectory from their lowly beginnings to their zeniths, and then enter into a downward trajectory towards bankruptcy, to restart the cycle again, or to elimination. The key transition point in this cycle has less to do with fluctuations in revenue and equity as much as it has to do with whether or not the organization has passed a tipping point: from one that has embraced and is pursuing its stated, valid objective, over to one that has begun to abandon those objectives, and devotes its energy instead to simply maintaining its existence, and the ranks of those in its upper echelons. This is one of the reasons why project management, as a discipline, represents such a profound modification of and upgrade to modern management science. By definition, project management is focused on attaining a documented scope of work. This scope becomes the narrative that the project team embraces and pursues, automatically defeating many of the pathologies that drive organizations past that very tipping point.

The enabler of *all* of the pathologies we've analyzed? The ubiquitous need for everyone to feel better about themselves. This is at the root of much destruction, subtle and overt, immediate impact, and delay. The common thread in all our analysis remains, that everybody's White Arrow is too high.

Socrates once queried one of his students about the inscription posted at the Temple of Apollo at Delphi, "Know Thyself." Had he seen it? Had he made the effort to understand its implications? To be so bold as to build off of Socrates, a further line of inquiry might have been, "Do you know – truly understand – the nature of the organizations to which you belong? Do you recognize the strategies employed by them to advance their objectives, and how those strategies point back to the narrative being employed? Is that narrative valid?"

The answers to these questions are knowable, and sometimes the answers aren't what we expect. Jesus of Nazareth once said "You will know them by their fruits."[2] Truly knowing ourselves, and our proper place within the ranks of the societies we associate with, or choose to belong to, as well as the nature of those societies, strongly influences, if not out and out determines, the decisions we make, the strategies we choose throughout the course of our lives.

Those choices determine our character. Those choices determine our destinies.

Notes

1 Plato, retrieved from *BrainyQuote*, http://www.brainyquote.com/quotes/quotes/p/plato164070. html#83rQrvPougL4TgZP.99, July 11, 2015.
2 *The Bible*, Matthew 7:16, English Standard Version.

Appendix

List of Hierarchical Strategies Addressed in the Book

Chapter	Name	Definition
1	Surviving	In extreme situations, predicating all ranks on demonstrated ability to help the group survive.
1	Narrative Veil	The notion that an organization exists and behaves based on reasons other than their stated objective.
2	Executive Angst Tolerance	Willingness from group leadership to allow (or even inflict) anxiety in the organization to induce better performance.
3	Forcing History	The tactic of carrying forward a canned strategy "solution" to present issues where it may or may not apply.
4	Tit-for-Tat	Responding to cooperation/defection strategies consistent with the other players.
4	"It's a jungle out there."	Acknowledging that the competitive environment of the group is unforgiving.
5	Bullying	Aggressive but informal or unauthorized enforcement of a group's ranking system.
7	Shield the Omega	A group response whenever any of their members – even the lowliest – are attacked from outside.
8	Invoking Victim	Within the three-arrow model, to claim that the accurate perception of one's low Black Arrow is due to forces outside their control, and in fair circumstances, their intrinsic value would be recognized as actually being rather high.
9	Teamwork/Helpful Ruse	In dysfunctional organizations, the tactic of presenting as desiring cooperation with the aspirant, while secretly pursuing a selfish agenda.
9	Humor/Submission Ruse	In dysfunctional organizations, the tactic of acting as enablers, seeking to make the act of participating in pursuing the group's goals more enjoyable, or less stressful.
9	Confrontation Ruse	In dysfunctional organizations, the tactic of testing others in order to evaluate where they see themselves in the organization's hierarchy.
9	Initiative Taking	An indication that a member of the organization is willing to abandon that group's norms in order to implement a novel way of achieving its goals.
9	Kissing Up and Kicking Down	In dysfunctional organizations, the act of inflating superiors' White Arrows while suppressing perceived inferiors' Grey Arrows, in order to prevent being displaced.

Chapter	Name	Definition
10	Nominal Strategy	To work on one's Black Arrow first, then Grey Arrow, then, reluctantly, the White Arrow.
10	Silent Veto	To agree to a group-wide course of action, and subsequently refuse to assist in its implementation.
10	Slow Roll	To agree to a group-wide course of action, and nominally participate in its implementation, but then deliberately withhold the level of participation needed for its success.
10	Maximize Storming	To take advantage of the nominal early teaming phase involving uncertainty among members, and introduce more conflict among members in order to delay the attainment of the performing phase.
11	Rank Impersonating	Low Black Arrows pretending to be their high Black Arrow counterparts.
11	Rank Cutting	Low Black Arrows slandering their high Black Arrow counterparts.
11	Arrow Resting	To know the group's minimum standards for allowing members to stay, and expending just enough effort to stay above that point.
11	Seagulling	To mistakenly jettison high performers while streamlining the organization.
11	Get Smart	Invest in the technology to keep the organization ahead.
11	Kaos	Espionage, or tamping down competitors' attempts at tech advancement.
11	Floor Shifting	Occurs when the target group undergoes duress, and responds by raising the minimum standards for membership in order to shed low performers.

Index